THE INTERSECTION OF RIGHTS AND REGULATION

Markets and the Law

Series Advisory Board:

Stefan Grundmann – Humboldt University of Berlin, Germany
Hans Micklitz – Bamberg Univeristy, Germany
James P. Nehf – Indiana University , USA
Iain Ramsay – York University, Canada
Charles Rickett – University of Queensland, Australia
Reiner Schulze – Münster University, Germany
Jules Stuyck – Katholieke Universiteit Leuven, Belgium
Stephen Weatherill – University of Oxford, UK
Thomas Wilhelmsson – University of Helsinki, Finland

Markets and the Law is concerned with the way the law interacts with the market through regulation, self-regulation and the impact of private law regimes. It looks at the impact of regional and international organizations (e.g. EC and WTO) and many of the works adopt a comparative approach and/or appeal to an international audience. Examples of subjects covered include trade laws, intellectual property, sales law, insurance, consumer law, banking, financial markets, labour law, environmental law and social regulation affecting the market as well as competition law. The series includes texts covering a broad area, monographs on focused issues, and collections of essays dealing with particular themes.

Other titles in the series

The Intersection of Rights and Regulation
New Directions in Sociolegal Scholarship

Edited by

BRONWEN MORGAN
University of Bristol, UK

Routledge
Taylor & Francis Group

LONDON AND NEW YORK

First published 2007 by Ashgate Publishing

Reissued 2018 by Routledge
2 Park Square, Milton Park, Abingdon, Oxon OX14 4RN
711 Third Avenue, New York, NY 10017, USA

Routledge is an imprint of the Taylor & Francis Group, an informa business

First issued in paperback 2018

A Library of Congress record exists under LC control number: 2007001514

Notice:
Product or corporate names may be trademarks or registered trademarks, and are used only for identification and explanation without intent to infringe.

Publisher's Note
The publisher has gone to great lengths to ensure the quality of this reprint but points out that some imperfections in the original copies may be apparent.

Disclaimer
The publisher has made every effort to trace copyright holders and welcomes correspondence from those they have been unable to contact.

ISBN 13: 978-0-815-39790-8 (hbk)
ISBN 13: 978-1-138-62106-0 (pbk)
ISBN 13: 978-1-351-14628-9 (ebk)

Contents

PART 3: POLITICS AND IDEOLOGIES: HYBRID DIALECTICS OF RIGHTS AND REGULATION

List of Tables and Figures

Notes on Contributors

Tola Amodu holds a PhD in Law from the London School of Economics, UK and is a member of the Public Law Team of the Law Commission for England and Wales.

Jeffrey R. Dudas is Assistant Professor of Political Science at the University of Connecticut, USA.

Amanda K. Baumle is an Assistant Professor in the Department of Sociology at the University of Houston, USA, and a J.D. graduate.

Laam Hae is a PhD candidate in Geography at Syracuse University, USA.

Erik Larson is an Assistant Professor of Sociology at Macalester College in Saint Paul, Minnesota, USA.

Orly Lobel is an Associate of Law at the University of San Diego School of Law, USA.

Bronwen Morgan is Professor of Socio-Legal Studies in the Faculty of Social Sciences and Law at the University of Bristol, UK.

Sundhya Pahuja is Associate Professor and Co-Director of the Law and Development Research Programme at the Institute for International Law and the Humanities at the Law School, University of Melbourne, Australia.

Galit A. Sarfaty is a PhD candidate in Anthropology at the University of Chicago, a J.D. graduate, and a 2007-2008 Visiting Scholar at The American Academy of Arts and Sciences.

Anders Walker is Assistant Professor of Law at the Saint Louis University School of Law, USA and holds a PhD in history.

Acknowledgements

This volume of essays originated in a workshop held in Oxford in July 2005 on the theme of this book. The workshop was a four-day Summer Institute for advanced postgraduate students and early career academics in 'law and society' and socio-legal studies (the terminology varies by academic location). This was the first of a consortium of three linked Institutes, all organized around the theme of the intersection of rights and regulation, and co-organized in sequence by myself and my colleagues Jonathan Klaaren of WITS University in Johannesburg, South Africa and Eve Darian-Smith of the Law and Society Programme, University of California at Santa Barbara, Amherst, USA. The second Summer Institute took place in Johannesburg, South Africa in July 2006, and the third will take place in Amherst, USA in June 2007. The contributors to this volume comprise nine of the 24 participants in the 2005 workshop at Oxford; these contributors met a second time over two days at the annual meeting of the Law and Society Association in Baltimore in July 2006 to revise and link their manuscripts.

Considerable thanks are due to a large number of people and institutions for the administrative, financial and intellectual support which generated and made possible this volume. The three Summer Institutes as a whole are supported by three-year financial grants from the Law and Society Association (which is based in the US but has an international membership base) and the US National Science Foundation (Grant SES-05-194-79). The 2005 Oxford Summer Institute also benefited from generous support from the University of Oxford Faculty of Law and its Centre for Socio-Legal Studies, the UK Socio-Legal Studies Association, and from the boards of two UK journals: the Journal of Law and Society, and Social and Legal Studies.

Excellent and congenial administrative support came from: the Law and Society Association Summer Institute Committee chaired by Mona Lynch; the Law and Society Association Executive Office in Amherst, Massachusetts, especially the inimitable Lissa Ganter, from Sudhir Krishnaswamy then in Oxford and now in India; from Maria Badeva of WITS University in Johannesburg, South Africa for website support; and from Tehseen Noorani in Bristol for invaluable editorial support.

Intellectually, many conversations and email exchanges have been enormously helpful: in particular the support of Jonathan Klaaren and Eve Darian-Smith who co-authored with me the original consortium proposal, participants in panels and roundtables that explored the theme in a preliminary and invigorating way (Javier Couso, Charles Gomez, Simon Halliday, Alexandra Huneeus and Alvaro Santo), and the 2005 Summer Institute Faculty (Tonya Brito, Elizabeth Boyle, David Campbell, Patricia Ewick, Chuck Epp, Denis Galligan, Anne Griffiths, George Lovell, David Sugarman, Annelise Riles and Patricia Tuitt). My new colleagues at Bristol have also given me valuable feedback, and a collaborative and congenial working environment which I greatly appreciate.

Finally, I would like to thank Peter Fitzpatrick, to whom this volume is dedicated. His unstinting and inspiring support for young scholars has sustained myself and countless others across the bridge from postgraduate study into an academic career. The existence of this volume can be traced back to the support and inspiration he gave me at the 1997 LSA Summer Institute in Madison, Wisconsin, support which continues until now. My enduring thanks to him, as to all those named here.

Bronwen Morgan
Bristol
November 2006

To Peter Fitzpatrick

Chapter 1

The Intersection of Rights and Regulation: New Directions in Sociolegal Scholarship

Bronwen Morgan

Introduction

Rights and regulation each provide a way of framing core preoccupations of sociolegal scholarship. Frequently there is a certain taken-for-granted resonance between particular areas of social life, and one or other of these two framing concepts. Take, for example, questions about law and equality as they arise in the context of race, class and gender. Problems of racial inequalities can be framed as a question of rights with relative ease. Responses to economic and class inequalities are commonly associated with regulatory regimes. Gender inequalities in the work force, on the other hand, seem to link to both rights and regulation, depending on whether we think about anti-discrimination rights or labour regulation. Of course, the degree to which these correlations are persuasive will be contingent on perspective, context and history. For example, correlations between economic *regulation* and race-based individual *rights* arguably make sense only if one accepts a particular, and contested, history of the emergence of civil rights in the 1940s in the United States (Goluboff, 2003).

This volume aims both to accept and explore such contingencies, and to use them to illuminate what we believe is a gap in the scholarship. Rights and regulation conjure up stereotypically different images of research foci, questions and topics. 'Rights scholarship' is concerned with mobilization, social change, questions of identity and culture, frequently taking the position of those who are disadvantaged or oppressed through judicial avenues, using claims of individualized entitlement as a point of departure. Regulation scholars are more typically concerned with questions of economic efficiency, the evaluation of results, rational design of institutions and bureaucratic or discretionary modes of pursuing generalized public interests.

Although these characterizations may exaggerate the differences between rights and regulation, the two are yoked more often in opposition than in concert, and regulation has often been framed as a social practice that restricts rights. Though initially plausible, however, there are ambiguities in this opposition. These ambiguities can be more clearly analysed if we disentangle four aspects of the above-stated differences between rights and regulation. The first is different strands in the scholarship concerning rights and regulation; the second, differences in the form and logic of the practices constituting rights and regulation; third, differences in the ideals or values pursued by rights and regulation; and finally, variation in the social groups who articulate their practices in terms of rights and regulation.

The chapters that follow untangle these four aspects of the rights/regulation interface in varying ways. Working backwards from the last, the wide range of topics covered in the volume illustrates the salience of the questions for a broad spectrum of social groups, ranging from groups involved in civil rights struggles, land use and urban planning, gender discrimination, indigenous peoples, economic development and workplace issues. In some cases the groups and actors appearing in the following chapters *themselves* articulate what they are doing in terms of rights or regulation. In other cases, rights and regulation are used by the authors as part of a scholarly framework that illuminates the practices *externally*. Now, as argued later in this chapter, rights and regulation tend to be associated with contrasting forms, logics, ideals and values. Yet these contrasts and oppositions may have several possible sources. They may reflect parallel scholarly dialogues (the first aspect of the rights/ regulation interface), they may be rooted in inherent formal or normative properties of rights and regulation (the second and third aspects of the interface), or they may arise from particular substantive political contexts that encourage groups to frame their own practices in a particular way – whether as rights-based or regulatory.

This book challenges stable oppositions between rights and regulation on all these fronts. It rests squarely in a particular tradition of law and society scholarship of interpretive qualitative empirical enquiry that contextualizes broad abstract claims about legal institutions and concepts, and often highlights ambiguities, contradictions and contingencies in their deployment. In particular, the volume shows how rights and regulation form overlapping and complementary aspects of processes of disputing and rule-elaboration that can be captured by two well-known triads – 'naming, blaming and claiming' and 'rule-making, monitoring and enforcement'. This approach both challenges the notion of contrasting logics of rights and regulation but also opens up interesting empirically-inspired questions at their intersection. Overall, we suggest there is a powerful, albeit varying, interdependency between rights and regulation: one that can be clarified by encouraging more work in regulatory scholarship on 'naming, claiming and blaming', and more work in rights scholarship on 'rule-making, monitoring and implementation'.

The remainder of this introduction proceeds in four parts. First, we sketch a brief intellectual history of the strands of scholarship that frame this introduction, presenting rights and regulation initially as parallel scholarly dialogues, and then viewing them through a broad lens of disputing as complementary and interdependent. Secondly, we elaborate a wide range of questions that focus on one or more of the four different aspects of the rights/regulation interface. We then provide an overview of the individual chapters, linking each to a subset of these questions. The chapters emerge from a striking variety of disciplinary approaches within law and society, including law, geography, sociology, political science, history and anthropology. As a result, they draw on the literature referenced in this opening chapter to varying degrees. Although each chapter uses additional strands of literature specific to its own topic, each also addresses its relationship to the questions posed by this introduction. Where that link is implicit, the overview of chapters provided in this opening contribution makes it explicit. Thus, the volume as a whole presents a range of work that engages with common questions, yet embeds each of the individual explorations in its own specific literature trajectory. By taking this approach, we hope to show that the force and interest of the questions posed in this introduction transcend pre-commitments to particular literatures and methodologies. The fourth and final part of the introduction takes a step in this direction by proposing three key themes that emerge cumulatively from the chapters and that suggest future research directions.

Intellectual History and Context

The context for this enquiry into the intersection of rights and regulation is that of empirically-grounded, sociolegal literature about these practices. Both adjectives are consciously intended to draw boundaries, placing some literature about rights and regulation beyond the imagined remit of the argument that follows. In particular, we do not directly engage with purely philosophical, conceptual or doctrinally-focused explorations (often a popular approach in rights studies), nor studies embedded in the law-and-economics tradition (popular in regulatory scholarship). Our starting point for understanding the trajectories catalysed by these two strands of literature is that there is a basic tension – even incompatibility – between the forms and logics underpinning rights and regulation. But this claim should not be read as an analytical claim about the *necessary* form of rights or regulation. Rather, it is a claim that this contrast can be observed in much sociolegal work that has explored empirically the social practices involved in claiming rights or exercising regulatory power.

To reiterate the substance of the contrast: rights capture individualized and deontologically justified entitlements while regulation implies a collectivist and consequentialist deployment of discretionary power. Or, as Orly Lobel puts it in her opening chapter, 'the regulation/rights dichotomy has remained pervasive in policy-making consciousness ... [illustrating] the divide between the administrative impulse to regulate the market and the adjudicative impulse to protect individual rights' (Lobel, this volume). The notion that rights and regulation have contrasting forms and logics makes most sense when understood as a contingent claim made in the context of a particular historical juncture: a basic commitment to Lockean liberalism and a free market, tempered by an interventionist welfare state, however minimalist. Rights, in this context, are common law rights, contract and property rights classically protected by courts and invoked to restrain the state. Regulation is something the state does that interferes with such rights. One could put this aphoristically, suggesting that regulation implies rule *by* law, while rights connote the rule *of* law.

However, a different historical-political perspective can reverse the political implications of rights and regulation in ways that blur an oppositional logic between them. Take for example, the situation when rights are invoked to make socio-economic and collective claims (rather than contract and property claims), and when regulation constitutes markets (rather than reshaping them or redistributing their effects). In this context, it is regulation that bolsters property and contract rights and mutes arbitrary state discretion. And socio-economic and collective rights claims are often fleshed out by positive programmes of state intervention: regulatory norms that establish minimum standards of provision in ways that some would argue entrenches upon individual liberties. The notion of contrasting forms and logics is considerably muddied here.

In the nine chapters that follow, we will see both the resonance of the liberal historical legacy and the challenges that unsettle it. The importance of empirical and historical context is a common thread throughout the volume. It is not the only way in which rights and regulation can be brought into more direct dialogue with each other. There have been nascent attempts to do so from a more law-based perspective. These approaches, some applying to private law rights (Collins, 1999), some to public law processes of judicial review (Hertogh and Halliday, 2004) and others spanning both (Parker et al., 2004), argue that patterns of exercising individual legal rights can be better understood by viewing their cumulative effect as a regulatory regime. But these studies impose a regulatory perspective on the exercise of legal rights: our intentions are broader in two ways. First, we aim to bring rights and regulation perspectives to bear *on each other*, and secondly, the work in this volume encompasses the social practices involved in both rights and regulation, even when they are not embedded in legal form. A useful reference point for the context we aim to establish here (albeit one with varying presence in the chapters themselves), can be constructed by drawing a broad-brush – and inevitably highly stylized – map of regulation and rights scholarship in the sociolegal field.

Reviewing a quarter-century of Anglo-Commonwealth-American scholarship in the two fields, one can identify, perhaps tendentiously, particular 'classics' that appear in the 1970s and 1980s, new contributions in the 1990s and fresh editions (or very closely related works) in the 2000s of the original 'classics' that confirm the enduring interest in both rights and regulation. This pattern is observable in a US context in respect of both rights and regulation, as well as in relation to an Anglo-Australian literature on regulation, as represented in Table 1.1.

These texts, along with many others in similar vein, have sparked lively debates that earlier on were conducted in relative parallel geographical isolation: the US literature being especially energized about rights and the Anglo-Australian scholarship about regulation. The geographical gulf is less marked in recent years. Sociolegal (as opposed to law-and-economics) scholarship on regulation crosses the Atlantic divide, particularly in the journal *Law and Policy* and in the growing interest in comparative work on the regulatory state that compares regulatory dynamics in a range of industrialized democracies (Kagan and Axelrad, 2000; Jordana and Levi-Faur, 2004; Ansell and Vogel, 2006). EU-US comparisons have also sparked increasing comparative scholarship on the judicialization of politics which deals to some degree with rights-claiming practices (Holmstrom, 1998; Stone Sweet, 2000; Keleman, 2006), and there is also a more general interest in rights scholarship within the US that ventures beyond US borders (Epp, 1998; Milner and Goldberg-Hiller and Milner, 2003).

Table 1.1 Common-law Trajectories of Sociolegal Rights and Regulation Literature

Regulation – US	Regulation: Anglo-Australian	Rights – US
Bardach and Kagan's 1981 *Going by the Book: A Study of Regulatory Unreasonableness*	Keith Hawkins' 1984 *Environment and Enforcement*	Stuart Scheingold's 1974 *The Politics of Rights*
Cass Sunstein's 1990 *Beyond the Rights Revolution: Reconceiving the Regulatory State*	Ayres and Braithwaite's 1992 *Responsive Regulation* and Julia Black's 1997 *Rules and Regulators*	Gerald Rosenberg's 1991 *The Hollow Hope* and Michael McCann's 1994 *Rights at Work*
Bardach and Kagan's 2002 *Going by the Book: A Study of Regulatory Unreasonableness* (reprinted with a new introduction)	Keith Hawkins' 2003 *Law as Last Resort*	Stuart Scheingold's 2004 *The Politics of Rights* (reprinted with a new introduction)

The question of a United Kingdom (UK) and EU-based rights literature is more fragmented. Despite two notable, widely spaced contributions (Harlow and Rawlings, 1992; Halliday and Schmidt, 2004), there is a relative absence in the European Union of the particular mix of empirical work and theoretical concerns that is taken here as a reference point. There was a plethora of empirical work in the 1970s and continuing into the 1980s, exploring various ways in which statutory entitlements crucial to civil liberties failed in practice to live up to their promise (Cain, 1979; Prosser, 1983; Sanders, 1987; Dixon et al., 1989). But in the absence of broadly worded guarantees of constitutional rights in the UK and its (possibly related) pragmatic, incremental legal culture, this literature did not engage much with the rhetorical force of rights as a universal claim.

There is also a large EU-based literature on *human* rights, particularly since the introduction of the UK Human Rights Act (1998). In the main, this falls outside the remit of this introduction insofar as it is conceptual literature that focuses on moral and politically normative criteria, or on legal doctrine, or a combination of the two (for example, Klug et al., 2005; McCrudden and Chambers, 1994). As far as empirical literature on human rights is concerned, there is a nascent focus on human rights statistics and democratic audit (Cingranelli, 1988; Jabine and Claude, 1992; Green, 2001; Hathaway, 2002). However, compared with studies which explore the broad institutional conditions that shape particular patterns of rights-claiming, this literature is more narrowly focused, using empirical analysis at a more applied level such as developing indicators for policy evaluation studies. There is also a venerable tradition of anthropology concerned with human rights and culture (Cowan, Dembour and Wilson, 2001; International Encyclopaedia of the Social Sciences vol. 10), although as compared with US-based anthropologically-rooted literature on rights, the micro-empirical analysis engages less with the conditions under which rights claims emerge and succeed, and more with relatively abstract discussions of universalism and relativism of a kind that pervade the normative conceptual literature.

Given the difficulty of drawing clear boundaries around the scope of either rights or regulation literature, we decided not to engage any further in a detailed literature review of transatlantic scholarship in rights and regulation. Especially as the chapters that follow themselves plumb a diverse range of literature, we thought it more useful to juxtapose briefly the early 'classic' monographs alluded to above in order to illustrate the divergent logics of rights and regulation. Scheingold argues (Dudas, 2004) that American political life is animated by a foundational faith in a rights-based politics which emerges at least in part as commitment to a 'myth of rights'. The myth of rights is grounded in the belief that litigation can evoke a declaration of rights from courts that once realized is tantamount to meaningful social change. This is a myth in two senses: it is a foundational narrative that motivates concrete practices, but it has elements of false promise. More specifically, the myth of rights concretely engenders repeated political mobilization in pursuit of progressive social change, even when those who do so experience significant practical limits to their activist goals. Such limits include problems with accessibility to litigation (particularly for those with few resources), and the limited room for radical decisions by a countermajoritarian institution that by its nature follows past precedent. Despite the negative effects of these obstacles on securing progressive change through litigating rights, Scheingold argues that the appeal of rights endures, and accounts for this in part by political culture and tradition, in part by institutional configurations that fragment coherent governmental decision-making.

Bardach and Kagan explore the regulatory dynamics in regulatory agencies that range from those that enforce environmental regulations, to quality control in food and drug manufacturing, to those that implement health and safety law. Their qualitative research focuses on the first-hand experience of enforcement officials at the 'street level' and those subject to regulation. They define 'regulatory unreasonableness', the core concept of the book, in the following way:

> A regulatory requirement is unreasonable if compliance would not yield the intended benefits ... or if compliance would entail costs that clearly exceed the resulting social benefits .... Basically, "unreasonableness" involves economic inefficiency (Bardach and Kagan, 1982, p. 6).

While Bardach and Kagan document both reasonable and unreasonable regulatory dynamics, on the opposite side of the Atlantic, Hawkins' exploration of regulatory enforcement dynamics in water pollution regulation under the purview of the UK Environment Agency finds a much more consistently consensual practice of negotiation and mutual adjustment. Both these monographs share a common emphasis in identifying varying regulatory styles (adversarial, heavy-handed, consensus-orientated, conciliatory) and trying to specify the conditions which produce one or another style. Bardach and Kagan argue that over-inclusive general rules, legalistic attitudes and 'predatory' political oversight pressures produce legalistic enforcement, while contexts with a less intense political and legal environment or very good leadership avoid unreasonableness, eliciting cooperation through a flexible mix of legal threat and professional judgment. Hawkins' findings of conciliatory strategies are explained by the moral ambivalence caused by lack of consensus about the social harm of pollution, and the related persistence of shared social norms that define only the most wilfully negligent breaches of regulations as 'morally deviant' and thus worthy of prosecution.

If we juxtapose these two strands, we can see two contrasts. First, rights have a stronger association with symbolic valency, with political mobilization and with a broader cultural consciousness than regulation, which focuses much more on efficiency and effectiveness. Relatedly, rights have a tendency to be understood by those who articulate and claim them as 'trumps', as guaranteed entitlements protected from the vicissitudes of politics. Of course, a large part of the work of sociolegal research on rights, from Scheingold through Rosenberg and onwards, is to document an empirical debunking of this hope. But what is striking is how much this hope persists at a general level, however hollow it may demonstrably turn out to be in specific sectors and at specific times.

Regulation, by contrast, is a practice that fits more comfortably within a culture of expectations that focuses on the exercise of discretion, albeit structured by rules to an extent. It is usually the patterns of bargaining occurring within that zone of discretion that are the object of study. Even in accounts which emphasize the discretion-structuring function that rules play within regulation, a contrast with rights is still visible. Ed Rubin, for example, reviews a recent book on regulating air pollution – Morag-Levine's *Chasing the Wind* (2003) – and contrasts 'common law standards, enforceable private rights and free market mechanisms' with 'administrative planning, agency action and regulation' (Rubin, 2005, p. 601). His discussion accepts that because the establishment of a free market requires legal rules, it makes sense to speak on occasion of 'market regulation'. But the existence of market regulation does not undermine the deeper contrast he draws between private rights and the greater political discretion associated with administrative regulation.

In order to challenge this contrast, it is helpful to stand back from the rights and regulation literature and think of both briefly from the broader perspective of disputing. In particular, this helps us step outside a view of either rights or regulation as enforceable *legal* interests. Instead, they appear as *social practices* articulating generalized claims upon the social order. These claims may or may not have specific legal implications, but rather constitute at most a call – sometimes an implicit one – for some kind of institutionalized response. This view resonates with Felstiner, Abel and Sarat's triad of 'naming, blaming and claiming' (Felstiner, Abel and Sarat, 1980). The well-known triad formulated by these authors captures the importance of the set of social practices that precede the formal articulation of a grievance. That formal articulation could emerge, we would argue, either as a rights claim or as a demand for regulation. Then to this well-known triad, we might add a further triad that can also be applied to claims (whether rights-based or embedded in regulation): rule-making, monitoring and enforcement. The effect of combining these triads can be illustrated by reference to gender inequality, a social issue which at the start of this introduction we suggested can be framed relatively easily from both rights and regulation perspectives.

Naming gender inequalities as a form of injustice is a crucial facet of grass-roots political organizing and feminist consciousness-raising that is a common constituent of many rights studies (Nielsen, 2000; Marshall, 2005). The construction or choice of appropriate subjects or practices to blame for this injustice shapes the agenda for the form in which the claim will finally emerge. For example, if deeply embedded social attitudes are selected as a key focus of blame, then a positive duty to combat gender inequality might be imposed by the government upon employers as a regulatory responsibility. By contrast, a focus on the discriminatory practices of 'bad apple' employers might be more likely to lead to framing the claim as an individual right not to be discriminated against. This last example, however, could also be framed as a regulatory responsibility. Only at the point when a sense of felt wrong is formulated as a specific *claim*, does it emerge clearly as either a call to enforce rights or a demand for regulation (or indeed another language of claim altogether).

Once articulated as either, however, both a right to equal treatment and a regulatory regime for achieving gender equality will require the articulation of specific rules, the mobilization of legal and political institutions in monitoring these rules, and the enforcement of such rules when those whom they target ignore their proscriptions.

Differences will still exist. For example, rights claims to gender equality may be likely to lead to rules created by judicial 'gap-filling' or to corporate training manuals, while regulation is more likely to create a government agency or commission to articulate detailed rules. Similarly, monitoring and enforcement will differ – for rights, it will be more decentralized, episodic and unpredictable, while for a regulatory regime, a more consciously articulated and proactive strategy of monitoring and enforcement is likely to develop, at least on paper. Indeed, one might argue that regulation and rights are consciously brought together by laws that provide simultaneously for rule-making and enforcement by regulatory agencies, on the one hand, and by lawsuits brought by those harmed by regulatory violations or by NGOs. Large numbers of regulatory statutes, in many different national seetings, grant beneficiaries the right to submit complaints about violations to a regulatory agency. In this sense, regulatory agencies might be considered institutions designed to enforce rights (regulatory entitlements) more proactively than courts, with the state bearing the burden and cost of gathering evidence, proving violations and ordering remedial and preventative measures (Kagan, 2004).

As this example illustrates, viewing social responses to gender inequality as part of a six-fold process of disputing (naming, blaming, claiming, rule-making, monitoring and enforcing) allows us to see regulation and rights as species of a common genre, rather than as contrasting forms and logics. True, this move depends to a certain degree on a rather functional understanding of these social practices, one that uses arguably unfamiliar terminology to describe empirical phenomena that we are used to speaking of much more contextually. It strips away, for the time being, a historical and contextual sense of the specificity of rights claims or the emergence of regulatory regimes. But we would argue that we gain much more than we lose in this process. We gain the ability to ask a range of questions that specify more precisely the possible interactions between rights and regulation, by focusing on different stages of the six-fold sequence common to both. And after reading the chapters that follow, we hope you will also gain some sense of the extent to which these very different social practices already overlap, of how much they speak to each other, and of whether they are capable of learning from each other.

Questions at the Intersection of Rights and Regulation

We view the questions that arise at the intersection of rights and regulation as typically doing one of two things. They may bring out a stage of 'claiming rights' or 'demanding regulation' that the literature in that area tends to neglect. Or they may frame an issue that is familiar within rights in terms of the language and concerns of regulation, and vice versa. In both types of cases, they provide a fresh perspective – sometimes on empirical aspects of the practices under study and sometimes on the conceptual angles used to analyse those practices.

First, several questions arise from considering the relationship between the naming, claiming and blaming phases of the emergence of rights on the one hand and regulation on the other. For example, in particular contexts, are there links between the ways in which political changes redefine the cultural meanings and boundaries of rights and of regulation? Does regulation possess the kind of independent discursive force that rights-talk has? – a fluid capacity to be exercised by a wide variety of groups in widely varying contexts, independently of whether it is encoded in legal form? We often think of rights as constituting individual (and perhaps also collective, but non-state) identities, while regulation expresses state-endorsed collective goals. But when, if at all, and how do rights express state-endorsed collective goals and when does regulation constitute identities? Can both rights and regulation shape social change even when they are not embodied in legal form, or does regulation depend more than rights on being legally embedded in order to shape events and practices?

These kinds of questions lead naturally to a consideration of the relationship between the concrete institutional forms taken by each of rights and regulation. For example, *do* the practices of rights and regulation in fact take contrasting forms as suggested by an initial consideration of the 'classics' in the fields? More specifically, to what extent does regulation deploy discretionary power shaped by technical expertise, while rights appear as clearly defined legal entitlements embodying ostensibly absolute ethical commitments? Do some kinds of rights necessitate particular types of regulatory systems: for example, does the rule-making that follows from fleshing out property rights necessarily require market-based regulation? Or does the rule-making that elaborates collective socio-economic rights necessarily entail highly discretionary political allocation of the distributive costs of providing such rights? Finally, does the increasing importance of non-state actors in regulatory enforcement complement or undermine notions of rights-based enforcement?

The direction of the set of questions in the last paragraph implies some possible tensions that could arise when exploring linkages between the concrete institutional forms of rights and regulation. Sometimes such tensions will arise from the shift from 'naming, blaming and claiming' to the more routine, often technocratic work of 'rule-making, monitoring and enforcement'. Interesting questions relating to complementarity arise here. For example, must rights catalyse the development of regulatory frameworks in order to go beyond having symbolic force? Would the 'hollow hope' that rights all too often offer be fleshed out if the study of rights routines incorporated insights from studies of regulatory compliance? Does regulation constrain social movements, de-radicalizing the political potential inherent in claiming rights, or does it facilitate long-term systemic change for those claims? How does regulatory implementation affect the ability of those benefiting from regulation to sustain rights-based political mobilization regarding the same issue? When do rights claims that catalyse regulatory frameworks end up pursuing non-rights based goals?

Many of these questions explore tensions that arise not only from the relationship between different stages of the disputing process, but also arise as a product of the specific political content animating rights claims and regulatory demands. How does the regulatory implementation of minority rights play out when the substantive political values underpinning the rights claims are bitterly contested? Or to what degree are viable regulatory regimes premised on social consensus about the current distribution of rights? Studies of regulatory regimes often focus on how they engender technocratic rationalities, while studies of rights regimes more often focus on how they shape (or fail to shape) popular consciousnesses. Reversing these tendencies generates interesting questions of how and when do rights regimes engender technocratic rationalities? And in what ways do regulatory regimes shape popular consciousnesses?

These questions give voice, we hope, to a fertile research agenda at the intersection of rights and regulation.

Overview of the Chapters

The chapters that follow engage with many of the questions articulated above. All of them take seriously the interdependency of rights and regulation, but many chapters focus more on one than on the other. Some chapters, particularly those in Part 1, generate questions about the intersection of the two internally within the compass of a particular chapter. In other cases, particularly in Part 3, the juxtaposition of rights and regulation is enhanced by reading the various chapters in relation to each other. The chapters also deal differently with the idea of contrasts between rights and regulation. Roughly, those in Part 1 give reasonable prominence to contrasts between rights and regulation in terms of form and logic, even while showing the limits of such contrasts. The chapters in Part 2 emphasize complementarity between rights and regulation, while those in Part 3 tend to highlight the tensions, ambiguities and contradictions that arise in fitting them together – suggesting a dialectical relationship between the two sets of social practices.

Part 1 opens with Orly Lobel's historical overview of US 'workplace law' to illustrate how certain alignments between form and substance can become taken-for-granted: specifically, linkages between rights and employment law on the one hand, and between regulation and labour law on the other hand. She tracks how minimum standards in occupational health and safety drew on a paradigmatic regulatory paradigm of a public administrative agency (the Occupational Safety and Health Administration) that issued general rules, while in anti-discrimination, individual private rights to litigate were the primary mechanism, buttressed by the supervisory role of an Equal Employment Opportunity Commission that could not issue binding rules. The chapter demonstrates the historical contingency of these alignments, and shows how more recent reforms are finding productive points of convergence between the forms and logics of regulation and rights. She carefully traces the ways in which political changes redefine the cultural meanings and boundaries of both rights and of regulation, bringing them into a more complementary relationship in each of the two areas of workplace law she describes. She also touches on the different ways in which regulatory regimes and rights-based claims can shape popular consciousness – partly by drawing on synergies between the increasing importance of non-state actors in both.

While Lobel's chapter relates squarely to both rights and regulation, the two chapters that follow each explore contrasting forms and logic from a starting point more firmly within one or other literature: rights for Amanda Baumle, and regulation for Tola Amodu. Both chapters, however, develop their starting point to investigate the intersection of the two. Baumle shows how rights discourse in online communities facilitates the articulation of gender discrimination claims in relation to large law firms, where the off-line organizational support for such claims is weak or non-existent. She tackles the contradiction implicit in the fact that despite the availability of some formal legal remedies, women lawyers rarely sue their employers, and often do not challenge discriminatory behaviour, even where it clearly exists. Her chapter explores what happens when rights discourse is employed to challenge inequality within an internet-based community – the 'Greedy Associates' website forum for US lawyers to discuss 'life as a lawyer'.

Baumle shows how the internet community provides a protected, semi-anonymous forum in which to engage in a range of both legal and lay discussion of discrimination in the workplace amongst professional lawyers. It thereby subverts many of the barriers that currently exist to challenging gender inequality in legal practice. Further, the community serves as a resource to bring public attention to bear upon law firms, creating external pressures which encourage a re-evaluation of both lay and legal understandings of prohibited gender discrimination. This is relevant to the question of under what conditions rights can shape social change even when they are not embodied in legal form. Online, the nexus of incentives and power relationships between attorneys in a law firm is altered in crucial ways that give rights claims more leverage than one would expect given the distribution of resources and organizational dynamics of the off-line world. Nonetheless, rights claims still seem to need to catalyze some form of regulatory framework in order to fulfil the potential of their symbolic force. In other words, rights still have a form of 'everyday regulatory dependency', even in cyberspace.

Tola Amodu's chapter constructs a somewhat similar sense of interdependency from the reverse direction: her chapter suggests what one might label the rights-dependency of regulatory frameworks. Her account of the historical development of land-use planning regulation in the UK shows how rights-based relationships between different actors laid the ground for the development of regulatory frameworks in this area. The rights involved here were individual property rights, encoded in bilateral planning agreements between a property owner and the local authority for the area. Property rights and planning regulation are classic examples of the 'contrasting forms and logics' alluded to earlier in this chapter. But these planning agreements, although initially a fragmented patchwork aimed at defining and protecting individual property rights, were moulded by creative central government officials over time to accommodate wide and diverse collective goals. Over a period of a decade, informal central government supervision of agreements evolved into a formal system of precedent, and eventually into an organized system of documented genres of permissible agreement types – in short, the regulatory basis of central planning law. This process gradually elided – at least in terms of institutional formal appearance – the line between 'public regulation' and 'private (property) rights'. Rights-based private law catalysed regulatory frameworks that moved significantly away from an individuated approach to the balancing of interests.

Amodu's chapter challenges the notion that an assertion of quasi-contractual and property rights necessitates a logic of market-based regulation. Moreover, she uncovers complementarities between rights and regulation by focusing on the important role of non-state actors in state-sponsored solutions – suggesting that such complementarity may exist where regulatory regimes are premised on relative social consensus regarding about the current distribution of rights. Relatedly, such circumstances may also foster the conditions for rights regimes to engender technocratic rationalities of a kind more commonly associated with regulatory dynamics.

Part 2 of the book develops the notion of complementarity between rights and regulation further, moving away from the nascent emergence of rights or regulatory frameworks, and focusing more on what happens in trying to implement and enforce their regimes. All three chapters in this part in fact take a *rights* regime, and explore the regulatory dimensions of attempts to flesh out and enforce that regime. The chapters allude to a wide range of scholarly perspectives that do not always use the language of regulatory literature. But when read together, they provide in effect a regulatory lens on the oft-noted danger that rights may all too often offer a 'hollow hope' (Rosenberg, 1991) to those who articulate their claims in its language. By grafting insights from studies of regulatory compliance into the study of rights, the institutional conditions for monitoring and enforcing the detail of rights claims can be more clearly understood. The chapters focus on different types of institutional contexts: from the internal organizational culture of The World Bank, to the effects of local political contexts in the US, to a consideration of how organizational culture and national political contexts intertwine on the global stage.

Galit Sarfaty's chapter identifies how the internalization of human rights within the World Bank faces difficulties created by 'interpretive gaps' between different interpretive communities within the Bank. Different disciplinary orientations lead to competing legal, economic and ethical views of what human rights mean and how they should be operationalized. Without a critical mass of 'translators' to help bridge these interpretive gaps, compliance with the human rights goal of the Bank is compromised. Indeed, this is arguably a case that illustrates how rights claims can, under certain conditions, catalyse a regulatory framework that ends up pursuing non-rights-based goals. The important condition here is a professional and organizational culture that is more comfortable with deploying discretionary power shaped by technical expertise than with clearly defined legal entitlements embodying relatively absolute ethical commitments. As a result, the strategies for rule-making, monitoring and implementation that develop within the Bank infuse rights with a functionalist orientation more often associated with regulation. Sarfaty's chapter thus implicitly raises the question of whether regulation contains social movements, deradicalising the political potential inherent in claiming rights, or whether it facilitates long-term systemic change for those claims.

Anders Walker's chapter addresses just this question somewhat more explicitly. Exploring two particular historical instances of civil rights politics in the US – school desegregation in the south and death penalty reform in the north – his chapter suggests that complementarities between regulation and rights may well facilitate long-term systemic change. He argues that legislative implementation of rights programmes that provide room for discretionary local adjustments are a crucial component of successfully protecting the rights of unpopular minorities. In essence, they build decentralized 'safety valves' that empower citizens at the local level to express opposition, without jeopardizing larger, state-wide mechanisms of rights implementation. Rather than prevent the public from expressing its will, they increase the transactional costs for doing so, facilitating larger, state-wide reform in the process. As a historian, Walker is sensitive to the contingency of such strategies, but tentatively suggests that they provide instances of a more abstracted model for tempering majoritarian political backlash against minority rights.

Erik Larson's chapter examines the emergence of indigenous rights in relation to the culture of global society. Drawing on world polity theory, he analyses the regulatory effects of these emergent rights on actors in the global system. By investigating newly developing rights, the chapter helps to address questions about whether rights can shape social change when not fully legally embodied. Larson assesses the ways in which ethical commitments and technical expertise interact in giving shape to these newly emergent rights, which have their origins in the interplay of nation-states, an international indigenous rights movement and global decision-making bodies. By analysing the effects of emerging indigenous rights on international bodies, states and the international indigenous rights movement itself, the chapter considers how the regulatory effects of rights influence social movements.

Sarfaty's and Walker's approaches to complementarity might be said to emphasize the salience of the structure of rule-making, monitoring and enforcement for fleshing out rights' capacity to forcefully 'name, claim and blame'. While Larson's chapter acknowledges this, he also stresses an inverse complementarity: the ways in which particular forms of 'naming, blaming and claiming' can foster new structures of rule-making, monitoring and enforcement. Indigenous rights claims in the global arena partially transform the tendency for nation-state centred rule-making, monitoring and enforcement. Larson links this to the capacity of the agency and sense of identity fostered by rights-claiming activities to *re-make* the typical regulatory strategies associated with fleshing out such rights.

While Part 2's complementarities between rights and regulation go in more than one direction, Part 3 foregrounds ambiguities, tensions and contradiction between the two forms of social practices. The chapters here share a sense with all those in the volume that there is mutual interdependence between rights and regulation, but the common thread here is a more *dialectical* conception of this interdependency. They also place particular emphasis on substantive politics – the ideals and values animating the practices – as a major constituent of how rights and regulation shape the social world. Mirroring Part 1, we have one contribution rooted in regulation (Laam Hae), and one in rights (Jeff Dudas), and conclude with Sundhya Pahuja's chapter that bridges both. But to a greater extent than Part 1, the chapters in Part 3 highlight conflict, political division, and internal contradictions.

Laam Hae's chapter examines conflicts in New York City over laws and regulations designed to police dance clubs, in the context of neoliberal urban planning policies at local government level since the late 1970s. She argues that these policies, as a 'mode of regulation', are tools through which the city government seeks to resolve ongoing contradictions in the 'creative destruction' catalysed by neoliberal urban capitalism, and, in doing so, to secure the continuation of neoliberal urbanization. The chapter focuses on the contradiction that has emerged between rights-based claims to a particular 'quality of life' on the one hand, and rights-based claims to preserve space for social dancing (that is, dance clubs), on the other. She argues that the historical trajectory of the New York cabaret law has gradually given priority to the former claims over the latter, leading to a decline of once prosperous subcultures in the city. Her chapter shows how an apparently vague and indeterminate right (claims to a particular 'quality of life') can be harnessed to – even created by – the regulatory dynamics of neoliberal urbanization. Under such conditions, its political force can trump that of more conventionally defined rights that lack an analogous regulatory infrastructure. The implication is that rights are dependent on the form that regulation takes, and in particular on the patterns of naturalization created by regulation.

Jeff Dudas explores how the goals of the New Right in the US have become tethered to a particular sort of rights talk – one that that is simultaneously focused on procedural equality and the ability of individuals to compete in the market, and yet also defends traditional hierarchies that have remained immune to the logic of the marketplace. This rights talk manipulates a dichotomy between equal rights and special rights, and in doing so, has regulatory effects that enact an exclusory normative vision, stigmatizing and marginalizing economically and culturally vulnerable minorities. These regulatory effects also constitute the identities of the speakers, who now imagine themselves not simply as defending their personal material interests but also as defending long-standing American values; not simply as reactionaries but as committed patriots. As a marker of identity, this regulatory facet of rights talk occurs independently of any specific legal dispute. It also highlights how practices of claiming rights confer positive identity *by virtue of* their negative regulatory dimension. From this perspective, the regulatory dimension of rights is constitutive of the very existence of rights. This dialectical perspective suggests a very different relationship from a complementary one that sees the regulatory dimension of rights as instrumental to their successful enforcement.

Sundhya Pahuja's chapter concludes with a consideration of the interpenetration and increasing convergence between human rights and development that poses an even more explicit challenge to visions of complementarity. Pahuja argues that it is useful to map development and international human rights onto the domains of 'regulation' and 'rights' respectively (although these domains are not typically explored in terms of the *sociolegal* literature on regulation and rights). Such a mapping has two implications. It shows how the increasing acceptance of this rapid merger represents an instance of 'the creeping transformation of a promised sphere of "rights" into a domain which may aptly be called "regulatory"' (Pahuja, chapter in this volume). This transformation threatens to subordinate rights to the forms and logic of the market, sealing their fate as sites of regulation rather than potential emancipation and increasing the likelihood of violent resistance to developmental transformation.

Secondly, the chapter engages with traditionally conceived notions of rights as emancipatory and regulation as restrictive, stressing instead the paradox of the regulatory dimension of human rights, while persisting with the notion that rights have a special character – related to that of law – that regulation lacks. Pahuja defends the need for a vision of political economy that depends on some degree of dissonance between the two vocabularies of claiming in order to preserve a useful, if fragile, space of politics. Perhaps more than any other chapter, Pahuja's argument suggests that regulatory implementation of a rights agenda will negatively affect the ability to sustain rights-based political mobilization. Indeed, her chapter brings the volume full circle from Lobel's optimism regarding the potential complementarities between rights and regulation. Instead, insisting on the incompatibilities inscribed in the mutual dependence of rights and regulation, Pahuja foregrounds the profound absence of social consensus about the current distribution of rights, and the challenge this poses to linking emancipatory goals to rights-based regulatory regimes.

Drawing the Threads Together

Three core insights can be drawn from this volume regarding the intersection of rights and regulation. The first, which might be called 'hybridity' for shorthand, emphasizes that rights and regulation interpenetrate one another in a manner that is shaped more by organizational and institutional dynamics than by inherently different logics. The second is that despite a frequent mutual interdependence between rights and regulation, rights possess a relatively stronger discursive power, particularly in relation to political mobilization and the constitution of identities and legal consciousnesses. Another way of putting this is to suggest that rights have a kind of independent discursive force that regulation lacks. The third insight is the increasing contingency of the political salience of rights and regulation, which arguably signals an underlying drift towards a pragmatic politics focused on 'what works'. These three insights open up an avenue for further research: are rights and regulation becoming important sites for displacing what once might have been directly ideological conflict in the democratic arena into the relatively technocratic interstices of disputing processes?

Hybridity

The clearest message common to the chapters in this volume is that the notion that regulation and rights are social practices with contrasting forms and logics is both politically and historically contingent. There is no general pattern of a link between rights and individualized, powerfully protected entitlements on the one hand, nor between collectivist, consequentially motivated deployment of discretionary power and regulation on the other hand. Rather, because the exercise of discretion in regulatory regimes is systematically patterned, and because the everyday implementation of even legally embedded rights is constrained by institutional realities, the two sets of practices often overlap and are mutually dependent. Moreover, the chapters' cumulative effects tend to decentre the state. Many of them focus less on formal, legally endowed institutional practices, and more on informal spaces and the role of non-state actors. From this perspective, local organizational and institutional dynamics are more powerfully constitutive of the relationship between rights and regulation than inherently different logics. Consequently, the relationship is highly contextual, as the variety in the different chapters illustrates.

Notwithstanding this variety, there is one important axis of variation. This concerns whether the relationship between rights and regulation is complementary or dialectical. Complementary understandings of the relationship between the two might envision that the capacity of rights-claiming to effectively articulate and address a sense of being wronged is strengthened by exploring its regulatory dimensions (Sarfaty's and Walker's chapters). Or they might include a sense that close attention to regulatory regimes can help us understand either how they are premised on and embedded in rights (Amodu's chapter), or create new social relations and bases upon which formal rights can be constructed (Larson's chapter).

Dialectical understandings of the relationship between rights and regulation, which are more prominent towards the end of the volume, are more inclined to stress the idea that regulation and rights are *necessarily* linked, as two sides of a coin might be, and yet at the same time to insist that this relationship creates tensions and contradictions which are capable of being politically exploited. This perspective is less optimistic about the possibilities for rights and regulation to complement each other, in part because of the second theme that emerges reasonably strongly: a sense that rights have a more powerful capacity to exercise an independent discursive force than regulation does.

Relative Discursive Power of Rights

The hybridity discussed above has important limits. Its insistence on mutual interdependency between rights and regulation, and on the organizational intermeshing of the two, arguably veers close to equating rights with interests (however clearly delineated). This, for many, is a misleading equation that misses a crucial aspect of rights: their deontological appeal to universal values – or, for value-agnostics, their more powerful rhetorical political appeal in terms of political mobilization. One might also express this as a greater capacity for rights discourse to exceed its organizational and institutional context than for regulatory frameworks.

This insight arguably underpins the idea that the first of the two triads we seek to bring together here is more easily associated with rights ('naming, blaming and claiming'), while the second triad allies more naturally with regulation ('rule-making, monitoring and implementation'). The 'naming, claiming and blaming' stages of disputing are by definition less systematically embedded in formal institutions and organizations devoted to resolving or preventing the wrongs at issue. Rights language can operate as a free-floating abstraction articulating such wrongs in a way that regulatory demands are less likely to. Hence we find it easier to flesh out ways in which rights can be elaborated and enforced through processes of rule-making, monitoring and interpretation than the reverse.

Rights more naturally appear to have *both* symbolic, discursive force, and a more mundane institutionalized dimension. A number of chapters have addressed that link, particularly those focusing on the complementarity of rights and regulation, or on questions of how rights struggles could secure long-term systemic change by integrating the compliance insights of regulation scholarship. But it takes arguably more imaginative work to extend the focus of regulation scholarship to the processes of 'naming, claiming and blaming' the social ills that catalyse regulatory responses. This may well flow from the sense of the greater discursive salience of rights, and at least one chapter in this volume – Pahuja's concluding chapter – explicitly defends the necessity to preserve this very difference, which she argues is not simply an analytical feature of rights, but a crucial moral facet of the very idea of rights.

Another response could be to challenge the assumption that rights have greater moral salience or independent discursive force than regulation. This could take the form, for example, of focusing more attention within regulation scholarship on issues of identity and political consciousness. Epistemic communities that share technical or scientific knowledge and professional commitments are a visible presence in regulatory scholarship. But where, if at all, in regulatory spaces do we find the analogy for a rights-based politics that universalizes issues, reforms existing political categories and helps build surprising coalitions (Milner and Goldberg-Hiller 2002)?

Increasing Contingency of the Political Salience of Rights and Regulation

As the last sentence indicates, this exercise of drawing common threads from the chapters is also intended to point towards future lines of research that could build on this volume. The third thread perhaps more than others points forward, building on an aspect of the chapters that is undoubtedly present in many chapters but is not systematically addressed by the structure of the book. This is the increasingly contingent link between the use of rights or regulation as a strategy or mechanism for achieving social change, and a particular political world view. One could say that rights and regulatory claims serve as barometers of changes in political economy over time. T.H. Marshall's famous argument about three phases of struggles for citizenship suggests just that in relation to rights: positing an early focus on civil (contractual and property) rights, moving into demands for civil and political rights, and finally to claims for social and economic rights (Marshall, 1950) – the last increasingly pervasive since the demise of actually existing Marxism. Since

Marshall wrote, still further categories of rights have proliferated, notably cultural rights and rights to self-determination.

Regulation too has shifted its political resonance. Once its connotations were part of the staple of social democratic interventionist welfare states, regulating not only prices and market access but also environmental, discrimination, and health and safety issues. But regulation more recently has become increasingly associated with stabilizing or disciplining market interactions, rather than modulating them or redistributing their outcomes. In the 2006 Oxford Handbook of Public Policy, regulation appears only in tandem with privatization, in a section discussing rationales of policy intervention (Scott, 2006). From this perspective, regulation is a stable and predictable means for protecting the individual property rights of corporate actors – a strategy for facilitating individual choice and exchange, rather than directly promoting substantively-defined collective goals.

But if new political resonances for both rights and regulation are proliferating, each new category of rights, or fresh resonance of regulation, overlays the existing ones. This creates an expanding menu of possible political salience, undermining the credibility of neat dichotomous oppositions. Once we might have suggested that rights claims act as constraints on state discretion while regulation allows the state to flex its muscles. Now, as the concluding chapter by Pahuja has argued, international financial institutions' regulatory policies constrain state discretion, making the state the object rather than the subject of regulation (for example, World Bank conditionality). Meanwhile, rights-based critiques of such policies open up avenues for re-energizing state discretion, making states the hope of, rather than a threat to, rights-claimers (for example, the United Nations' claim to reclaim state regulatory autonomy for social programmes by stressing the legal obligations of states that have entered into international treaties protecting social and economic human rights).

The muddy nature of the political salience of rights and regulation may mirror the increasing muddiness of ideological cleavages more generally, signalling an underlying drift towards a pragmatic politics focused on 'what works'. There is something rather striking about the increasing pervasiveness of both rights and regulation in political life more generally. They displace what once might have been directly ideological conflict in the democratic arena, channelling it into the relatively technocratic interstices of disputing processes that operate ostensibly independently from politics. Consider how surprising it would have been to observers in the 1970s to predict that the World Bank in the new century would be calling for the establishment of regulatory agencies the world over as part of essential services reform – or that the European Court of Justice would be interpreting and enforcing the details of a right to a healthy environment.

The triads are once again helpful in suggesting what is happening here. The World Bank's enthusiasm for regulation arguably demonstrates just the kind of rhetorical and symbolic appeal that we earlier speculated might only accrue to rights. We could analyse this enthusiasm in terms of an attempt to name a felt wrong, blame a wrongdoer and articulate it as a formal claim. Noting that the Bank is calling for *independent* regulators, not for the return of powerful state discretion, we see that the felt wrong is that of politically arbitrary behaviour, and the wrongdoer is the politician who exercises unstructured discretion. We could also view the entry of the European Court of Justice into the business of interpreting the right to a healthy environment as providing detailed rules for structuring state discretion from a position independent of everyday political accountability pressures, one which can be monitored and enforced without recourse to politics.

Seen from this perspective, both rights and regulation have become markers of *non-majoritarian* governance; both limit the scope of democratic politics for influencing trajectories of social change. This does not make them any less political, as many if not all of the chapters in this volume have insisted. But it does alter the location of politics, the language in which it is conducted, and the accessibility of opportunities to participate in it. Future research could explore the extent to which current directions in rights claims and regulatory demands, and particularly frameworks where the two intersect, catalyse a flight from politics. Do interdependent frameworks of rights and regulation remove issues from collective control? Do they de-emphasize dissent and conflict, whether through the neutral expertise focus of regulation or by virtue of the ethical value consensus underpinning a rights claim?

Exploring the specificities of how the two interact can be done through the lens of the two triads. Where interdependent structures of rights and regulation are shaped primarily by concerns of rule-making, monitoring and enforcement, a drift to technocratic governance may be pervasive. Where the original animating sense of a felt wrong still has strong purchase – the 'naming, blaming and claiming' dimension of interdependent structures of rights and regulation – the political dimension may be more visible and salient.

Of course, both these dynamics will often be present at the same time: that is, a growing tendency for rights and regulation to intersect in technocratic ways, and intensifying political controversy over just that intersection. A technically opaque yet highly politicized system of governance could be a recipe for instability – or it could be a precondition for reinvigorating increasingly stale perceptions of the social value of the rule of law. Whatever direction actual political events take, the scholarly juxtaposition of the social practices of claiming rights and enforcing regulation can provide a helpful framework for elaborating a research agenda that reintegrates these hitherto disparate strands of sociolegal scholarship.

PART 1
Rights and Regulation:
Contrasting Forms and Logics?

Chapter 2

Form and Substance in Labour Market Policies

Orly Lobel[1]

The history of legal thought since the turn of the century is the history of the decline of a particular set of distinctions – those that, taken together, constitute the liberal way of thinking about the social world. Those distinctions are state/society, public/private, individual/group, right/power, property/sovereignty, contract/tort, law/policy, legislature/ judiciary, objective/subjective, reason/fiat, freedom/coercion (Kennedy, 1982).

Introduction

In the recent history of declining dichotomies in legal thought, the regulation/rights dichotomy has remained pervasive in policy-making consciousness. In particular, the field of employment and labour law serves as a good illustration of the divide between the administrative impulse to regulate the market and the adjudicative impulse to protect individual rights. Employment law is concerned with both individual relationships and with macro market policy. A rights framework in employment law has focused on the individual entitlements of either workers or employers. In contrast, the focus of social regulation of economic markets has been the overall welfare-maximization in the labour market, taking a utilitarian approach to each individual case in order to achieve macro-ends. Further, while the idiom of rights is universal and deontological, regulation has largely been understood as consequentialist and instrumentalist. Finally, while regulation is traditionally thought to require bureaucratic control and expertise, rights have been developed as the subject of general adjudication.

Workplace law and policy straddle between these two senses of micro entitlements and macro social engineering of market relations. The field constitutes a myriad of norms and doctrines ranging from constitutional law principles, through statutory legislation, to common law doctrines developed by both state and federal courts. There are often overlapping norms, protections and remedies. Moreover, enforcement schemes widely vary, ranging from individual litigation to government enforcement. By and large, the starting point of all contexts of work law is contractual relations supplemented with doctrines and statutory protections. Over the twentieth century however, American work law has been fragmented into distinct areas of 'employment

---

1   I would like to thank Bronwen Morgan and the other participants of the Oxford Summer Institute of Law and Society (2005) for invaluable input.

protection law', 'labour law', 'employment discrimination' and the tax-orientated 'employee benefits law'.[2] Each subfield is dominated by a particular idea of the law – government regulation, privatized collective action, individual rights and contractual duties. More than simply substantive divisions, these sub-categories reveal historical developments in regulatory theory and practice, as they vary in the public and private mechanisms each undertakes as means for social control. In other words, the sub-fields of work law correspond with ideas about modes of effective and legitimate social regulation, creating contrived form/substance alignments. While some questions have been resolved through legislation, others areas developed through ad hoc adjudication. Similarly, while some areas are federally regulated, others are controlled by state law. For example, statutory regulation of employment relations begun with the states' worker compensation systems in the late nineteenth century, while a federal system concerned with preventative regulation of occupational risk was established only in the second half of the twentieth century. Finally, while some issues are addressed through an elaborate regulatory scheme, other contexts are set out to be resolved through individual entitlement claiming. In particular, this chapter will contrast the context of workplace safety, enforced by a public administrative agency relying on the framework of regulation, with anti-discrimination claims, enforced primarily by private litigation using the framework of rights.

This chapter argues that while form/substance alignments between rights and regulation are historically contingent, they have in some cases distorted and limited the possibilities of social justice reform. The chapter describes how the framework of minimum standards in employment regulation, focusing in particular on the context of minimum occupational safety requirements, contrasts with the framework of employment anti-discrimination rights-based litigation. Furthermore, the chapter explores ways in which the next generation of anti-discrimination strategies and risk regulation strategies in a new labour market era are finding points of convergence between these categories of policies. As other chapters in this volume suggest, there are ways in which the rights and regulation frameworks intersect to allow hybrid institutional designs that are better suited in addressing complex socio-economic realties than each framework alone.

The two administrative agencies that were founded around the same time a half a century ago to administer workplace safety and equality were each envisioned as embodying different roles, which flowed from the dichotomy of regulation/rights. In the first area, the Occupational Safety and Health Administration (OSHA) was established as a paradigmatic regulatory agency. Its mandate was to promulgate rules and to strictly enforce them through inspections and fines. By contrast, in the area of anti-discrimination, the equal employment opportunity commission (EEOC) was constituted as the guardian of individual rights of non-discrimination. It was not given the power to issue binding rules but rather its role was to investigate, litigate, and resolve individual cases in which the rights of equal protection at work were breached. The rights/regulation distinction that developed in these policy areas are pervasive in workplace policies. Yet, increasingly, the limits of each framework alone are striking. Regulation is considered entrenched and rules have the quality of

---

2   See also Lobel (2006).

quickly becoming obsolete. By contrast, rights are understood to last the test of time. Unlike regulatory rules that are codified in statutory law, rights develop incrementally, in better sync with changing social realities. Because of its universal quality, the language of rights has also proven more politically salient than regulation discourse, mobilizing more social movements around issues such as non-discrimination than occupational safety. On the other hand, rights often lack the backup of a structured administration to ensure their enforcement. The gap between the declared rights and the continued reality of lack of their realization can be counter-productive and result in disenchantment and scepticism about the power of law to bring change. The final section of the paper will discuss recent developments, indicating that increasingly both OSHA and the EEOC are finding the separation between rights and regulation limiting and inadequate and are experimenting with ways to bring the two worlds of regulation and rights together. The sub-fields of work law reveal the contingencies and challenges of institutional design. Today, as agencies increasingly focus on the role of non-state actors in effectively advancing policy goals, the forms of rights and regulation have become less distinct and policy makers are finding new ways to draw on the strength of both frameworks for better implementation.

Whose Rights? A Brief History of American Work Law

Employment relations in the USA are constantly evolving as society's values and economic conditions change. In turn, employment law has been characterized as a hotchpotch of common law doctrines, statutes, administrative regulation and rights (Finkin, 2003, 413). These laws have been developed incrementally, in a fractured way, often in response to moments of heightened labour market unrest. Originally, American employment law followed the English common law of master and servant. Accordingly, the feudal notion of a presumed one year job security was followed in the early phases of the founding American colonies. Yet, during the mid-nineteenth century, the idea of freedom of contract proved dominant in industrializing America. By the end of the nineteenth century, with no exception, all-American states adopted a presumption of at-will employment, in which the employment relationship could be terminated by either side at any point and for any reason. The at-will regime fit well with a *laissez faire* capitalist ideology that informed American courts during the late nineteenth century and early twentieth century. Famously known for lending its name to a defining phase in American adjudication, *Lochner v New York* was a 1905 case in which the US Supreme Court struck down a New York State law prohibiting bakers from working more than 60 hours a week. The Lochner Court declared: 'The right to purchase or to sell labour is part of the liberty protected by [the Fourteenth] Amendment, unless there are circumstances which exclude the right' (*Lochner v New York* 1905, 53). The *Lochner* era signified the courts' insistence that the constitutional rights of freedom of contract and property meant no regulation by government. Between 1905 and 1935, contract and property rights were used to justify the striking down of protective laws designed to improve worker health and safety as well as to enable collective bargaining and union membership. The court granted injunctions against labour strikes and struck down laws making it a crime to fire an employee because of union membership, all in reliance upon the notions of constitutional rights. Incrementally, however, the notion of absolute freedoms and property rights was challenged both by new economic realities and by developments in legal thought. The Great Depression presented new dire economic conditions that made it difficult for a continued faith in the invisible hand of the free market and in the stable coherent concept of absolute rights. Mass unemployment and wage deflation brought a public call for government intervention in the economy. Consequently, the New Deal government rejected the individualistic, formalist approach to market relationships and introduced macro social engineering through comprehensive regulation of collective bargaining. President Roosevelt's goals were to revive the vitality of the market by getting people back to work, raising employment conditions, and thereby reinvigorating private consumption. At the same time, in legal thought, the legal realists destabilized the idea that 'a right' mandated particular distributional results. The realists showed how property rights were in effect a bundle of relationships between differently situated people with different interests, rather than a unified object (Radin, 1938; Grey, 1980; Penner, 1996). Realist understandings further developed the notion that rights are indeterminate, historically contingent, and indeed, subject to manipulation by those who are better positioned to have an effect on legal interpretation and enforcement (Tushnet, 1984). Thus, the New Deal era signified a transformative moment in American law, in which the market was to be reordered and questions of 'whose rights' in employment relations were to be opened up for government resolution. Enacted in 1935, the National Labour Relations Act (NLRA) was considered a revolution in the regulation of work (National Labour Relations Act 1935).

The NLRA signified a new era of direct state intervention in regulating market relations. The act provided a framework for union organizing, collective bargaining and industrial peace that was aimed to simultaneously improve work relations and work conditions. The main hope was that the NLRA framework of collective bargaining would render the market more equitable, and would, at the same time, reduce conflict among labour and management. Moreover, preceding the Civil Rights Act of 1964, the courts in interpreting the NLRA established a standard for non-discrimination of workers by unions. Despite an omission in the NLRA of an anti-discrimination standard, the courts developed an implicit duty of the labour union to represent fairly each of the workers in the bargaining unit (*Steele v Louisville and N.R. Co.* 1944).[3] The same New Deal period also established a floor for individual employment relations. For the residual context of non-unionized workplaces, the Fair Labour Standards Act enacted in 1938 mandated a federal minimum wage and overtime compensation for work exceeding 40 hours per week.

Collective bargaining was meant to allow negotiation and coordination of work relations through the concerted action of workers. However, in order for it to be effective, bargaining had to be based on an elaborate set of procedural conditions, including the methods of electing unions, selecting representatives and providing for dispute resolution. Ironically, the notion of a 'right to work' was appropriated

---

3   (1944) 323 U.S. 192. The rule of fair representation was further applied to the NLRA, in *Ford Motor Co. v. Huffman* (1953) 345 U.S. 330.

by anti-union campaigns seeking to bar unionization. By 1947, over a dozen states passed 'right to work' laws, which generally outlaw union security clauses and are designed to curtail the ability of unions to expand membership through closed shop requirements for newly hired workers (Gall, 1988). Most recently, the number of unionized workers has dropped to less than 8 per cent of the private sector labour force (Bureau of Labour Statistics, 2004). Like in the prior era of formalist notions of property 'rights' trumping government regulation, the 'right to work' campaigns reveal how the language of rights can be adopted by competing political agendas and from various employer/employee perspectives:

> Since supporters of right to work laws regard unions as monopolistic forces, their decline is seen as a positive contribution to efficient market functioning. From that premise, it logically follows that right to work laws promote economic growth and further policy discussion is moot. Unionists, however, dispute that 'free markets' always lead to distributive outcomes consistent with our general notions of social fairness ... [T]he NLRA lent itself to conflicting policy aims; on the one hand, the ends of wealth redistribution and increased consumer demand required worker solidarity, while on the other hand, the goal of individual liberty respected the workers' decision to join a company union or no union. Right to work laws are an iteration of the enduring American theme of individual interests versus state compulsion (Hogler, 2005, 137).

Fraught with tension and resistance, the collective framework never met its promise of an overall reordering of market relations. Ironically, at least part of the decline of collective bargaining is the result of the regulation/rights dichotomy which was embodied in the NLRA itself. While the NLRA meant to provide protection to workers who sought to unionize, it also protected the right of individual workers not to join unions. In the decades that followed, unionization had reached its peak and continues today a steady and dramatic downward trend. By the mid-1960s, the hope that collective bargaining would establish the primary mode of regulating employment relations was fading. Unionization was in decline and a majority of workers in the American labour market were without collective representation.

The contest over what receives legal recognition as a 'right to work' reflects the broader dilemmas embedded in employment policy. With the decline of collective bargaining as the primary mode of regulating work relations, subsequent years brought more labour and employment law legislation. In contrast to the New Deal political call for labour reform, the civil rights movement of the 1960s called for equality in the workplace using not the collective unity language of former decades but the language of equal protection rights for the individuals of particular identity groups. In 1964, Title VII was enacted, prohibiting employment discrimination based on race, sex, colour, religion, and national origin. During this period, rights discourse captured the popular imagination and mobilized social action. Title VII established the Equal Employment Opportunity Commission as an independent administrative agency to support and promote the act. In the years that followed, more legislative initiatives resulted in more anti-discrimination statutes, including the Age Discrimination in Employment Act (ADEA), the Americans with Disability Act (ADA), and parallel state laws pertaining to equality at work. The Great Society Congress of the mid-1960 and early 1970s enacted dozens of laws designed to protect workers, consumers and citizens in their market interactions. In those years, new economic and social regulation – including the Clean Air Act, the Clean Water Act, the Safe Drinking Water Act, the Resource Conservation and Recovery Act, the Comprehensive Environmental Response, Compensation, and Liability Act, the Toxic Substances Control Act, the Food, Drug and Cosmetic Act, the Atomic Energy Act, the Consumer Product Safety Act, the Federal Hazardous Substances Act, the motor vehicle safety laws and the Occupational Safety and Health Act (the OSH Act) – was passed by the Federal legislature (see Sunstein, 1990). The OSH Act enacted in 1970 authorized the newly founded Occupational Safety and Health Administration (OSHA) to regulate toxins so as 'to assure[], to the extent feasible ... that no employee will suffer material impairment of health or functional capacity.'

The following sections introduce some of the differences between the two agencies, the EEOC, founded to protect the right of equal employment, and OSHA, founded to regulate the field of workplace safety. Two different modes of reasoning were developed in the subfields of individual employment safety protections and employment anti-discrimination. The regulation of occupational risk largely followed a regulatory logic, while employment discrimination developed upon a rights-based model. As will be evident, both frameworks are only lately benefiting from a more interrelated discussion between rights advocacy and economic reasoning. Interestingly, while each of these subfields has a different point of departure, there have been points of convergence in recent years building upon both the strength and weaknesses of regulation and rights.

Decoupled Frames of Safety and Equality: Rights without Regulation; Regulation without Rights

The Regulatory Model: Safety Regulation and OSHA

The regulation of safety since the 1970s has been typified by regulatory command-and-control. The Occupational Safety and Health Administration (OSHA) was founded in 1970 with the mission to ensure safety for every working man and woman. While this mandate could have been understood as granting individual absolute rights to safety (as with the prevailing understanding of equality rights), the agency and the courts have understood the mandate as requiring a regulatory approach which must take a balanced and limited approach to occupational safety. The language of the OSH Act itself speaks of 'feasibility', 'reasonability', 'appropriate standards', pointing to the demands of compromises between economic considerations of workplace production and the interest of safety. In practice, OSHA's work is divided into two phases – rule-making and enforcement. First, the agency must promulgate safety and health standards that address various hazards in workplaces. Second, OSHA's compliance officers perform inspections of the workplaces. If a violation is detected, the compliance officers issue citations and impose fines on the employer.

OSHA's rule-making activities have been some of the most contested among agency action in the USA. In fact, with few exceptions, virtually every standard that OSHA attempted to promulgate has been attacked in court, often by both employer and worker groups. OSHA's practice of adopting substantive rules and enforcing these rules invariably on all firms has perpetuated the image of an agency that is insensitive to the costs of its regulatory demands. These realities of top-down detailed regulation and zealous enforcement have led to intense resistance by industry. The Act requires the agency to establish permitted levels of risk and OSHA standards are subject to judicial review under the Administrative Procedure Act. In the landmark *Benzene* case, the Fifth Circuit invalidated OSHA's standard for safe toxic exposure, stating that the agency failed to quantify the benefits that would be achieved by reducing permissible benzene exposure from 10ppm to 1ppm (*Indus. Union Dept. v Am. Petroleum Inst.* 1980). The Supreme Court, upholding the decision, stated that before the agency could issue a standard, it must determine that the standard is 'reasonably necessary and appropriate to remedy a significant risk of material health impairment'. The decision exemplifies the distance between the scrutiny that the courts use in the case of safety regulation and the alternative notion of a universal 'right to safety', which arguably could have included not only 'significant risks' but any risks, not only 'material health impairments' but any health hazard, and not only what is 'reasonably necessary' but any action that could remedy the wrong of occupational safety and health risks.

The judicial review terms of reasonableness and appropriateness remain contested. In a subsequent case after *Benzene*, the Supreme Court rejected a strict cost-benefit requirement on the agency's rule-making process, observing that:

> Congress itself defined the basic relationship between costs and benefits, by placing the 'benefit' of worker health above all other considerations save those making attainment of this 'benefit' unachievable … cost-benefit analysis by OSHA is not required by the statute because feasibility analysis is (*Indus. Union Dept. v Am. Petroleum Inst.* 1980, *supra* notes 14, 2490).

The tension between the right to a safe workplace and the inherent need to take economic considerations into account is clear in this decision. In the next major toxin exposure case before the Federal Supreme Court, the Court in fact rejected a strict cost-benefit requirement but emphasized that 'feasibility' includes economic feasibility (*Am. Textile Mfrs. Inst., Inc. v Donovan*, 1981). The Court defined feasibility as 'capable of being done, executed or effected.' The Court emphasize that a feasibility standard was more protective than a cost-benefit requirement because it placed the health of workers above all other considerations but for those that would make the regulation unattainable.

In subsequent years and still today, these definitions and requirements have been debated in the political arena, in adjudication and in scholarly writing. For example, in a case in which OSHA's attempt to regulate air contaminant standards for 428 toxic substances, the court struck down the new standards because the agency failed to prove 'significant risk' posed by each substance and failed to establish the 'technological and economic feasibility' for the regulation of each substance. In addition to intense judicial review, Congress as well has moved to limit OSHA's capacity to regulate safety. Most recently, Congress revoked the much anticipated ergonomics standards on which the agency had been working for years. This was the first time Congress used its power under the Congressional Review Act of 1996, which allows Congress to consider regulations once they are enacted by administrative agencies. These cases and conflicts illustrate the highly contested field of occupational risk regulation and the pervasive limitations that have been incrementally imposed on the agency under the regulatory mandate it was given. The impact of judicial review, private resistance, and new legislative hurdles on issuing administrative rules have all burdened and ossified administrative rule-making in general and OSHA's standard setting activities in particular (Comprehensive Regulatory Reform Act 1995; see also Mashaw, 1996; Jordan, 2000). As a result, while in some areas detailed standards have produced little safety improvement, other areas, posing significant risks, have been left dangerously unregulated (for example, see Viscusi, 1983).[4]

The second major function of OSHA as a regulatory agency is enforcement of safety compliance. At the same time that regulatory rule-making has presented a myriad of challenges, regulatory enforcement has similarly proven to have large limitations. The agency's role of enforcement through inspection has been highly difficult and contested. OSHA's enforcement practices are traditionally top-down random wall-to-wall inspections, seeking violations of its substantive rules in various worksites, followed by prosecution and sanctions. Compared to the vast amount of workplaces OSHA is required to monitor, the resources of the agency are greatly limited. With a staff of little over 2,000 employees, today's OSHA is in charge of the safety of more than one hundred and fifteen million American workers at over eight million worksites (AFL-CIO, 2004). The agency has relatively few inspectors and limited capacities to deter private firms in order to ensure compliance. In effect, the agency can only inspect a fraction of the workplaces with which it is charged and employers rarely view the possibility of enforcement as a real threat to their operations. Similarly, the sanctions in the case of safety violations are limited and are generally not enough to alter behaviour post-inspection (Lobel, 2005). In practice, fines are routinely decreased after negotiation and citations are often downgraded from 'wilful violations' to less severe citations (Barstow, 2003, A1). Most importantly, enforcement has been challenged as counter-productive when firms become increasingly averse to working with the agency toward mutually beneficial results (Lobel, 2005). Indeed, studies indicate that repeat inspections have only modest effects on compliance with OSHA standards (Weil, 1992). Often, firms engage in merely temporary fixes rather than undergoing systemic sustainable changes in their risk management (Simon and Sparrow, 1997, 6–7).

In the early years of the OSH Act, despite these significant limitations of operating solely within the regulatory framework of rule-making and inspection, the regulation of risk largely focused on the desirability of top-down rules framing the debate in cost-benefit terms. Other aspects of the legal process, including the crucial stages of implementation and the ways in which government can diversify its interaction with regulated parties remained relatively undeveloped. Indeed, OSHA is a particularly interesting example in understanding the limits of a regulatory framework alone because, as we explored, since the agency's establishment within the US Labour

---

4   Viscusi argues that while OSHA regulates standards with little benefits, it does not regulate the significant risks of carcinogenic substances.

Department in the early 1970s, the agency and its regulatory practices have been the source of controversy and conflict. The agency is considered the paradigm of regulation. In political debates, the agency has been described as cultivating 'a culture of regulatory excess that eats away at the vitality of our economy' (Hutchison, 1995). In academic circles, OSHA has been described as the paradigmatic case of bureaucratic failure and regulatory unreasonableness (Bardach and Kagan, 1982). Nevertheless, the perception of an omnipresent agency does not reflect the reality of a highly under-staffed and under-funded agency. Occupational injury and disease rates remain relatively high (Afl-Cio 13th Annual Report on Occupational Safety, *supra* note 18). Despite the severity of occupational related care, exceeding two hundred billion dollars per year, government spending on workplace safety has never reached the levels of other social issues and OSHA's budget continues to steadily decline (Goldstein and Cohen, 2004). Although OSHA received wide regulatory authority, the legislative mandate provides the agency scarce resources to carry through the regulations and actively enforce them.

The Rights Model: The EEOC and Workplace Anti-Discrimination Policy

Founded through the Civil Rights Act of 1964, the equal employment opportunity commission (EEOC) was entrusted with the enforcement of Title VII, the leading law on workplace non-discrimination. Title VII applies to private employers, labour unions and employment agencies, and prohibits discrimination in recruitment, hiring, wages, assignment, promotions, benefits, discipline, discharge, layoffs and almost all other aspects of work relations (history of the EEOC). Similarly to OSHA, the EEOC has struggled for power vis-à-vis the Federal Supreme Court and Congress. Unlike OSHA however, the EEOC did not receive rule making power under Title VII. Instead, the EEOC issues 'guidelines' that are considered non-binding.

In 1972, the Equal Employment Opportunity Act was enacted and Congress amended Title VII to grant the EEOC prosecutorial power (42 USC § 2000e-5 (f) (1) 1991). Yet, it still denied the EEOC the authority to issue binding regulation under Title VII. Demonstrative of the historical contingency in the structures of regulatory authority, in 1978 the EEOC received the power to issue binding rules and regulations under the Age Discrimination in Employment Act (ADEA). Similarly, in 1990, with the enactment of Americans with Disabilities Act (ADA), the EEOC was granted the authority to issue binding regulations under the ADA (Age Discrimination in Employment Act of 1967, 29 USC § 628 (1988); ADA, 42 USC §§ 12101-12213 (1990). Thus, today the EEOC lacks regulatory authority in the context of Title VII, while having rule-making powers in the context of the ADEA and the ADA.

In the early days of the EEOC, the Supreme Court tended to defer to its guidelines as an expert agency. In 1971, in the famous case of *Griggs*, which laid the foundation of disparate impact discrimination theory, Chief Justice Burger relied on the EEOC's guideline that interpreted Title VII to permit only intrinsically business related screening tests for job applicants (*Griggs v Duke Power* 1971, 433). The Chief Justice stated that 'the administrative interpretation of the Act by the enforcing agency is entitled to great deference. Since the Act and its legislative history support the Commission's construction, this affords good reason to treat the guidelines as expressing the will of Congress' (*Griggs v Duke Power* 1971, 433–4). In subsequent decisions, however, instead of giving 'great deference' as the Court did in Griggs, the Court declared that when enacting Title VII Congress had not given the EEOC power to promulgate rules or regulations and as such the courts may properly 'accord less weight to such guidelines than to administrative regulations which Congress has declared shall have the force of law' (*Griggs v Duke Power* 1971, 141). This minimal deference has led commentators to argue that '[i]n the area of federal anti-discrimination law, the US Supreme Court often prefers to "chart its own course" rather than to defer to Equal Employment Opportunity Commission ("EEOC" of "Commission") regulations and guidance interpreting these laws' (Hart, 2006). Indeed, Congress has several times passed legislation that overrules certain Supreme Court decisions in disagreement with EEOC guidelines (*History of the EEOC*; ADEA of 1967; ADA, 1990). It should be noted however, that even though the EEOC Guidelines on Title VII have no legal authority, private parties tend to pay close attention to their guidance. This again blurs the lines between binding rules under a traditional regulatory approach and other administrative activities under a rights orientated approach.

The area of anti-discrimination, similarly to risk regulation, presents deep doctrinal uncertainty about the scope of statutory protection. The declaration that every working man and woman has the right to equality in the workplace fails to solve the details of prohibited discriminatory behaviour. Moreover, the idea that rights provide absolute protection and are not subject to balance with cost, as compared for example with the regulatory framework of occupation safety, is largely misleading. For example, in ADA litigation, courts find themselves in the difficult position of having to consider public safety concerns, costs and effects of large accommodation demands (Issacharoff and Nelson, 2001; Jolls, 2001). Similarly, the courts have had to develop doctrines that give substance to the defence of bona fide occupational qualification (BFOQ), which serves as the most direct exception to Title VII and the ADEA (42 USC § 2,000e-2(e)). The BFOQ allows employers to explicitly disqualify certain classes of applicants when such exclusion is 'reasonably necessary to the normal operation of that particular business' (29 USC § 623(f)(1)). Clearly, as the case law in these contexts readily reveals, the framing of legal policies in terms of rights, rather than regulation, does not exclude the necessity to further define, balance and compile detailed rules about the meaning of the protective legislation. The questions brought before the courts in the discrimination area demonstrate a wide interpretive gap between the declaration of equal rights and the implementation of these rights in particular contexts. Courts have been widely diverse in their holdings and various social claims and interests in the field of workplace anti-discrimination have often reached strategic bargaining and adversarial stalemates, rather than positive, collaborative steps toward the goal of equal employment.

On the enforcement side, the EEOC was set up to be the gatekeeper for processing all charges of discrimination under Title VII. Any individual claimant who believes their rights were infringed under Title VII must go through the mandatory step of filing with the EEOC before they are issued a 'right-to-sue' letter by the EEOC (Civil Rights Act of 1964 § 706, 78 stat: 259–61). The EEOC investigates the charge and determines whether there is probable cause of Title VII violation. The idea behind this complicated procedural requirement before filing suit is that plaintiffs would be encouraged to reach conciliation and resolve the dispute without litigation. Similarly, the remedies provided in Title VII also reflect an intermediate ground between fully-fledged private litigation of civil disputes and a more regulatory administrative approach. Title VII empowers workers to vindicate their legal rights as private claimants, yet the public interest of encouraging settlement and eliminating discrimination at large led the legislature to cap monetary remedies, while allowing for attorney fees (as a way of encouraging private claiming of rights) as well as reinstatement (as a way of ensuring the return of a minority group to the workplace with the aim to incrementally create more equitable workplaces). Moreover, the courts have encouraged arbitration arrangements by authorizing the practice of employers that require employees to sign a contractual obligation to arbitrate even when the worker has a statutory claim under Title VII (for example, see *Gilmer v Interstate Johnson Lane Corp.*, 1991). Thus, despite setting up Title VII enforcement as a court litigated rights framework, courts regularly defer to private dispute resolution.

In sum, successful strategies for realizing the rights to equality have been complex and non-evident. Even though Title VII was set up as an individual rights litigation framework, it has evolved to a far more multi-dimensional system. In light of these developments, many have begun to question the limited role of the EEOC as the regulatory agency authorized to enforce anti-discrimination laws. As others have identified in this volume, rights discourse is recognized by social movements as a mobilizing and consciousness-raising strategy. Yet, in order to reach meaningful reform, rights require regulatory structures in order to be effectively implemented. Inevitably, in action, there is a need to set priorities and recognize trade-offs among different goals and problems. Rights speak in a language of urgency and immediacy and present themselves in absolute terms. Unlike rights which have this imperative quality, regulation embodies the language of compromise. Regulatory rule making is couched in questions about economic efficiency. Because of the practical juxtaposition between rights and regulation, it is highly fruitful for agencies and courts to recognize the perils and promises of each of these two sets of frameworks.

Systemic Approaches to Safety and Equality

The workplace is fraught with struggles and inequality. Almost an inherent characteristic of the separation between ownership and labour, adversarial interests between employers and employees is an ongoing reality. However, policy makers are increasingly recognizing potential synergies and points in which interests can align with the right set of incentives. As described above, the Great Society era, from the mid-1960s onwards, brought established new federal administrative agencies. The design and operation of these agencies corresponded roughly with the two approaches/fields of normative ordering that flow from the paradigms of regulation and of rights. Yet each of these frames by themselves has proven limiting in reaching the policies they were designed to promote. Moreover, the nature of work itself has changed in various ways (see generally, Lobel, 2003). The adoption of more contingent, flexible, lean and outsourced employment is a major trend of today's labour market. Closely connected is the ongoing process of workforce globalization, including capital flows to developing countries and widespread migration flows of workers from poor countries to developed countries like the US and the UK. Finally, the move to higher technology production in some sectors, as well as the increase in the service sectors, has again presented new realities to employment relationships. The new workplace is thus marked by increased diversity in production and heterogeneity of workforces, a shift from goods to services, and a decrease in the percentage of workers employed in stable full-time jobs. All of these new realities further exacerbate the limitations in using a single framework for policy-making in each employment law subfield. Because the workforce and the labour market today are intensely diverse, complex and dynamic, there is a need to diversify the approaches of law and the legal process.

'Cooperation instead of adversarialism' has been the motto of administrative agencies in the past decade. Government agencies such as OSHA and the EEOC are experimenting with shifts from extensive elaboration of prohibitive standards and high rates of inspection to facilitation of self-regulation and programs of collaborative, semi-voluntary compliance. Both agencies are focusing more today on implementation and compliance, which in turn dynamically give content and change the initial frames of regulation and rights.

In response to the limitations of each of the settings under which OSHA and the EEOC have been operating, as well as a response to the changing nature of work, both agencies have in fact been moving closer in their practices. As will be elaborated below, both OSHA and the EEOC have been experimenting with new policies and forms of action with the goal of better addressing the nature of the new world of work. Indeed, these agencies are not alone in the development of the principles of administrative governance and the role of the regulatory state. Recent years have brought fundamental transformations in the range of possibilities for governmental action. Both in practice and in legal research, there has been a growing interest in the possibilities of third way approaches to regulation and public action in the new political economy. Policy makers recognize that a better understanding of the comparative advantages of different institutional mechanisms and the breadth of the legal process spectrum will increase the effectiveness of policies in most, if not all, legal fields. In effect, a diverse range of contemporary social challenges, including work relations, safety and health, consumption, equal protection, welfare and sustainable economies can benefit from an integrated analysis through the perspective of public/private partnership, regulatory theory and administrative governance (Lobel, 2004a). In the article, *The Renew Deal: The Fall of Regulation and the Rise of Governance*, I have argued that a new governance paradigm is emerging that ties together recent developments in the political economy with advances in legal and democratic theory. The article describes the organizing principles of the governance model, consisting of increased participation of non-state actors, public/private collaboration, diversity and competition, decentralization and subsidiarity, integration of policy domains, flexibility and non-coerciveness ('soft law'), adaptability and learning, and finally, legal orchestration. These features are then considered in three leading domains of governance – new workplace policies, civic environmentalism, and cyberdemocracy. I further argue that new governance is purposely and ingeniously designed as a hybrid of different frames, drawing together elements from rival schools of thought and critical insights concerning both regulatory and market failures. Through the pragmatic synthesis of legal approaches, the emerging governance model confronts the false dilemma between 'regulation' and 'rights' in the abstract. In a subsequent article, *Setting the Agenda for New Governance Research*, I further refine the theory of new governance, elaborating on the continuing relationship between alternative and hybrid models of regulation, rights and the legal process (Lobel, 2004b).

The previously sharp divide between regulatory and rights frameworks has become more hybrid with the advent of second generation anti-discrimination strategies and new forms of workplace risk prevention in the new era. While each agency began its path from a very different stance, both agencies have been exploring the possibilities of relying more on cooperative problem-solving than on either top-down regulation or individual rights litigation. These agencies, like many others, are currently exploring the possibilities of administrative governance in an effort to rethink their traditional administrative roles:

> Public agencies encourage local institutions to solve problems by examining their own practices in relation to common metrics and by comparing themselves to their most successful peers. Problem solving operates through direct involvement of affected and responsible individuals. Information about performance drives this process. Its production and disclosure enable problems to be identified, performance to be compared, pressure for change to mount, and the rules themselves to be revised. Public bodies coordinate, encourage, and hold accountable these participatory, data-driven problem solving processes (Sturm, 2006, 268).

In response to the inadequacies of traditional regulatory approaches to safety and health regulation, OSHA recently officially declared a move away from 'command and control' regulatory strategies toward more collaborative partnerships. The agency is developing compliance assistance activities, a range of cooperative programs and the general promotion of 'a safety and health culture' through education and training, public/private alliances, and structural impact. In its early days of existence, OSHA promulgated hundreds of pages of regulation (Fleming, 1996). In effect, OSHA adopted existing industry standards. Rules were often too complex, vague, needlessly detailed, or simply unsuited to fit the realities of production and work (McGarity and Shapiro, 1993, 42). Increasingly, there has been a proven disconnect between compliance with substantive rules and the safety of workers. Standards frequently diverge from the major sources of fatalities and injuries in the workplace (for example, see Mendeloff, 1984, 353). In effect, even with perfect compliance with existing regulations, industrial safety studies predict that uniform occupational safety regulation can only prevent less than 25 per cent of occupational injury (Centers for Disease Control and Prevention, 1992, cited in Haas (2003, 205–206) at fn. 10). Rather than a result of any particular violation of existing OSHA standards, workplace accidents are most often attributable to defects in planning, internal communication, definition of responsibilities and authority, deficiencies in training, inadequate supervision, and an overarching absence of a *culture* of safety

(Bacow, 1980; Braithwaite, 1985).[5] OSHA, fraught with budgetary constraints, political resistance and a weak legal mandate, is now building on these insights. The agency is also setting out to change its regulatory image and to revive its public legitimacy by using the language of cooperation and partnership. It now speaks of the importance of prevention through the promotion of compliance cultures rather than adversarial top-down citations of hazards by the agency.

In 2004, John Henshaw, then heading OSHA, declared 'OSHA is not just a regulatory agency anymore' (Henshaw, 2004). OSHA thus increasingly emphasizes its educational and compliance assistance programs (OSH Law Committee, 2005). In practice, the agency is expanding programs under its 'Office of Cooperative Programs', that offer a safe haven from regulatory enforcement in return for a showing of self-improvement by participating firms. Firm are required to adopt internal safety programs and to conduct an analysis of safety hazards as they occur. Moreover, OSHA has also expanded its general outreach activities, encouraging the development of shared voluntary guidelines and the dissemination of information. Similarly, OSHA and other regulatory agencies increasingly issue non-binding policy statements or 'good guidance' (Lobel, 2004a, *supra* note 42). These roles are much closer to the EEOC framework of guidelines and education than to OSHA's traditional rule-making and inspection activities.

The risk however is that cooperative initiatives can also signify a decline in the political commitment to public regulation of the new workplace. Here, questions about implementation and how they relate to rights and protections become particularly crucial. A broader repertoire of agency tools in fact allows better targeting and use of the on-going availability of traditional government sanctions. An agency strapped for resources, facing a shrinking budget and extensive regulatory resistance, can in fact *upgrade* its traditional enforcement levels with sophisticated targeting and escalated sanctions, leveraging limited resources by the introduction of innovative comprehensive governance techniques. However, merely relying on positive incentives and giving up the use of coercive government sanctions risks a permissive regime that fails to deter bad faith violators. A repeated failure has been the absence of worker participation programs to improve safety. In order to adequately ensure that cooperative prevention will not be a subterfuge for regulatory evasion, employees must also be given voice and power to claim their rights to a safe environment (Lobel, 2005, *supra* note 19). Similarly, with increased transparency and public data, private actors will be able to make informed choices that consider responsible safety records. For example, reporters, consumers, sub-contractors, suppliers and workers can investigate where it was riskiest to work and whether the agency is effectively pursuing recalcitrant actors. OSHA reports that many firms that participate in their cooperative programs now require their subcontractors to also meet the elevated safety standards (Government Accountability Office, 2004, *supra* note 28). The hope is that more firms, including subcontractors, will have incentives to improve their safety practices if they are widely published. Ongoing monitoring and research of the effectiveness of these processes by the agency remains essential.

---

5   Mendeloff found that violations accounted for 13–19 per cent of 645 fatality cases that he studied.

In the realm of anti-discrimination, commentators have suggested a parallel move from an entrenched framework of individual rights claiming to a more robust set of strategies for increasing workplace equity. On the one hand, the idea of rights as universal and as 'trumps' of other interests has mobilized much interest and social debate in the area of anti-discrimination policy. Debates about the value and meanings of workplace equality have been central to the political and legal arenas, much more so than questions about regulating workplace safety. This is indeed exemplary of the notion, expressed in other chapters in this volume, that rights have the quality of political salience. On the other hand, the idea the rights are self-executing, with a declaration and individual relief, has proven to be problematic. Rights in fact signify bundles of interests and correlative powers that must receive further meaning through struggle, interpretation, and context. In light of ongoing inequalities in many area of the labour market under the rights litigation framework, many have begun to question whether the goal of anti-discrimination policies is to solve individual disputes, or rather, to promote more structural changes in the economy at large. For example, Susan Sturm has argued that providing an affirmative defence in employment discrimination litigation for employers who attempt to promote equality can have a positive effect in 'encourage[ing] the development of a dynamic regulatory regime through ongoing interaction between general legal norms and workplace problem solving' (Sturm, 2001, 489). Sturm warns against the pure rights litigation approach in employment discrimination, which she sees as inadequate in addressing the '[c]ognitive bias, structures of decision making, and patterns of interaction [that] have replaced deliberate racism and sexism as the frontier of much continued inequality' (Sturm, 2001, 460).

Even more recently, Julie Suk argues that 'if the goal of anti-discrimination law is to pursue a substantive vision of equality, greater regulation by the administrative state is warranted ... [R]egulation by the administrative state is an important and underused tool for achieving the principles of distributive justice embedded in antidiscrimination law' (Suk, 2006, 407). While rights in the courts are analysed as the search for violation and correction of past wrongs, administrative agencies can potentially take a broader approach of distributive justice, and future change. Agencies thus tend to be more proactive than courts that are reactive. Suk thus argues that 'regulation by administrative agencies is better suited to a society's collective pursuit of equality than tort-like lawsuits. With legal doctrines such as disparate impact, hostile environment, and reasonable accommodation, regulatory standards set by agencies are more appropriate, as such standards can be aimed at eradicating inequality prospectively rather than remedying specific harms after they have already occurred' (Suk, 2006, *supra* note 57). Taking a comparative perspective, the American EEOC powers are weak. Suk for example compares the EEOC to the British Equal Opportunities Commission (EOC) which has both investigative and rule making powers: 'The Government envisioned an EOC that would address industry-wide and institutional problems of discrimination, rather than remedy individual unlawful acts' (Suk, 2006, *supra* note 57). The British agency also has greater administrative enforcement powers, and is designed to study the market, collect information and promote industry-wide change. Suk thus argues in favour of a shift toward more 'regulatory approaches to discrimination and inequality', wherein 'Once the duties of employers in antidiscrimination law are understood through the lens of distributive justice, it is up to the administrative state to regulate and eradicate group-based inequalities' (Suk, 2006, *supra* note 57).

The EEOC has been slow in moving in that direction. It has however increased the number of guidelines that provide structural guidance to private industry, focusing on ex ante prevention and elimination of discriminatory practices, rather than ex-post rights dispute resolution. For example, in its sexual harassment guidelines, the EEOC states:

> Prevention is the best tool for the elimination of sexual harassment. An employer should take all steps necessary to prevent sexual harassment from occurring, such as affirmatively raising the subject, expressing strong disapproval, developing appropriate sanctions, informing employees of their right to raise and how to raise the issue of harassment under Title VII, and developing methods to sensitize all concerned (29 C.F. R. § 604.11(f)).

The agency has also recently compiled a Task Force Report on 'best' private sector Equal Employment Opportunity Policies, Programs, and practices in the private sector (Jones, 1998; Zaring, 2006). According to the task force's chair:

> While the Commission is primarily a law enforcement agency responsible for compliance with the specific laws that we enforce, the Commission also has an important role in facilitating voluntary compliance through education, training, outreach, and policy guidance. A primary goal of the Task Force was to promote voluntary compliance. This was the aim of its examination of business practices that are consistent with employers' business priorities (usually producing quality goods or services and turning a profit) as well as with their EEO obligations and diversity objectives. We anticipated that employers would take this opportunity to showcase those policies, programs, and practices of which they are particularly proud. The Task Force also set out to catalogue its findings so that they would be useful to employers, especially smaller and medium-sized employers that are less likely to employ professional personnel and legal staffs to address these concerns internally (Jones, 1998, *supra* note 62).

In general, the EEOC has been developing its practices of alternative dispute resolution, education, outreach and technical assistance (Jones, 1998, *supra* note 62). In the past decade, similar to OSHA's strategic planning, the EEOC has announced its focus on the promotion of equal opportunity and prevention of discrimination through education and outreach, voluntary resolution of disputes where appropriate and possible, and, as a last resort, strong and fair enforcement through litigation (Jones, 1998, *supra* note 62). Similarly to OSHA's focus on cooperative compliance, a caveat for these developments is that cooperation should not serve as a mask for merely symbolic changes and ongoing inequalities. To that end, the EEOC Task Force describes a 'best' practice as one that ensures management and employee communication and produces positive results. The challenge in the next decade will be for the agency to indeed research and monitor these initiatives and to honestly report and learn from their comparative effectiveness in the promotion of workplace equality.

Conclusion

The area of work law administration reveals ways in which the frameworks of regulation and rights developed separately yet are being brought together through new efforts to diversify policy reform strategies in the new economy. In the two contexts of workplace discrimination and occupational safety, the key questions today are about the right balance between cooperative versus coercive styles of regulation and law enforcement. Second generation anti-discrimination strategies and second-generation risk prevention initiatives are finding points of convergence and illuminate how form/substance alignments, between rights/regulation as mechanisms and as ideologies are contingent and keeping them separate can be distorting for effective policy reform. Traditionally, law suits by individual employees are used to enforce 'rights' while agency enforcement was understood as 'regulatory acts'. Yet, today rights are viewed as more multidimensional and they are understood as a bundle of powers and goals. Their normative power can contribute to sustaining ongoing reforms, learning processes and innovation in regulatory mechanisms, while new developments in regulatory theory and practice can effectuate rights and render their promise meaningful.

Chapter 3

Lawyers Using Rights Discourse in an Internet Community: Challenging and Redefining Gender Discrimination in the Legal Practice

Amanda K. Baumle[1]

Introduction

Law and society scholars have noted that rights discourse often has the power to mobilize groups and effect change, even where regulation fails to do so (Scheingold, 1974; McCann, 1994; Marshall and Barclay, 2003). The value of rights language is such that in the absence of a legal remedy, reference to a 'right' can still serve to mobilize and unite individuals in a common cause (Scheingold, 1974). This chapter explores the manner in which attorneys use rights discourse to challenge gender inequality in the workplace, and demonstrates that even those trained in the law will rely on nonexistent legal remedies to challenge perceived discrimination. Further, their use of rights discourse in the context of an Internet community evidences the potential to generate new rights and regulation regarding gender discrimination and harassment in the workplace.

Prior research has repeatedly documented the existence of gender inequality, discrimination and harassment in the legal practice, an occupation that remains male-dominated both in terms of numbers and organizational culture (Epstein, 1970; Rosenberg et al., 1993; Pierce, 1995). Gender stereotyping, sex discrimination and sexual harassment are all actionable under Title VII of the United States Civil Rights Act of 1965, as well as under many state laws. Despite the availability of legal remedies, however, women attorneys rarely sue their employers and often do not challenge discriminatory behaviour. This seemingly contradictory situation is examined in this chapter, where lawyers fail to employ the legal system to assert rights on their own behalf. In particular, the manner in which attorneys use (or fail to use) the law when opposing gender inequality in their employment is explored

---

1 I would like to thank a number of individuals who read and commented on earlier drafts of this research and/or who provided guidance during the formation of this research agenda, including Sarah N. Gatson, Dudley L. Poston Jr, Mark Fossett, Barbara Sharf, Nancy Plankey Videla, Joan Manley and Bronwen Morgan.

in order to determine whether the law can be activated to challenge, and perhaps change, gender relations in the legal practice.

If attorneys decline to use formal litigation to challenge gender inequality, the law can nonetheless still serve as a useful tool for women attorneys. Generalized notions of rights are flexible and can be transformed by the oppressed into symbols for mobilization and for change (Bourdieu, 1991; Lee, 2001). Bourdieu (1991) observes that language is a source of symbolic power, in addition to being a means of communication, which is deployed by individuals in a manner dependent on the particular situated context; thus individuals can adapt language to advance their own interests in political or social pursuits. Consequently, Lee contends that 'linguistic agency [that is, the ability to define words in new ways] ... provides an alternative to the relentless search for legal remedy' (2001, 869). In particular, as noted by Omi and Winant (1994), when movements by the oppressed advancing new understandings of racial (or gender) hegemony gain significant momentum, those in power are forced to a compromise and, thus, to a rearticulation of hegemony. When this happens, both the specific definitions of racial or gender identities are reformed, as well as the relationships between those identities. Drawing upon these notions, I examine whether attorneys might be able to call upon generalized notions of legal rights in order to mobilize individuals to pressure for change within law firm practices, forcing a rearticulation of gender identities and relationships within the legal practice.

Specifically, the use of legal discourse by members of the Greedy Associates Internet community is analysed in order to ascertain whether the website community could serve as a medium for change. I explore how the Internet community allows attorneys to assert claims to 'legal rights', as well as possible methods of instigating change through appeals to legal rights. Prior research examining the power of legal discourse has, at times, examined the role of attorneys in helping the oppressed to formulate their claims (see Sarat and Felstiner, 1988; McCann, 1994); this chapter, however, focuses on how attorneys can activate legal discourse on their own behalf.

Defining 'Gender Discrimination'

Throughout this chapter, I reference gender inequality in the legal practice and discuss different means of using the law to challenge existing inequalities. In doing so, the notion of 'discrimination' is either implicitly or explicitly present in my discussions of inequality, work done by prior researchers, and the way that members of the Greedy Associates community discuss inequality. It is useful, therefore, to provide a framework for understanding what it meant by discrimination in the context of this work, as its nesting in the law and society literature might prompt an assumption of a narrow, legalistic definition of discrimination. Discrimination, however, remains a very fluid concept, despite a wealth of literature from varying disciplines which has attempted to provide the term with a concrete definition (Baumle and Fossett, 2005). This fluidity is mirrored in the way that courts, lawyers, sociologists, politicians and various other laypersons discuss discrimination, and it is this definitional malleability which imbues the notion of discrimination with a great deal of power for prompting change. If what constitutes discrimination cannot be definitively set forth, then it is constantly vulnerable to challenges and rearticulation, serving as a powerful linguistic tool for change.

Sociologists have offered a range of definitions of discrimination that differ in the extent to which they identify characteristics of the discriminator, specify the intent of the discriminator, require a motivation for discrimination, specify groups or categories subject to discrimination or require a particular outcome of discrimination (whether it is positive or negative). Levin and Levin, for instance, suggest that discrimination consists of 'differential or unequal treatment of the members of some group or category on the basis of their group membership rather than on the basis of their individual qualities' (1982, 51). This definition does not require that the discriminator be motivated by prejudice or negative affect; instead, the discriminator could be motivated by group interest. In addition, the definition does not provide any guidance as to the type of group which can be the object of discrimination; the group could be a racial minority or majority, or it could also be individuals who graduated from a particular institution. One can see, therefore, that this definition is very general if it is applied strictly as stated; one would assume that Levin and Levin intended for the definition to cover differential treatment on the basis of an ascribed characteristic, although it is not specifically indicated.

Feagin and Eckberg, on the other hand, have provided a definition of discrimination that is much more narrowly tailored. They contend that discrimination consists of 'practices and actions of dominant race-ethnic groups that have a differential and negative impact on subordinate race-ethnic groups' (1980, 9). This definition, unlike Levin and Levin's, clearly intends to identify actions as discriminatory only if they are taken by dominant race and ethnic groups against minority groups. They specify only that the actions must have a negative impact on minority groups, regardless of the intent of the actors. Thus, Feagin and Eckberg's definition stands in stark contrast with Levin and Levin's in that it identifies a clear 'bad actor' – majority race and ethnic groups. In addition, actions taken by minority groups against majority groups apparently would not be considered discrimination under Feagin and Eckberg's definition, regardless of negative outcome or intent.

These two sociological definitions of discrimination highlight some of the lack of consensus of a clear definition of discrimination existing within just the sociological literature. As mentioned previously, definitions vary as well in other disciplines (Baumle and Fossett, 2005). A number of reasons could attribute to the lack of consensus concerning a single definition of discrimination. The overarching reason is likely attributable to the fact that viewing an act as discriminatory will differ according to race, gender, socioeconomic background, and political motivations. Further, power differentials will determine whose definition of discrimination gains dominance within the legal system. One can see simply by examining Feagin and Eckberg's definition of discrimination that definitions of discrimination can be powerfully influenced by academic or political interests. Defining discrimination as existing only in actions taken by a member of a majority racial group against a minority racial group disregards the fact that race discrimination can occur in the reverse situation, as well as within a racial group (see, for example, instances in which African-Americans of darker phenotype have asserted discrimination by those of lighter skin). In addition, Feagin and Eckberg's definition does not acknowledge discrimination on the basis of gender, age, disability, or other protected classes. Thus, the definition advanced by Feagin and Eckberg is clearly proffered for a particular purpose, rather than as a broad definition of the practice of discrimination.

Within the legal system itself, individuals also advocate varying interpretations of the concept of discrimination. Most laypersons would likely expect that statutes prohibiting discrimination, such as Title VII of the Civil Rights Act of 1964, would contain a precise definition of what constitutes discrimination. However this is not the case. Title VII prohibits employment decisions based on certain group characteristics, including race, colour, religion, sex and national origin. It further identifies some specific discriminatory acts, such as failing to hire, promote, or increase the wages of an individual because of membership in a protected group (Title VII Section 703 [a] 1964). After this general list of prohibited acts, title VII includes vague language noting that it will be unlawful 'otherwise to discriminate;' the statute fails, however, to set forth a specific definition of what it means to discriminate. The lack of a specific definition is undoubtedly attributable in large part to the difficulty in operationalizing an acceptable, encompassing definition of what it means to discriminate (as highlighted in the above discussion of sociological definitions of discrimination). Consequently, it has been left to lawyers and judges to shape the meaning of 'discrimination', with differing perspectives vying for ratification.

For instance, many contend that the definition of discrimination that has prevailed in sex discrimination decisions has been dictated by the male-dominated judicial system (MacKinnon, 1979; Baer, 1999; Nelson and Bridges, 1999). Nelson and Bridges (1999) note that the concept of comparable worth failed as a result of the judicial system accepting the unsubstantiated evidence that the market, rather than discrimination, determines pay differences between men and women. By embracing this perspective, the court accepted the definition of discrimination (or lack thereof) that was advanced by the male-dominated bureaucracy. In this manner, courts began to place barriers on what types of so-called structural inequalities fall under the definitional umbrella of 'discrimination'. Similarly, Baer (1999) and MacKinnon (1979) note that the burden of what constitutes sexual harassment has been very difficult to meet for women in large part due to the fact that white men are those who have been in the position to define what constitutes 'discrimination' in these situations. As a result, women find that many situations that create seemingly intolerable working situations are not considered 'discrimination' or 'harassment' under the law. All of these factors indicate that discrimination definitions differ in part due to who has the power to render the final decision concerning the definition, whose interests will be protected by the definition, and the race, gender and class of those individuals.

Consequently, throughout this chapter the definition of discrimination is very much determined by the context in which it is discussed, as well as the characteristics of the individual invoking its use. At times, discrimination refers to actions that could potentially be actionable under state or federal law. But discrimination, as has been discussed, is broader than what has been recognized by the judicial system. In fact, Title VII itself is quite broad in setting forth what constitutes discrimination, and it is only judicial interpretation of the statute that has narrowly curtailed rights under this law. As a result, what constitutes actionable gender inequality under the statutes perhaps exceeds what has been currently recognized by the courts. Further, what attorneys recognize as being unfair workplace practices clearly exceeds what has been recognized under the law. As will be highlighted in the following analyses of attorneys' discussions, although attorneys might look to the law in raising objections to workplace behaviour, they frequently move beyond recognized prohibited behaviour. They employ legal discourse to step outside of the formally recognized definition of discrimination and, thereby, implicitly suggest its rearticulation (Bourdieu and Thompson, 1991; Omi and Winant, 1994). The ability to both work within recognized definitions of gender discrimination, and to push those boundaries, is thus explored throughout this work. It is important, however, to bear in mind that attorneys, like laypersons, invoke idealistic notions of discrimination that are perhaps more comparable to Levin and Levin's broad sociological notion of discrimination, than the courts' narrow interpretations of gender discrimination.

Internet Ethnography

The Internet has opened up a new realm of research opportunities for social scientists, both through the increased accessibility of databases and information sources, and through the development of online communities which have created more easily accessible field research sites. As a result, a growing number of individuals are engaging in the practice of 'cyber ethnography' – or 'the study of humans in virtual communities and networked environments' (Mizrach). Cyber ethnographies focus on the idea that 'the new ... communities are no longer defined by geographic or even semiotic (ethnic/religious/linguistic) boundaries. Instead, communities are being constructed in cyberspace on the basis of common affiliative interests, transcending boundaries of class, nation, race, gender and language' (Mizrach).[2] Visualizing an online community as an actual place where a social scientist can 'observe, visit, stay and go', has prompted researchers in the field to query to what extent traditional ethnographic methods can be transplanted to the study of online communities (Jones, 1999, 17).

Traditional ethnographic methods rely on the notion that there is a particular community to be studied, to which an individual can be admitted and expelled, and for which there are particular guiding principles or laws. Communities need not have geographic boundaries, as individuals who share common interests can constitute a community, in addition to those who share a physical location (Fernback, 1999). Gatson and Zweerink (2000) determined that a fan-based website constituted a community due to practices such as: 1) the presence of criteria for authentic group membership; 2) group members defining rules or laws that set forth the protocol for

---

2   Although online communities offer some methods of deconstructing these boundaries, many argue that individuals bring offline identities and understandings with them when they enter online communities (Warhol, 1999; Kendall, 2000; Kendall, 2002). As a result, the concept of the Internet as a utopian society, where gender, race, class and geography are irrelevant, overstates the ability to escape offline identities.

proper group interaction; 3) members engaging in the patrolling of the boundaries of the community in order to expel those who do not belong and/or who violate rules for proper behaviour, and 4) engaging in political practices, such as encouraging members to unite for charitable causes or to promote the development of a diverse group membership in the community. Similar types of practices have occurred in the Greedy Associates field site, rendering it appropriate for the use of ethnographic field research.[3]

Thus, my study adapts the elements of traditional ethnographic field research to 'a largely [or totally] unseen group of subjects' (Gatson and Zweerink, 2000, 107–108), who can be observed only through their disembodied online interactions. Specifically, I engaged in participant observation of the field site, employing ethnographic techniques to gain an understanding of the background of the participants, the content of the website and the frequency of its use. During my period of observation, I never posted messages within the community, but participated as a 'lurker' at the website – reading the message threads, without commenting. The findings of my participant observation are combined with a content analysis of the messages posted to the website, in order to produce the research results.

The content analysis centred around messages selected from those created between the dates of August 1999 (when the website was created) and March (2005); from the creation of the website until 24 October 2004, members of the website community had posted 21,940 messages to the Greedy Associates board. In completing the content analysis, I operationalized my key variables, selected posts using the search tool made available at the website, and coded data according to the categories I had constructed to measure my key variables.

The Field Research Site

The message boards of the website www.greedyassociates.com serve as the site for this study's field research. The Greedy Associates website, copyrighted in 2000, is a 'site dedicated to providing a forum for discussing issues concerning life as a lawyer' ('About Us' at www.greedyassociates.com). The site contains a job board, resources for individuals seeking jobs or preparing to apply to law schools, legal research resources and – most importantly for the purposes of this study – message boards addressing issues concerning law firm life and practice. The actual stated 'goal' of the website community is to 'provide Internet services such as an Internet "public square" where people can discuss issues relating to the practice of law' ('Privacy Policy' at www.greedyassociates.com).

The Greedy Associates message board is a threaded message board, in which posts are organized by topic. An individual can create a new topic or reply to an old one. By clicking on the subject line of any message, one is brought to the content of that particular message, as well as to all messages that came before and after on the same subject line. Each message is also numbered in the order in which it

---

3   For a more extensive discussion of the development of the community and interactions within this community, see Baumle (2005).

was posted, beginning with the first message ever posted on the website as message number one. A search engine allows the user to search the message board for posts containing particular phrases or names, as well as to search by message number.

The messages themselves on the Greedy Associates board concern questions regarding firm salaries, billable hour requirements and working environments. Both attorneys and law students utilize the message board in their hunt for an 'ideal' legal position. Through the use of the message boards, individuals are able to anonymously post information about the firms for which they work, or wish to work. Visitors to the board are, then, able to exchange knowledge regarding issues that are of concern in the employer selection process.

The Greedy Associates website was created in the year 1999,[4] a year marked by large salary increases for lawyers throughout much of the country. Law firms on the West Coast initiated these salary hikes, attributable in part to their success in representing Internet start-up companies. Once some firms began to offer salaries $30,000 to $50,000 above what other firms were offering to incoming attorneys, many other firms felt compelled to match these salary raises in order to compete for top candidates. The Internet was ablaze with rumours concerning which law firms might join suit with the West Coast firms in the salary wars. It was during this period that the Greedy Associates website was born. The website offered law students and attorneys a source to obtain information concerning the status of the salary raises at firms throughout the country.

Despite its temporal connections with the 1999–2000 salary raises, the Greedy website contains no history of the forces compelling the creation of the site or the identification of its 'webmasters'. Following the creation of the website, the message board was increasingly home to messages that leaned towards an examination of complaints associated with the legal practice in general, or practice at a particular firm. These discussions have included addressing issues such as attitudes towards women or racial minorities, and working conditions.

The transformation of an online forum from an informational source to a community focused on broader aspects of its members' lives is a common phenomenon online (Sharf, 1997; Gatson and Zweerink, 2000); Rheingold observed that 'a continuing theme throughout the history of CMC [Computer-Mediated Community] is the way people adapt technologies designed for one purpose to suit their own, very different, communication needs' (1993, 7). The Greedy Associates community has certainly embraced this concept. Although the community originated to exchange salary information and other information concerning costs and benefits of employment at particular firms, the community members have transformed the forum to better accommodate their own requirements. Contrary to the usual depiction of attorneys as focused solely on the acquisition of wealth, as embodied in the website's self-deprecating name, the attorneys instead took control of the medium provided to them by the forum to express their viewpoints on a wide variety of issues relating to law firm life. At the Greedy Associates forum, the members discuss items including ethical dilemmas, discrimination, negotiating relationships in law firms,

---

4   The website name has a 2000 copyright, although the first post is dated August 1999.

disillusionment with the legal practice and wistful longings of finding a meaningful legal career or of leaving the practice altogether.

Over the past 6 years of its existence, Greedy Associates has grown to a sizeable community. Although the website does not maintain a 'counter' which tracks usage or members, a rough estimate of participants can be discerned from a review of data provided by the website www.alexa.com. Alexa is a web information service developed by www.amazon.com which provides a search and data toolbar to its users and, in return, collects information about Internet traffic and use from those who employ its toolbar. As part of its analysis of Internet traffic, Alexa developed a measure of 'reach' for websites that ascertains the number of users of the site; reach can be 'expressed as the percentage of all Internet users who visit a given site' (www.alexa.com). The three month average reach for the greedyassociates.com website for October 2004 was 2.8 per cent; this is the average of the daily reach figures over a three month period and means that if random samples of one million Internet users were taken, one would find on average that 28,000 of them visit www. greedyassociates.com on a given day.

Membership in the Greedy Associates community is, at first appearance, very open; this openness brings with it both benefits and challenges to the researcher. No action need be taken by individuals in order to have full access to peruse all of the messages of the website. Someone can, therefore, 'lurk' at the website for an unlimited period of time, without ever revealing their presence or providing any information about themselves. If an individual wishes to post a message at the website, he or she can do so simply by registering as a new user of the site. The registration process consists of entering a user name, password and a working email address. The registrant is not required to provide any demographic information, such as gender, race, age or geographic location. Further, the individual need not provide any information connected with their status in the legal community, such as whether they are in fact an attorney, an associate or partner, or their area of practice.

The secrecy surrounding the identity of the online participants and their characteristics posed some concern for this study. Ideally, when researching gender inequality in the legal practice, one would wish to know the gender of the individuals posting particular comments onto the website. The gender of the participants would certainly be of interest in determining the number of women who participate in the forum and, thus, could be expected to be exposed to a movement occurring on the website. Further, the gender of community members could be relevant in examining how gender affects whether members value litigation as a means to address gender inequality, or whether men or women are more likely to use legal discourse in the community.

Ultimately, however, the gender of the community members is perhaps less important than might at first be indicated. The gender of an individual who makes a particular post is less significant than the fact that the message has been publicized, and will perhaps affect the actions of other community members and/or employers. For instance, assume one community member posts a message that describes a practice of gender discrimination in a particular law firm. The research questions raised by this post concern, primarily, what type of response the message receives both inside and outside of the community. Do other community members encourage litigation as a means to redress the harm? Do they use legal discourse to assert the right to a working environment free of discrimination? Do employers respond to the message by denying the practice of gender discrimination, or offering a remedy? In answering these questions, the gender of those responding is less pertinent than the fact that the discourse has entered the community and has prompted a response of some kind. Both men and women in the community are equally likely, then, to be exposed to both the original post and the subsequent responses; those men and women might choose to respond online or might choose to refrain. The discourse, nonetheless, has the potential to affect their personal and work lives, regardless of their participation or knowledge of the gender of the community members. As a result, the gender of the participants becomes less pertinent than the content of the interactions themselves.

Nonetheless, I have attempted to identify the gender of respondents throughout this work, in order to provide some context for the responses. If the individual self-identifies a gender, this gender was reported.[5] Further, a gender was reported if the individual's username reflects a strong indication of a particular gender (for example, a name such as 'HoustonLawGirl' would suggest a female identity). When individuals do not self-identify, I have attempted to determine gender through the analysis of various verbal cues. Warhol notes that a researcher may 'only rely on posters' self-representation (and on self-perpetuating stereotypes of the masculine behaviour of men and the feminine behaviour of women) to draw conclusions about the sex of persons who write Internet messages' (1999, 94). In particular, some researchers have contended that differing communication styles can pose challenges to females seeking entrance into male-dominated communities, as well as males seeking entrance to female-dominated communities (Sharf, 1997; Warhol, 1999; Baym, 2000; Kendall, 2000). At the same time, however, community 'culture', so to speak, can influence the conversational style used by members. In other words, women might choose to use masculine styles in some communities, and men might employ feminine styles in others (Warhol, 1999; Kendall, 2000). As a result, it becomes difficult to identify the gender of an individual posting a message if the online community is dominated by one type of conversational style, since all community members, regardless of gender, might choose to adopt this style. Observations to date indicate that the conversational style at the Greedy Associates website is not dominated by a 'masculine' or 'feminine' style; rather some members express conversational styles that possess characteristics of each. This could provide some indication that there is a gender balance of sorts within the community which has not permitted one style to take hold. There are potential obstacles to labelling an individual as male based simply on 'conversational style', however, when one is studying a community based around a profession that is dominated by

---

5　Even if the individual does self-identify, there is always room for doubt, since the Internet allows for a disembodiment which can result in individuals engaging in gender switching (O'Farrell and Vallone, 1999; Kendall, 2002). Researchers studying members of website communities both online and offline have found, however, that gender switching does not occur often and, when it does, the members often reveal their true identity over the course of time (Kendall, 2002).

aggressive conversational styles. As a result, I have attempted to identify the gender of participants when the individuals have self-identified or when gender is readily discernable based on context; I have been more cautious in labelling individuals as male or female based simply on conversational style.

Employing the above-described techniques, I have attempted to draw some conclusions concerning the gender breakdown of participants in the Greedy Associates community. I reviewed all posts made during the work week starting 28 February 2005 and ending 4 March 2005. Of all of the messages posted to the community, approximately 47 per cent of the authors could be identified as men, 25 per cent as women, and 28 per cent were undetermined (see Table 3.1). This initial finding seems to suggest a dominance of men participating in the community. When individuals who make repeat posts are removed, however, 27 per cent of the community participants were men, 24 per cent women and 48 per cent undetermined. One can see that men comprise a much larger portion of individuals who make multiple posts during the week (61 per cent), resulting in the total number of posts made by individuals identified as male being larger than that of those identified as female. Individuals with an undetermined gender comprised the greatest number of all individuals posting at the site, but these individuals were much less likely to make repeated posts. Consequently, individuals who can be identified as men do dominate the overall number of messages, but they do not seem to comprise a greater number of actual participants in the community.

Table 3.1 Gender of Community Members Posting During One Week

Gender	Men	Women	Undetermined
% of Total Posts	46.8%	24.7%	28.5%
% of Individuals	27.3%	24.2%	48.5%
% of Repeat Posters	61.4%	25%	13.6%

The similarity between the percentages of individuals identified as men and as women parallels findings of other studies of online participation, where women were found to engage in online interactions in numbers either roughly similar to men, or in greater numbers (Gatson and Zweerink, 2004b; Ross et al., 2005). At the same time, however, communities that are not focused on feminine issues are frequently dominated by men in terms of participation, as men might use their social power to control and dominate the interactions (Wasserman and Richmond-Abbott, 2005). This could discourage repeated postings by women, resulting in women being more likely to 'lurk', reading responses but posting messages of their own less frequently.

Attorneys Using Rights Discourse to Effect Change

Many view the law as a powerful force for change, exemplified by the civil rights movement in which repeated appeals to the law (as opposed to simply the existence of the law on the books) assisted in bringing about victories for minority groups. Due to this perceived entitlement to a kind of 'justice' present in natural law, the oppressed often call upon the law in attempts to challenge both intolerance and oppression. Karst notes that 'equality has been a rallying cry' (1989, 1) in the US, that not only serves to unite the oppressed, but provides a basis for legal challenge in order to effectuate change. He observes that Americans appear to have great faith in the ability of the law to enforce notions of egalitarianism.

Americans' invocation of the language of equality or legal rights when challenging those in power suggests that individuals' understandings of the way law works can be as important – or perhaps more important – as the law on the books if such understanding is used to mobilize the oppressed (Marshall and Barclay, 2003). Law is mobilized when a desire is transformed into a demand as an assertion of rights (McCann, 1994); this demand parallels the claiming stage of the dispute process (Felstiner et al., 1980–81). Assertions of rights can 'give rise to rights consciousness so that individuals and groups may imagine and act in light of rights that have not been formally recognized or enforced' (McCann, 1994, 7; see also Marshall and Barclay, 2003). Legal consciousness (or rights consciousness), therefore, 'refers to the ongoing, dynamic process of constructing one's understanding of, and relationship to, the social world through use of legal conventions and discourses' (McCann, 1994, 7). The legal consciousness of both laypersons and lawyers might be based on perceptions of the law, rather than the reality of it; nonetheless, this consciousness is an integral component in the process of making a claim for change.

The efficacy of using rights discourse as a tool for change is often debated. Critical legal scholars contend that equality cannot be achieved through the law, arguing that even engaging in rights discourse is inconsistent with the goal of social change. Although legal victories can temporarily energize a social movement, critical legal scholars argue that reliance on legal remedies and the assertion of rights ultimately results in the legitimization of existing inequalities and repression (Altman, 1990; Schneider, 1990; Crenshaw, 1988). This legitimization occurs because when rights discourse is employed, the social movement of the disadvantaged is organized 'according to the law's boundaries and, in turn [is] bound by its conceptual limitations' (Crenshaw, 1988, 108). As a result, the legitimacy of the current social order is never truly challenged because the oppressed choose to operate within their oppressor's system of law. Thus, when women attempt to challenge gender inequality through the use of legal discourse, they must do so by appealing to legal notions steeped in the male dominance of the legal system. Those who write the laws, argue the cases, and interpret the laws have been, and remain, predominantly male (Baer, 1999; Rhode, 2001); critical legal scholars, therefore, maintain that women who draw upon rights discourse are legitimating the male hierarchy by choosing to operate within the legal system.

Rights discourse not only legitimates the legal system of the oppressors, but Tushnet (1984) contends that it fails to effect change because rights discourse limits the ability of its users to step back and truly examine the current problem; instead, the 'real demands, experiences, and concerns' of the oppressed are absorbed into a 'vacuous and indeterminate discourse' (Tushnet 1984). As a result, the oppressed lose touch with their original objectives as they attempt to fit their problems into a rights category. Similarly, legal doctrines permit multiple interpretations, so that the law can be twisted to fit one's own particular perspective (Unger, 1989; Altman, 1990). Given the malleability of the law, critical legal scholars argue that it is difficult for individuals to truly mobilize behind a claim of rights, since their oppressors can turn the same claim to right against the oppressed. The language of law is too easily manipulated to the will of the one who wields it, and the interpretation of those with the most power is likely to triumph. The ability to twist the law in this manner leads some to the difficult conclusion that 'because everything can be defended, nothing can' (Unger, 1989, p. 8), resulting in the law serving little or no utility in effecting change.

Despite these noted weaknesses, many advocate the use of rights discourse to challenge oppression. Proponents of liberal legal and political philosophy contend that when the law is applied faithfully by the government, the dominant values of individual liberty will prevail (Altman, 1990). Altman argues that liberalism can accommodate the critical legal scholars' critiques, contending that although law cannot serve as the sole recourse for the oppressed, the law can be employed as a significant resource for protecting people from intolerance and oppression.

Crenshaw (1988), for instance, acknowledges the critical legal scholars' arguments that rights rhetoric is of limited usefulness in effecting change. Nonetheless, Crenshaw contends that the critical legal scholars' view fails to take into account the powerful role that rights discourse has played in social movements, such as how the civil rights movement mobilized minorities and assisted in creating new demands for rights. By discrediting the utility of rights discourse, then, the critical legal scholars might unintentionally disempower the oppressed by removing this method of challenging the dominant culture. Specifically, critical legal scholars deconstruct rights discourse, yet offer no alternative strategy for producing change (Altman, 1990; Crenshaw, 1988).

Crenshaw (1988) and Altman (1990) posit that there is no alternative strategy and, as a result, the oppressed should turn to the law as a method for challenging the dominant social order. Schneider (1990) supports this viewpoint, contending that the critical legal scholars focus only on the limits of rights, rather than the possibilities offered by rights discourse. She emphasizes that rights discourse can affirm human values, enhance political growth, and assist in the development of a collective identity; all of these elements can prove invaluable to a political struggle.

How, then, can a claim to right be transformed into an effective weapon in a political movement? Rights discourse can be a particularly effective tool for the disadvantaged, as such discourse appeals to the dominant ideology and, as a result, is more likely to be accepted as legitimate (Crenshaw, 1988). One manner of producing change, therefore, is to expose a contradiction between the dominant ideology (such as the American notion of equality) and reality (the fact that inequality exists). By utilizing rights discourse, 'powerless people can sometimes trigger ... a crisis by challenging an institution internally, that is, by using its own logic against it'

(Crenshaw, 1988, p. 111). When such a discrepancy is exposed, the damage to the dominant ideology can be of such a nature that the dominant group will desire to repair the inequality in order to maintain its vision of equality (Crenshaw, 1988). As a result, rights discourse can be an effective mode of change because it calls upon the dominant ideology of equality and natural rights and can elicit a desire to correct situations contrary to these notions.

Scheingold notes that the rhetoric of rights plays an important role in political discourse, as it brings values embodied in the American Constitution into politics. Individuals engaged in mobilization efforts often 'speak in terms of rights that are violated, obligations unfulfilled, punishment of the guilty, vindication of the innocent' (Scheingold, 1974, p. 44). Even when a right has not been authoritatively established by the judicial or legislative process, an assertion of rights is 'not simply empty rhetoric' (Scheingold, 1974, pp. 44–45). Rights rhetoric calls upon moral norms, compelling the listener to support and defend the cause in order to support and defend the accompanying moral norm. Mobilization efforts are thereby 'made possible by the presence of rights in American society' (Scheingold, 1974, p. 83). Once again, whether the right has been recognized by the legislative or judicial system is unimportant; the belief system of rights influences social change. Thus, the success of a rights assertion lies more in its association with social justice than in its having been recognized by an authority as protected. Rights discourse can, then, be a powerful weapon for the disadvantaged; 'legal and constitutional processes might not be able to neutralize power relationships', but 'the authoritative declaration of a right can be viewed as the beginning of a political process in which power relationships loom large and immediate' (Scheingold, 1974, p. 85).

In the case of gender inequality in the legal profession, women attorneys are not necessarily dealing with making changes within American society as a whole, but within the law firm environment. As the notion of rights is engrained within the law, perhaps mobilization through the use of rights discourse is nowhere more appropriate than in the legal practice, where attorneys might be able to bring about change by using the very logic of the legal system against itself. This chapter examines how attorneys within the Greedy Associates community use rights discourse to challenge their employers, in order to ascertain whether such discourse could be an effective means for women to challenge gender inequality in the legal practice.

As noted by Marshall and Barclay (2003), one's view of whether the law can serve as a successful tool for change depends in part on one's own experiences with the law, perceptions of the law and hopes for what the law should be. Ewick and Silbey (1998) observe that individuals typically relate to the law in one of three manners: they are before the law (awed by its majesty and legitimacy); with the law (utilizing it when it favours them, and treating it like a game); or against the law (cynical and distrustful of its implementation). The particular mode of legal consciousness one adopts tends to be associated with social status, with those who are less powerful tending to be 'against the law'. In this regard, Nielsen (2000) found that women who were more likely to experience harassment on the street were less supportive of legislation prohibiting this very harassment. Similarly, women in the legal community might bear a less optimistic view of the utility of legal discourse for bringing about change. It is doubtless that the particular legal consciousness of the members of the website community will play an important role in determining whether they choose to mobilize the law to challenge inequality, or whether they view the law as an ineffective tool for change.

Legal Mobilization in the Greedy Associates Community

McCann (1994) examined the use of legal mobilization in the pay equity movement, and concluded that legal mobilization can be an important factor in producing change, especially if utilized during the movement building stage. The Greedy Associates community, therefore, might provide a fertile environment for movement-building to occur through legal mobilization. Indeed, other employees have utilized computer networks to challenge employer practices (Wellman et al., 1996). For instance, university professors in Israel employed computerized messaging to organize a nationwide strike (Pliskin and Romm, 1994). Similarly, union activists and labour organizers are able to use the Internet to 'denounce irresponsible corporations or to announce their own efforts to curtail them' (Warf and Grimes, 1997, 265). The potential for this type of activity results in management 'fear[ing] that [computer networks] will threaten control by accelerating the flow of (mis)information, including rumours, complaints, jokes, and subversive communications' (Finholt and Sproull (1990), cited in Wellman et al. (1996, 226). In one large corporation, women organized a computerized conference in order to discuss their careers; in response, management monitored the conversation due to fear of demands for unionization or affirmative action (Zuboff, 1988). These fears compelled one corporation to go so far as to shut down a company-sponsored 'Gripenet' when the employees began to use this medium to challenge corporate practices (Emmett, 1982).

Just as in other employee movements initiated on the Internet, the Greedy Associates community could prove a successful means by which to challenge employer practices. The use of rights discourse might, in fact, prove better adapted to the needs of women attorneys when such discourse is used in an Internet community. Through the Internet, there is the ability to reinforce hegemonic discourse, as individuals' racism and sexism accompany them into an online environment (Warf and Grimes, 1997). At the same time, however, the Internet has the capacity to create counterhegemonic discourse, 'challenging established systems of domination and legitimizing and publicizing political claims by the powerless and marginalized' (Warf and Grimes, 1997, p. 260). This possibility becomes particularly significant for individuals who are unable to openly articulate their demands offline (Warf and Grimes, 1997).

Associate attorneys in general, as well as women associates in particular, certainly fall into this category of individuals; voicing claims through litigation has been heretofore ineffective, and making claims either formally or informally could endanger their careers. As a result, the Greedy Associates community might prove an effective ground for creating counterhegemonic discourse regarding definitions and understandings of gender inequality and discrimination. By employing rights and legal discourse in the community, community members are able to challenge employer practices under the shelter of anonymity. As examined in this chapter, attorneys' use of legal discourse both embraces formal understandings of gender discrimination and introduces new, broader concepts of discrimination. By using legal discourse within the community to label employer behaviour as discriminatory, community members are able to bring pressure to bear on employers, even in situations where employer actions fall outside the realm of legally recognized prohibited behaviour.

Greedy Associates Using Rights Discourse to Challenge Working Conditions

Although members of the web community rarely mention a definite intent to sue their employers, they do engage in rights discourse, both through the suggestion of legal action and through challenging law firms to respond to their claims. The fact that the board, initially created as a forum to discuss firm salary hikes, has morphed into a place in which associates assert rights claims regarding working conditions bodes well for the prospect of women attorneys using the board to challenge gender discrimination. In this section, I explore the use of legal discourse to challenge working conditions generally, as well as gender discrimination in particular.

One of the most common complaints made by attorneys is that working conditions are incompatible with maintaining a normal family and social life. Hours are long, the pressure is high and many associates report feeling under-appreciated. Interestingly, however, associates at the Greedy Associate website frequently assert that they have a 'right' to better working conditions, despite their sizeable monetary compensation. One individual suggested that associates should 'grin and bear it', rather than complain about their working conditions, because they are well compensated for their troubles (dvadar 8,188 11/8/01). Another attorney quickly lashed back, questioning,

> Are you implying that associates at biglaw firms should be grateful for the job they have and the pay they get, regardless of conditions. I know we're not working in a coal mine but don't you think that employees in an industry have the right to demand better pay and better conditions?" (Paper Pusher 8197 11/08/01, emphasis added).

Similarly, another attorney bemoans the lifestyle difficulties created by long hours and billable hour requirements, stating that,

> firms ... are never truthful enough about the difficult choices that one is compelled to make between having a normal and meaningful life and being a highly prized contributor to the firm. Yes of course, one does not get paid the big bucks for nothing in return, but how much is enough .... Humane working conditions (generously defined) do not have to be so hopelessly at odds with big bucks (Corporate Diva 5724 7/26/01).

In this manner, the attorney implies that law firms misrepresent working conditions, and are violating the right to 'humane working conditions', thereby suggesting that there is some natural right to humane conditions that is not currently being met in the legal field.

The issue of layoffs within law firms created a great deal of controversy in the board community, as layoffs were uncommon in the legal field until recent years. In response to allegations that layoffs were implemented in an unfair manner, a board member stated:

> Not sure what [the firm's] current policy is on managing poor performers and denying retention bonuses, but ... listening to the stories (here, from friends and in the papers) of how random lay-offs were, the so-called "under performers" probably do have a right to more than [the firm] is giving if the firm didn't follow its policies. They are more likely entitled to the "retention" bonuses if the lay-offs were due to mismanagement and over-hiring because (can they really be this dumb) the layoffs were a product of the success of the bonus program. How can it make sense to say to an associate, "we'll pay you to forego other opportunities" and then say "because you didn't leave, we're cutting you and you have no right to the bonus that kept you here?' This seems so obvious that I bet anyone without a JD (a juror) would see the injustice (ssalum 8353 11/14/01, emphasis added).

This board member asserts a claim of rights against the law firm on behalf of the terminated associates, relying upon legal discourse and logic, as well as claims of rights and entitlement. The attorney claims that terminated employees perhaps have a right, or are entitled, to additional payment, suggesting a legal obligation; they then drive home the point by indicating that a juror would be able to recognize the rights violations that occurred. Another attorney asserted that law firms violated a *quasi-*legal obligation to employees by engaging in layoffs at all, arguing that:

> Many of these firms (especially in the last few years) just about promised associates job security. Don't you think that these layoffs are to some extent a breach of faith (of course it wasn't contractual or otherwise enforceable). Don't you think that there was an understanding at biglaw firms, a sort of implied quid pro quo. I always thought that if you are a biglaw associate and you bust your ass, then although you might not make partner, you will still have job security until you get passed over (barring some egregious behavior) (Paper Pusher 8197 11/08/01).

This attorney readily acknowledged that there was no 'contractual' or 'enforceable' obligation between the law firms and the associates who were the victims of layoffs. Nonetheless, the individual suggests that there was an 'implied quid pro quo' and that the firm engaged in a 'breach of faith' – the phrasing definitely connoting a legal claim. The attorney has, therefore, both denied the existence of a formal right and, simultaneously, used legal language to assert that very right.

Attorneys in the community seem to be more reluctant to use legal discourse in order to demand a remedy for claims connected with gender inequality; this hesitancy is perhaps due to a perception that the law, in general, has been ineffectual in assisting women in dealing with gender discrimination and harassment issues. Quinn (2000) observes that women are often hesitant not only to use legal discourse to demand a remedy for sexual harassment, but also fail to label sexual harassment as 'sexual harassment'. When women do not use legal terminology to name their harm, Quinn argues that they disempower the law, both as a tool to seek a remedy and as a discursive power. The law has discursive power, regardless of whether a claim for remedy is made; by labelling an action as 'sexual harassment', a woman can call upon the power of the law to cause the action to cease, even if she never files a formal complaint (Quinn, 2000). Whether the law is being used as a discursive tool, or as a formal method of pursuing a remedy, it is important that the individual name the harm in legal terms. If one fails to do so, 'the law is immobilized both ideologically and instrumentally' (Quinn, 2000, 1155). Consequently, if attorneys are reluctant to label gender inequality in legal terms, the law cannot be used in its discursive form to challenge the inequality.

When examining the use of legal discourse in the Greedy Associates community, therefore, it becomes important to examine whether attorneys use legal terms both in identifying harms, as well as in making a claim for remedy. When discussing gender issues, community members are much more likely to use legal discourse when labelling a harm than in demanding a right. In one case, which exemplifies many others, a female attorney announced to community members: 'I am facing a sexual harassment problem' (bostonlawgirl 20,465 7/8/04). It is important to recognize that by merely calling inappropriate behaviour 'sexual harassment', community members are using legal discourse to challenge the behaviour. When an offence is characterized by legal terminology, it imbues the claim with legal authority and places pressure on the offender to transform his or her behaviour; this is true regardless of whether a formal claim for remedy is made (Quinn, 2000).

At times, attorneys take this process a step further by not simply using legal terminology to label a harm, but in assessing the legality of particular behaviour. For instance, a male attorney argued that one woman's experiences with her employer might not be harassment, claiming 'just because you subjectively feel uncomfortable doesn't make it sexual harassment' (eyestrain 20,466 7/8/04). In response, another attorney states:

> WRONG. Note the first word of the EEOC's definition of sexual harassment: "*Unwelcome* sexual advances ... constitutes sexual harassment when submission to or rejection of this conduct explicitly or implicitly affects an individual's employment, unreasonably interferes with an individual's work performance or creates an intimidating, hostile or offensive work environment.' Yes, there is an objective element to consider, but what you said is just wrong (Boxer 20471 7/08/04).

This exchange indicates the easy manner by which attorneys fall into the use of legal discourse in discussing workplace issues. The first individual attempts to make a blanket legal statement in assessing how a woman should proceed in dealing with harassing behaviour. Note that this is different from a layperson's argument of what does or does not constitute sexual harassment; the attorney is clearly referring to the necessary elements to establish a sexual harassment claim, rather than simply offering up an opinion about whether the behaviour should be generally considered to be harassing. In response, another attorney refers to a specific right contained on the books, when they cite a portion of the EEOC guidelines on harassment. Engaging in a debate concerning the legality of the alleged behaviour is an important method of establishing the legitimacy of a complaint and, thereby, placing pressure on an employer to provide a remedy.

In one of the discussions concerning the retention of attractive female associates with poor work records, one male attorney contended that 'what is being described ... is mean spirited, and actionable by the ["unattractive"] woman if she so chooses' (roveresq 8,050 11/6/01). This observation prompted a debate among the community members concerning whether a cause of action exists when women who are not considered attractive, or do not use their attractiveness to play sexual 'games' with partners, are terminated. One attorney asserted that 'the mere existence of a gamey environment probably violates Title VII ... and in all likelihood eliminates any real possibility of women at the firm being treated in a manner similar to men' (game face 8,062 11/6/01). The attorney goes on, however, to state that an actual lawsuit would likely fail and/or damage an attorney's career, but nonetheless reemphasizes that 'it sounds as if there is [sic] clear violations of Title VII going on' (game face 8,062 11/6/01). Once again, therefore, the intent of many of the attorneys in analysing whether a valid legal claim exists appears to be less about encouraging litigation, than about determining whether a situation can be legitimately labelled as a rights violation. The power in these exchanges lies more in the ability to cast suspicion on the legality of a firm's behaviour, and perhaps prompt a response, than in encouraging a lawsuit.

Similarly, when attorneys describe situations which they claim 'sound like' title VII violations (see, for example, ssalum 8,084 11/7/01; Mistress Stern 15,745 11/7/02), their words have the dual function of perhaps suggesting that litigation be pursued, as well as framing the employer's behaviour in terms of the violation of a right. In other words, even if litigation is never pursued (as is largely the case) and even if the author never considers litigation a viable option, the mere labelling of behaviour as a 'Title VII violation' has a power unto itself. A law firm has been described to the legal community as a law violator and, whether an actual law has been violated, pressure is placed on the firm to respond in some manner to the accusation. One male attorney, in fact, makes note of this reality, contending that the firm involved in the questionable layoff practices 'HAS become the talk of the legal associate and student community and the taint will last for years to come' (S&S Survivor 7,967 11/5/01). Another individual, directing a response to a partner of the same firm, voiced a similar observation, stating that:

> Now a day doesn't pass when I don't hear something about how this firm sucks, how I bet wrong in law school (I had "other options"), how embarrassed I must be after last year [when the terminations occurred] ... So go back to working with our defunct IT department to figure out who is really on this board and get off our backs. Or better yet, why don't you try to restore some decency to this firm. Don't blame greedy associates for [the firm's] problems (Voice From Hell 11831 03/19/02).

This message reveals how critiques of the legality of a firm's behaviours can serve to damage the firm's reputation in the legal community, as well as the power of the legal discourse to prompt exchanges between partners and associates. In this message, the associate is able to deflect the partner's accusations that the website community is responsible for the firm's poor reputation, and instead assert that the firm itself must remedy the damage it has inflicted on its own reputation.

Not only is legal discourse employed in terms of an employer's need to comply with the law, but website members at times use legal discourse to describe the legal obligations of the participants in gender discrimination disputes. For instance, during a conversation concerning sexual harassment at a firm, one attorney advised the victim: 'The other alternative is to report him. You may have a duty to yourself, the firm and other potential victims' (BaggedIt 20,524 7/13/04, emphasis added). By phrasing a response in terms of 'duty', the attorney conjures up images of legal rights and obligations; the presence of a 'duty' to others is an essential element in establishing many legal claims. Through the use of this term, the attorney suggests a legal obligation on the part of the victim to challenge gender discrimination, in addition to a legal obligation on the part of the employer to remedy the discrimination.

Greedy Associates Use Legal Discourse to Assert the Right Use Legal Discourse

Attorneys' use of legal discourse within the website community has been wide-reaching, encompassing situations in which community members clearly assert non-existent legal rights. Faced with restrictions on their ability to post messages about their firms, attorneys in the community jumped to the apparently instinctual conclusion that they must have a right to engage in such activity, labelling the firms' prohibitions as 'censorship' and violations of First Amendment rights. One attorney implored 'isn't there a 1st amendment thing so long as I don't do it from within the building? Does this bother anyone?' (S&S Survivor 8,088 11/7/01). Another responded in horror, 'ARE YOU KIDDING???!!!! This is terrible. Is [the firm] that afraid of the truth .... Definitely a free speech issue, although you can continue to write whatever you want, but I suppose they can just fire you' (randomassociate 8,100 11/7/01). Notably, this attorney begins by expressing shock at the firms' actions and readily invokes the notion of free speech, but then admits that the firm can fire individuals if they operate in violation of the firm's orders.

The attorney's ultimate conclusion that firms have the 'right' to terminate employees who violate no-posting rules is perhaps the more realistic of the attorney's two responses to law firm 'censorship'. One attorney derided those calling upon the First Amendment, stating, 'you went to law school? you only have first amendment rights for prior restraint by gov't. say what you want where you want, but there may be consequences' (ishbaal 8,089 11/7/01). This attorney is certainly correct. After an employee was terminated by his employer for maintaining a website with questionable content, Lewis Maltby, director of the American Civil Liberties Union's Workplace Rights office, explained that the First Amendment protects an individual's right to present his or her opinion on a website, but does not prevent a private employer from terminating the employee due to the website content (Silberman, 1998). Maltby observed, 'You should take a passport when you enter the private sector, because you leave your rights as an American citizen behind. Once you go into the private sector, the Constitution doesn't exist. You have no constitutional rights.'[6]

Nonetheless, attorneys who have been well-trained in the law instinctively called upon the First Amendment when faced with limitations placed upon their speech by law firms. Further, another invoked the First Amendment's reference to freedom of association, claiming that it afforded attorneys protection against law firm attacks on website posting:

---

6 Although the First Amendment offers no protection in this case, the National Labor Relations Act might provide some protection of collective employee action.

Thanks G [reedy] A [ssociates], this makes the board more than a pure gossip arena, more like the information age water cooler. Damn, if only law firms could figure out how to get around that First Amendment freedom of association loophole (Shearmanditched 9783 12/14/01).

This reliance upon rights discourse is, therefore, a strong enough force that even attorneys who know of the law's inability to equalize all playing grounds will resort to imagined legal protection in the face of oppression. Scheingold (1974) and Crenshaw (1988) both acknowledge that legal discourse can be a powerful mode for change, even when the rights referenced have not been authoritatively established by the legislative or judicial system. The ability to argue for rights where none exist is important in seeking to effect social change; if attorneys are to be successful in using legal discourse on behalf of women attorneys, they must be able to refer to both legally recognized rights (notions of equality and anti-discrimination), as well as rights that have yet to be placed into formal law.

In addition, the debates that erupted over the 'censorship' issue demonstrate a strong commitment to the community as a forum to voice complaints against employers, and perhaps compel a response. One attorney noted the power of the website in providing a community that allows attorneys to challenge partners' decisions, such as this one, stating that 'forums like this can hold dishonest partners accountable when we are otherwise powerless' (shearmanditched 9,783 12/14/01). In particular, attorneys posting at the website are able to use the power of legal discourse in an attempt to publicize disfavoured firm practices, such as gender discrimination and sexual harassment, and perhaps effectuate change.

The above examples demonstrate that members of the Greedy Associates community use rights discourse and legal language to describe rights violations, make demands for remedies, and to imply an obligation to challenge discrimination. The use of rights and legal discourse in all of these manners can place pressure on an employer to investigate, respond to, and perhaps remedy behaviours. Further, the use of the web community for this type of interaction has become so commonplace that at times such discourse dominates the board, as opposed to conversations regarding law firm salaries. The website, therefore, shows promise as a forum in which attorneys can assert rights claims against law firms and, perhaps, prompt change in gender relations.

Conclusion

Results indicate that attorneys are already engaging in attempts to mobilize and effect change in Internet communities through the use of legal discourse, suggesting that this medium could serve as a vehicle for women attorneys to organize and perhaps alter existing inequalities in the legal practice. Legal discourse is an important means to challenge inequality, as it imbues claims with the authority of the law, lending an air of legitimacy to assertions of gender discrimination. Notably, community members label gender inequality as discriminatory even when the law has not clearly prohibited particular acts. This is significant on a number of levels. First, it emphasizes the fact that attorneys will often resort to legal discourse to assert claims to rights in a manner quite similar to laypersons. Despite their particular training in the law, attorneys will call upon general notions of equality to assert a claim to rights that do not exist on the books; this type of rights consciousness has been frequently discussed in terms of laypersons (Karst, 1989; Marshall and Barclay, 2003), but not in the context of those trained in the law.

Second, the use of legal discourse to broadly label inequalities as discrimination is significant in that it takes a step towards redefining current conceptions of gender discrimination. These results have emphasized that the experiences and understandings of lawyers, in addition to laypersons, are at odds with current judicial and management interpretations of gender discrimination law. In other words, there is not simply a disconnect that exists between judicial interpretation of the law and lay understandings of gender discrimination or harassment. Those attorneys who have been trained in the field of law experience the same lack of connection between their everyday experiences with gender inequality and the remedies and rights afforded them by the formal litigation process. Consequently, when attorneys use legal discourse to label practices as gender discrimination that have heretofore not been formally recognized as such, they both emphasize the current disconnect between the law and workplace experience, and begin to suggest a reformulation of gender discrimination. Legal discourse can be a particularly effective tool to use towards this end, as it allows attorneys to use a system embraced by their oppressors, as attorneys, as a vehicle for change.

Legal discourse on its own, however, would perhaps be an ineffective method for change, as it carries with it many of the same costs as litigation. The discourse becomes more valuable when used within the Greedy Associates community. Community members are able to bypass many of the obstacles set in place by management and other associates, and find a voice to challenge inequalities. In particular, the anonymity the community provides its users enables them to challenge gender discrimination without endangering their employment or their status with their colleagues. Notably, it is not simply female associates who are empowered, but male associates as well. Men who are unable to challenge partners regarding oppressive, hyper-masculine practices in the workplace are more apt to do so (and have done so) in an anonymous environment.

In addition, the community allows attorneys to engage in a dialogue about gender inequality, both with one another and with those in positions of power. In other words, the community does not simply provide a forum for voicing complaints, but permits the response of others – those of an opposite gender, those whose experience with discrimination provides special insight, and those who are in management positions. Marshall (2005) observes that some employers train employees on how to encourage victims to raise issues concerning discrimination and harassment, and to arrive at possible solutions. She notes that 'strategies such as these mobilize already existing gossip networks that disseminate valuable information' (Marshall, 2005, 119). In much the same way, interactions occurring in the Greedy Associates community could result in mobilizing against gender inequality through the use of 'existing gossip networks' which encourage the raising of issues of inequality, as well as the exploration of possible solutions. These solutions have thus far ranged from litigation to the use of legal discourse to thoughts of unionization, as well as less overt strategies (one-on-one confrontation, using grievance procedures and so on).

The community also permits direct claims to employers, and hosts employers' responses to these claims. Lee suggests that in the face of hate speech, 'placing the perpetrator and victim in a hypothetically solidaristic, communicative relationship (as members of a common speech community) rather than in an adversarial juridical relationship (as legal persons)' provides a stronger possibility for change (2001, 874). This would be the case especially when the dominant group suffers sanctions through public exposure from failing to engage in a dialogue with the oppressed (Lee, 2001). The Greedy Associates community provides a forum for attorneys to use legal discourse to assert rights against their employers, and permits employers the opportunity to respond, thereby initiating an open dialogue (see Baumle, 2005 for discussion of employer response to attorney claims). Although this dialogue is still adversarial in nature, it is removed from the formal legal process and law firms face potential sanctions from the public by failing to respond to associate claims. As a result, law firms must take the potential for public exposure into account in making the decision of whether and how to respond to associates claims of rights violations.

In addition to engaging in semi-protected, anonymous challenges to employer actions, the public nature of the website community further permits attorneys to use the threat of media exposure as an added weapon against their employers. Community members have noted the importance of the media in advancing the community's claims against employers. One male attorney described the media intervention in a particular dispute, stating that:

> Tom Adcock from the N[ew] Y[ork] L[aw] J[ournal] did a good job but sounds like someone quickly shut him up. Maybe if the W[all] S[treet] J[ournal] or the N[ew] Y[ork] T [imes] wants a crack they should try and see if these whiners are real. If you have some idea how we could move this discussion off of this board and give it to some authority to investigate the firm's employment, sexual harassment and general ethical practices, then speak up and the rest of us will wait for the results of the investigation (*S&S Survivor* 8168 11/08/01).

At a later date, the same male attorney encouraged the media to investigate the practices at a law firm, stating that:

> Bottom line, let the N [ew] Y [ork] L [aw] J [ournal] or W [all] S [treet] J [ournal] take a free walk around, form their own opinion, and call it a day (9187; 12/03/01).

Using the community to invite media investigation is, therefore, viewed as an additional source of power for attorneys in the community.

And the media do visit the Greedy Associates website to obtain the 'inside scoop' about law firm activities. Some reporters visit the website to actively solicit responses on particular issues. For instance, one New York reporter stated, 'I'm a legal reporter at Bloomberg News, trolling the message board for stories. Here's my contact info if you've got one' (oldskoolgreedy 14,561 8/28/02). Another reporter echoed the invitation, soliciting community members to 'Call me any time. Confidentiality guaranteed' (Thomas Adcock 14,620 9/4/02). In response to an article published about a firm which drew on comments in the community, one community member stated, 'I want to thank [the author] for giving a voice to those who had not had one. I know firsthand that there have been problems at this firm for a long time ... I take solace in the fact that these slimy partners are finally getting the bad press they deserve' (friendofassoc 7,766 11/1/01).

Community members not only welcome the media for the potential to open a more public dialogue on controversies, but also take note of the power of the media to place pressure on offending law firms. As one attorney aptly summarized, it is '[i]nteresting that those disguised [firm] partners jump up to attack us when we have something to say, but run for cover when it's a reporter' (S&S Survivor 9,801 12/14/01). This individual goes on to essentially implore the media to pressure law firms to respond more publicly to associate complaints, stating '[w]e never said everything that we hear was confirmed three times over. That is why we asked [the firm], over and over again, to invite a third party in to look at the facts. How far to push that point is now also mostly in the hands of journalists' (S&S Survivor 9,801 12/14/01).

Perhaps, therefore, the efficacy of the Greedy Associates website in eliciting change for women attorneys is dependent in part on the public pressuring of firms for responses to associates' claims of rights violations. Claims of sexual harassment and other law violations have a significant potential to damage a law firm's reputation. By using legal discourse to lend an air of legitimacy to claims, members of the community can both prompt employer response, and perhaps encourage an alteration in gender practices in law firms. If statements within the community itself do not serve as a powerful enough force, the media will perhaps amplify the voices of community members, serving to bring the issue of gender discrimination into the court of public opinion.

Chapter 4

Rights as the Seeds of Regulation in UK Land-Use Planning

Tola Amodu[1]

Introduction

This chapter argues that an appreciation of the history of UK land-use planning regulation illuminates important ways in which rights can play a powerful role in shaping the evolution and implementation of regulatory practices. Understandings of regulation often fail to acknowledge the role of rights, beyond a limited perception of them as a form of private regulatory enforcement form, low in cost to government (Calabresi and Melamed, 1972; Breyer, 1982; Baldwin and Cave, 1999, 51–52).[2] Rather, discussions of regulation more usually locate it as a state-based, public activity, taking place within an economic or political context where governments are encouraging or directing behaviour – sometimes by using law and sometimes without recourse to law (Ogus, 1994). Much debate in regulatory scholarship discourse revolves around an appreciation of the limitations of legalism. This is true of the specific criticisms of regulatory enforcement (Yeager, 1991) and command and control strategies as informed by the compliance literature (Bardach and Kagan, 1982; Hawkins, 1984; Hutter, 1997), as well as for the more general literature that implicates law as a source of, rather than a solution to regulatory deficits (Teubner, 1987). Where law is considered a regulatory resource, its function in public regulation has been seen as one that '… encodes [the] principles, and instrumentalities, of the welfare state' (Black, 2002, 24). This is a perspective that in its public emphasis, brackets private law – and it is private law, and the common law in particular, that encodes rights and obligations. Public regulation, despite the asserted collapse of the public/private divide, remains on this reading a product of legislation rather than the common law and one that is weakened rather than sustained by conceptions of rights. Rights in this context tend to be seen as a hindrance to regulation rather than a resource (Reiss, 1974).

Rights conceptions can underpin and inform regulatory activity, however. Sometimes this occurs when the government attempts to use established common law principles for regulatory purposes. It can result in the redefinition or reconstruction

1   My thanks to all of the participants, both faculty and students, at the LSA Summer Institute, and to Professor Colin Scott, for comments and criticisms.
2   This is not to suggest, however, that the enforcement of rights does not require the institutional support of the state, as Calabresi and Melamed (1972) emphasize.

of those principles. In this chapter I explore how regulation is effected in the context of land-use planning control, in part through the manipulation of rights-based conceptions which have informed the foundation for one part of that regime. In land-use planning regulation in England and Wales, the planning agreement constitutes a part of the regulatory structure and has done so since the advent of a cohesive system of town and country planning control in the early twentieth century. Yet whilst the instrument is largely a statutory construct, it has its roots in the individuated form associated with contract and land law and has provided central government with the means to regulate and indeed manipulate ostensibly locally negotiated bilateral relations. These agreements have become a useful tool in shaping the public regulation of land-use activity. Thus, the instrument of the agreement and the individuated construct it represented came to be controlled by central government to secure largely collective ends. This chapter will be used to show how in the early stages in the creation of a planning control system, regulation was achieved through co-opting and distorting, or subverting, these rights-based conceptions through the calibration of information resources to deliver other more centrally determined instrumental ends.

The government has harnessed the regulatory capacities of land law and contractual principles articulated in common law, through a sponsoring of those constructs in the creation of planning agreements as mechanisms for restricting and regulating land-use development. The principles of contract provided the basis for formalizing the use of negotiated solutions to regulate the impact of development activity. Whilst contracting has been seen as a privatizing of state control without the provision of commensurate mechanisms of oversight, in the land-use planning context at least, this analysis is flawed to the extent that many different forms of oversight have evolved to regulate practice. These regulatory effects are defined through interaction and negotiation that enhances rather than diminishes the government's capacities. I argue here that regulation by the government is characterized by a process of experimentation, which consolidates its limited capacities of oversight to regulate agreements. This is far removed from some contemporary understandings of regulatory contracting that view the practice as potentially difficult for the government to regulate by reason primarily of the insulation from third party involvement.[3]

Local authorities used agreements as a form of development control in the embryonic stages of town and country planning. Landowners could agree with local planning authorities to restrict development activity by imposing covenants that bound the original covenanter who entered into the agreement but also their successors in title. The statutory form of the planning agreement overcame the limitations of land law by providing the vires for the planning authority to enforce the covenant against successors in title to the original landowner notwithstanding that it neither retained nor had an interest in adjoining land benefiting from the covenant. Covenants in planning agreements thus ran with the land and through the individuated form the

---

3   Law and economics scholars, for example, tend not to favour a use of contracting for regulatory ends, for reason of the hierarchical element introduced that carries with it a prospect of hold-out and uncertainty (see Pritchard, 1983).

collective goals pertaining to the promotion and protection of community interests affected by individual landowner activity could be secured.

In this chapter I consider how during the early stages of the evolution of town and country planning control, private rights concepts were used for regulatory purposes. In the era 1909–43 (which I define as the pre-modern era), notions of covenant and agreement were co-opted by central government in the quest for effective regulatory solutions. The result was one, as we shall see, that reformulated the notion of private rights into a more public regulatory ideal that gave a prominence to those aside from the parties to the agreement in the regulatory scene. Through the adoption of a series of techniques, public officials moulded a use of agreement to conform to the central regulatory ideal; one that sought to control the effects of land-use development so that it met with public rather than private objectives. These techniques, which ranged from the provision of individual advice and guidance to the systematic construction of a regime for the approval of all drafts, were to become increasingly formalized and enacted ultimately through statute in 1943. In essence they capture the progression towards a redefining of the individuated form as a regulatory tool, which third party actors could themselves shape.

The Regulatory Challenges of Controlling Land-Use

Town and country planning control can be defined as a problem of regulating rights. The rights associated with land use and development are circumscribed by collective concerns. Public policy considerations seek to constrain the impacts of land-use activities that have environmental, technological or economic effects. Through the planning system, both central and local government has a vested interest in ensuring land-use development accords with local, regional and national demands for economic and environmental sustainability. The planning system functions primarily through a form of licensing whereby appropriate development is sanctioned by the grant of planning permission. The bundle of rights and interests that constitute and characterize the legal estate are redefined and ultimately regulated by the law of town and country planning in so far as the use and development of land has the potential to impact upon the aesthetic and amenity considerations of the wider community.

Here regulation can be viewed as a discrete mode of governmental activity facilitating as much as promoting the achievement of broad policy objectives through a process of continual appraisal that often invokes multiple forms of ordering and control.[4] The rise of the 'regulatory state' (Loughlin and Scott, 1990; Majone, 1994) could be interpreted as defining the existence of a pragmatic opportunistic state that is more concerned with policy practice than legal instruments. Yet in the context of land-use development control, legal norms form an integral part of the regulatory landscape and frame and structure regulatory activity. In land-use development control in England and Wales, contractual practices are used as regulatory mechanisms and in turn are regulated in the process. Here planning agreements are

---

4   Black conceptualizes regulation as 'the intentional activity of attempting to control, order or influence the behaviour of others' (Black, 2002, p. 1), and it is a definition applied here.

used for policy ends and can be moulded by others aside from the parties to the agreement – especially central government. Through regulation, agreements acquire much broader policy attributes and objectives imposed by the government which undercut and to an extent undermine an ordering of the rights and interests of the parties to negotiate locally efficient land-use development control solutions. The result may be a restriction of the capacity of landowners and planning authorities to agree with what may seem to them to be appropriate land-use control solutions, through a process of third party intervention. Thus, the common law conceptions founding the notion of contract and land interests are rewritten as regulatory tools by the state.

Using Contracting Practices in Land-Use Planning

The use of planning agreements provides insight into the many regulatory techniques that have been used to regulate a legal instrument and in turn produce regulatory effects. This strategy implicates a changing constellation of actors that can range from government officials to individuals. Here regulation is associated both with the micro-level activity of controlling land-use activity locally and the broader aim of successive governments to achieve and maintain a level of coherence and integrity within the planning system overall. Agreements are regulated not only by the understandings of the parties involved, the planning authority and developer or landowner, but also by more distant parties.

The embryonic stages of the practice illustrate perhaps most easily the functioning of agreements in their purest local form. During this period, however, central government constructed the foundations for exercising further oversight by in effect creating a culture of dependency and compliance on the part of both local planning authorities and individual landowners. This involved various policy actors and led ultimately to a system of express oversight in the form of ministerial consent. The preparatory work was characterized by a degree of experimentation as to the boundaries of regulation. Essentially this period can be seen as a testing ground for various regulatory strategies in the quest for effective control. It is suggestive of a somewhat different orientation towards directive oversight or command where express mechanisms of control become effective through a process of subtle induction.

This history indicates also that the use in the public domain of contracting for regulatory ends is not necessarily, as has been asserted, a postmodern regulatory form coinciding with an increasing complexity of state activity and an interdependence between public and private bodies of the late twentieth century (Edgeworth, 2003). In the context of land-use control, the device of contract, traditionally associated with the exercise of individuated rights and interests, is used by the government to regulate development activity and in doing so permit more flexible land-use planning solutions. The contracting practices of others are harnessed by the government to secure collective objectives in such a way so as to make community interests almost dependent upon individual rights. The agreements made between the individual actors have given rise to a form of public regulation that accords with and is shaped by public policy concerns, and in doing so generates community benefits. Planning agreements are statutory contracts, entered into by the planning authority and landowner or developer for the purposes of restricting or regulating the use or development of land. They have been used to provide tangible benefits to the local community whether in terms of the provision of public facilities or financial payments. The practice occurs within a context of shifting dependency relations as between central government, the Local Planning Authority and the developer, where none has sufficient capacity or resources alone to bring its instrumental goals to fruition. Central government seeks to give some overall coherence to land-use development activity throughout the jurisdiction, as the planning authority seeks to regulate land-use activity within its area and landowners exercise the right (in the form of the grant of planning permission) to undertake lawful development.

Contracting practices have regulatory effects that not only bind the parties to the agreement but accommodate the objectives of third parties, especially the government, which established the planning framework. Through a process of definition and redefinition agreements have been ordered to reflect the changing policy objectives of the planning system itself. This poses a challenge to those who indicate that contracting practices cause inherent difficulties in terms of central oversight where the government is not a party to the contract, making it unsuited to securing public policy objectives (Collins, 1999). In the land-use planning context many different forms of oversight have evolved to regulate agreements that are characterized by an ongoing process of experimentation on the part of the government. These include a use of informal advice and guidance, through to formalization and even the restructuring of the planning framework so as to engender actor dependency. The regulatory effects are defined through iterative processes of interaction and negotiation that enhance rather than diminish the government's capacities.

Bilateral agreements are a continuing facet of land-use control in England and Wales and illustrate how a legal instrument shapes and is shaped by both legal and policy concerns which give rise to regulatory effects. Agreements have a long history deriving from the early twentieth century when they were used locally as an informal solution to the pressing need to control urban expansion and to order land-use development in the absence of a comprehensive and coherent system.[5] The practice became embedded within the institutional fabric of planning space, evolving simultaneously with the fluid demands of central government. The use of agreements was given statutory recognition as a 'free standing' regulatory instrument in 1932 (Town and Country Planning Act Section 34 1932). Before then the practice was integral to the operation of the planning scheme, a more general mechanism of land-use control. Agreements supplemented a decision-making frame that was initially highly fragmented but subject to varying, and at times intensive, forms of central oversight. Planning agreements were seen as valuable instruments where the government could use the capacity of other actors to restrict their conduct to beneficial effect for the local community. Over time the instrument was used to control on-site activity by defining the form of the particular development and also to secure the provision of off-site infrastructure that would benefit the community as a whole. The latter function

---

5   Dating from as early as 1909.

is not uncontroversial (Department of the Environment Property Advisory Group, 1981; Grant, 1982). Through the flexibility that the practice engendered the quality of development proposals was enhanced. Infrastructure deficiencies (both on- or off-site highways or drainage works) were overcome and localities were compensated for the potentially adverse impacts of development. The latter, commonly known as planning gains are most often associated with large-scale developments and can include the provision of public open spaces or community facilities unrelated to the development proposal itself. Illustrations of these include the provision of community facilities in connection with residential or commercial developments. Agreements functioned to define and regulate those aspects of development that cannot be secured easily through the imposition of planning conditions on a grant of planning permission. These binding agreements, which are enforceable against successors in title, are made for the most part between Local Planning Authority and landowner or developer to restrict or enhance a development proposal. In more recent times landowners gained the capacity to give binding unilateral undertakings regarding the use or development of land.[6]

The use of agreements illustrates how the government effectively harnesses an individuated market instrument used by the parties to negotiate efficient solutions and to deliver improved collective outcomes. This is achieved in part by introducing further margins of flexibility into a development control system already characterized by the exercise of discretion by public authorities and elements of negotiation and bargaining. As I will show, the history of planning agreements is indicative of the adoption of a level of regulatory variety or hybridity by central government and its officials.

Regulation in this context can be viewed as a process that combines cooperation and contestation in addition to direction such as to generate what are at times effective outcomes. Understandings of regulation include but often transcend the more limited vision of 'command and control' pointing to an early awareness on successive governments' parts of the significance to regulatory control of interactions between public and private actors, where order or control is brokered or negotiated rather than imposed. The actors present in the policy space often tacitly establish frameworks for ordering and their participation shapes the regulatory form and substance. Regulation is constructed through a process of negotiation that sets the bounds of both the thinkable and the possible through an iterative dialogue, which can compensate for the participatory deficits that the government may experience when seeking to regulate the activity of others.

Negotiating Regulation: The Case of Planning Agreements

Planning by agreement exemplifies the coexistence of public and private interests, that structure development activity on both horizontal and vertical axes (that is the mutual or lateral and the hierarchical) against which are mapped the competing time

---

6   Under the provisions of Section 12 of the Planning and Compensation Act 1991, agreements and unilateral undertakings became redesignated as planning obligations.

frames of past, present and future. Planning controls are directed towards both past and present development activity, remedying the unacceptable whilst promoting those land use and development activities considered beneficial to society. Agreements are used to facilitate these objectives through a process of structured negotiation, where the Local Planning Authority and developer settle the terms intrinsic to the particular development. The parties themselves assume responsibility for negotiating solutions and in doing so achieve effective local land-use control. An internal system of enforceable rules is created that has the effect of regulating certain aspects of development control.

The practice implicates also multiple *dramatis personae* in the regulation of ostensibly bilateral relations, including those having a more general vested interest in land-use activity. Most notably this has included the government and its officials, rival developers, professional actors and local objectors. Each had competing, if dissonant, rationalities, whether landowner or developer, lawyer, planner or central official and brought with them a different perspective on the normative questions of the function of planning and its regulation. The perspectives changed over time and were influenced by the environment in which they operated and the instrumental goals colouring the evolution of their respective profession or interest grouping. Here the various actors present participated in a process of reinterpretation of underlying principles forming the basis for legitimating negotiation and bargaining, which led to an institutionalizing of certain practices. The ensuing turf battles led sometimes to a restructuring of the regulatory practices (Dezalay and Garth, 1995, 1–21). The involvement of professional actors functioned to regulate the lateral dealings as between the parties to the agreement, and allowed central government to the exercise further hierarchical control. The participation of civil servants gave rise to the existence of more reflexive regulatory forms deriving from their participation and interaction. The base premise remained however, that cooperation is to be preferred initially to command-based deterrence.

Central government archives indicate the evolution of the forms of oversight adopted by it in relation to agreements. This narrative shows the adoption of an array of different techniques, which are centred upon the collection and dissemination of information. Governmental records retained under the Public Records Act 1958 (as amended) and the commentary of contemporaneous legal textbooks provide insight into this aspect. The records of government include minutes of civil servants, cabinet papers, consultation responses and the working papers of specialist working parties. These are retained by the National Archives, an executive agency and government department. Under the provisions of the 1958 Act, the government's departmental and administrative records selected for preservation are required to be made available (subject to certain exemptions made on grounds of confidentiality) for public inspection after 30 years from the date the records were created (Public Records Act Section 1 1967; Public Records Act Section 10 Schedule 1 1958).[7] A reliance on documentary reportage can never provide a complete picture and the reader must exercise a level of caution in critically assessing the text against known facts of the

---

7   Originally, the period was 50 years under Section 5(1) of the 1958 Public Records Act.

period. The task is to establish a credible account of the regulatory developments historically.

These texts highlight the strategies of government in its endeavour to maintain a level of congruence between a use of agreements and the evolving planning system. The National Archives allude to the culture of government organization and the working of the Whitehall machine by showing how the government represented its regulatory position. They link also policy statements to the legislative provisions.

During the pre-modern era the government deployed a number of strategies other than command. These included persuasion, encouragement, education and instruction. All were founded upon the use of information as a regulatory resource. The production of information and the brokering of alternative systems of interpretation at variance with the express statutory provisions were developed to give complex and convoluted meanings to ostensibly straightforward legislative provisions and in the process of doing so generate further opportunities for control. Through the process of interaction and negotiation, a climate was created where dependency flourished and the government and its officials promulgated and legitimated favoured interpretations that in turn enhanced regulatory control.

The legal provisions became a valuable, if contested, resource to be used and manipulated by the key actors to secure regulatory advantage. Through dialogue the various actors during the course of that evolving process tested different interpretations. Essentially the Archives record the mediation of legal and political processes by central government in the quest for effective regulation. This is a history that highlights functional changes in regulatory intent (moving from local solutions to accommodating centrally imposed goals) and more importantly the variable participation of numerous players (each with variable levels of capacity and influence) in the regulatory arena.

During the pre-modern era, the regulation of agreements assumed considerable significance for the government and its officials – as much as the parties to the instrument. Here regulation is signified by a more inclusive orientation that captures an interdependence between public and private actors and shifts the emphasis away from central government control as the sole province of regulation. The government remains a key actor within the regulatory space but is reliant upon others as much as itself to secure effective results. During the pre-modern era the dichotomy between the individuated rational instrumentalism, commonly associated with contracting activity and collective policy objectives are secured through both lateral dealings and hierarchical oversight in a way that cuts across the regulatory space. Here contractual rights and interests were manipulated by the government to secure collective objectives and regulatory practices became a product of this strategy. In the next section I outline the embryonic development of the practice of using planning agreements to illustrate this.

Planning Agreements in the Pre-Modern Era

Although a statutory construct, it was from common law and equitable principles (especially those of contract and land law) in addition to the earlier public health legislation that the conceptual base for the use of agreements was drawn. The practice was devised so that the parties themselves assumed responsibility for negotiating solutions and in doing so achieved effective land-use control. In this era, lacking in a comprehensive planning system, negotiated solutions were often the only ones available to address the effects of post-industrialization. Thus, through the device of agreement the planning authority acquired rights to enforce those obligations made by the landowner as a means to regulate land-use activity, often in exchange for the grant of development rights. Whilst originally included within the town-planning scheme, a form of statutory zoning, agreements were given independent statutory recognition under Section 34 of the 1932 Town and Country Planning Act.

Section 34 provides few clues as to the mechanisms by which the practice was regulated nor do the provisions limit its use. It states:

Where any person is willing to agree with any such authority as is mentioned in Subsection (2) of this section that his land or any part thereof, shall, so far as his interest in the land enables him to bind it, be made subject, either permanently or for a specified period, to conditions restricting the planning, development, or use thereof in any manner in which those matters may be dealt with by or under a scheme, the authority may, if they think fit, enter into an agreement with him to that effect, and shall have power to enforce the agreement against persons deriving title under him in the like manner and to the like extent as if the authority were possessed of, or interested in, adjacent land and as if the agreement had been entered into for the benefit of that adjacent land.

Ostensibly agreements could be entered into for any purpose provided these are consistent with the lawful exercise of public powers. Reference to the Archives indicates however, the existence of an alternative regulatory narrative, which had been in the process of construction by central government officials since at least 1909. Various policy strategies were being used to monitor and oversee the practice that would be honed to perfection by the creation of a statutory system of oversight in 1943.

Central Regulation through the Calibration of Control

During the pre-modern era the significance of agreements as instruments of land-use control was recognized by central government. They were important especially in controlling land-use development activity in the rural areas because at that time general planning controls were for the most part confined to the urban areas or those areas in the course of development. Agreements were key regulatory instruments in the provision of large tracts of land for the purposes of recreation.[8] At this early stage agreements had the advantage of formalizing arrangements with the consent of the landowner, as opposed to the directive tool of the planning scheme that often could be viewed as a form of zoning verging on the state expropriation of rights. Nevertheless, the practice of agreement was subject to scrutiny in part to ensure that local authorities exercised their powers properly. It was a time when public

---

8   Illustrations can be found in respect of Aintree racecourse and the Clivedon Estate owned by Viscount Astor.

authorities had limited experience of executing land-use development functions and the central government sought to protect individual landowners as far as possible from the perceived possibility of abuses of power. The climate was one of instability and change where central government sought to pave the way for further regulatory intervention in land-use activity as a means to combat the product of rapid technological and environmental changes. A use of agreement, whilst significant, had to accord with overall central objectives. Regulation of the practice was achieved through the calibration of informal strategies that included the dissemination of information and the provisions of advice and guidance.

The use of consensus and cooperation were the prime mechanisms by which planning agreements were regulated. Consensus had a dual significance, as that of regulating local land-use activity and as a source of meta-regulation, where government could control the contracting parties remotely. Before 1932, central officials regulated agreements in the course of checking and approving planning schemes. The scheme-making procedure was particularly detailed and incorporated both parliamentary scrutiny and potentially administrative enquiry where objections were raised. Both became a regulatory resource from which to shape the practice. Central officials also provided more general advice to planning authorities which regulated the latter's activities including the conclusion of agreements. For those agreements not part of a scheme, the capacity of civil servants to regulate the practice was even greater. In cases affecting high profile agents or sites of strategic importance, civil servants held meetings with landowners and local authorities in person. An illustration of this is the agreement relating to Lord Astor's Cliveden estate. The first agreement referred to in the 11th Annual report of the Ministry of Health (1930) related to the reservation of a stretch of land along the Thames river as private open space and the erection of dwellings for tenants of the estate including agricultural workers. It provided for the local authority to purchase the reserved land at open market value. Ministry files show that meetings were held with both the landowner's advisers (including Professor Abercrombie, a past president of the Town Planning Institute and an eminent practitioner in the domain), and a representative of the local authority, at the Ministry (TNA: HLG 52/592 1933). Together professional actors and civil servants defined the practice and the process of local negotiations. Status, interest and the authority of these actors (who for the most part were not legally qualified) in combination were an important regulatory resource. Policy practices defined the legal provisions. The fragmented nature of planning control at this stage contributed to the creation of a climate of dependency upon central government (and thus easier control) which in combination with the presence of powerful professional actors and landowners enhanced central regulatory capacities.

With the enactment of the 1932 Town and Country Planning Act, agreements were seen as both an alternative to the complex scheme procedure and as complementary to it. The Ministry of Health (the lead Department for land-use control at the time) seems to have encouraged their use in circumstances related to rural planning and preservation (a primary objective of the 1932 legislation). The Seventeenth Annual Report of the Ministry of Health emphasized the practical significance of agreements in 'preserv[ing] a stretch of the country' and retaining agricultural uses of land (Ministry of Health, 1936). The instrument was perceived as a mechanism by which the individual liberty of the landowner could be moulded to central government's will, albeit subtly whilst still retaining a veneer of landowner autonomy. By now Government was concerned to record and monitor the practice. Civil servants compiled a series of files to record the form and substance of agreements. They assembled precedent books on planning questions from the early 1930s until 1943 (TNA: HLG 95/52 1932).[9] The books contained details of the clauses contained in agreements, and those considered acceptable were distributed among planning authorities. By assisting planning authorities in applying land-use control mechanisms, central government secured a measure of purchase to engender future reliance and thus control. Local authorities seeking direction or eager to demonstrate their local initiatives submitted copies of their drafts to the Ministry, although this was not a statutory requirement. Those documents sent were considered by the Ministry and those most in accord with the civil servant's perception of appropriateness, disseminated to other authorities. The ostensibly benevolent promotion of best practice served as an effective regulatory device, enhancing the central government's authority and its ability to generate a policy-driven regulatory system. In this way systematic attempts were made to compile a picture of what were considered to be significant agreements by civil servants at the time. The agreements selected were listed according to subject matter, date and authority (where relevant), with a brief explanation of the decision, and where appropriate cross-referenced according to the scheme files. Gradually, through the dissemination of appropriate precedents, a coherent centrally-ordered regulatory system was created that attempted to confine the ambit of the statutory provisions by limiting a use of agreements when a scheme had been made. The increasing dependency of planning authorities on central government (not least because of its creation of a new and ostensibly comprehensive framework for town and country planning) no doubt assisted in establishing discrete mechanisms of control. Central government was not averse, however, to sending Ministry officials from the regional offices 'into the field', to undertake covert fact finding so as to gather more information, whilst they were providing practical assistance (TNA: HLG 71/267 1942–47).

The dissemination of precedents permitted the generation of a normative regulatory system confining agreements. Central officials, through a process of informal approval and the selection of drafts, initiated 'best practice' procedures that would be further institutionalized subsequently. Policy rather than strict legal interpretation informed official thinking and the regulatory process. By late 1933, agreements were viewed as the preferred way to secure land-use restrictions and in particular the prevention of building. Ministry files show that for agreements made under the 1932 Act, 'the main object ... is really to provide for special circumstances of a particular case which make some variation of the scheme provisions desirable, which it would be inconvenient to incorporate in the body of the scheme' (TNA: HLG 71/267 1942–47, Pepler to Hill 27 January 1933). Over time the Ministry began to exercise clear oversight by giving 'authoritative' advice as to the lawfulness or otherwise of local authority proposals, even in the absence of any statutory requirement to obtain ministerial consent. Civil servants made systematic efforts to coordinate and control

---

9 The precedent book contains some 58 cases.

the use of agreements through the use of precedents. Officials checked agreements during the course of considering draft schemes, and sometimes as a consequence they were revised or rejected. Regulatory efficacy was assisted by the configuration of the emerging system of agency for determining planning proposals, which gave local authorities new powers and made them further dependent upon central government for advice regarding how these were exercisable. Civil servants, in assuming a role of protector of the individual landowner against a 'bad bargain', promoted a vision of the practice which was more limited than the statutory provisions.

The techniques adopted indicate the extent of central input, notwithstanding an absence of any express oversight mechanism. By monitoring agreements, central officials in the Ministry of Health seem to have effectively controlled not only landowner and local authority dealings but relations *inter se* between branches of the government, and even specialists including legal counsel. Commenting on another agreement in a memorandum, civil servants note, '[t]he first is an amateur production which gives rise to all kinds of difficulties. Most of it appeared in a draft agreement ... sent to us by the Treasury Solicitor. We persuaded the latter to abandon the draft and accept an alternative form' (TNA: HLG 52/592 1933, Hill to Gibbon 23 November 1933). The centripetal pull of the government's non-legal actors appears to have prevailed, overriding the knowledge of others. This is something to which the planning authority became complicit through its own dependency on central government with the introduction of further statutory land-use planning controls and the technical innovations associated with this. By defining the limits of the practice, the Ministry lay the foundation for further intervention, which is formalized by the 1943 legislation. For the pre-modern era, planning authorities, with the assistance of the Ministry, achieve their local goals and targets through the negotiation of agreements with landowners, partly because these coincide with central ideals (the Ministry having developed a series of supporting stratagems where their ideals converge). For central government, in this embryonic phase few other regulatory solutions to land-use planning problems exist, hence the importance of agreements. Central officials (who were mostly legally unqualified) defined the parameters and legal effects of the instrument, thus establishing the trend for further centralizing tactics. By 1940, it would seem that a de facto consent system was being operated. By 1942, officers at the Ministry were systematically viewing draft agreements (TNA: HLG 95/52). The use of the tool was in turn being further integrated into the statutory (and increasingly comprehensive) system of control. Using agreements where the objective could be achieved through other statutory means was discouraged.[10] All of this occurred without statutory sanction.

Fostering a Climate of Regulatory Responsibility

The use of planning agreements during the early 1900s shows that the harnessing of contracting practices for public purposes has a long heritage and is not peculiar to

---

10 And thus risk the local authority paying compensation. By 1942 advice was given that agreements were to be considered '... in cases only where their object cannot be readily served by the planning scheme' (TNA: HLG 95/52 Berkhampsted and Tring 91601/223/501B).

the dilemmas of the late twentieth century. In the pre-modern era the regulation of planning agreements is achieved through the bilateral relations of the parties as much as through a calibration of informal controls centred around the use and production of information by the central government. Regulating the practice does not seem particularly problematic and this is no doubt assisted by the configuration of the policy space itself, which in this early stage can be characterized as one receptive to regulatory innovation. The creation of novel instruments such as planning agreements in combination with the uncertainties associated with the introduction of a new regime to regulate land use gave central government enhanced capacities of control, especially over planning authorities. It appears also to have made the parties to be regulated more cautious and receptive to central influence. Thus, the history of planning agreements in the pre-modern era suggests that in appropriate contexts a use of contractual practices for regulatory purposes is not inherently problematic.

Here regulation assumes a number of forms ranging from encouragement and advice to central direction. One of the most significant aspects of the pre-modern era is the preparatory work undertaken by central government to foster a climate of regulatory order and responsibility. The regulatory architecture being constructed transcends distinctions between law and policy with regulatory effects being determined through the adoption of policy strategies. It paves the way for a use by central government of formal oversight in the form of the introduction of a statutory mechanism of express consent, effectively by facilitating the introduction and calibration of direction. A use of agreements is shaped for the most part by the interventions of central and other influential actors rather than the planning authority or landowner and even less so by the application of legal principles. This is achieved through inducing local authority dependency upon central advice and opinion.

Perhaps paradoxically public regulation is secured, however, through the manipulation of common law forms. Contracting practices and land law principles are moulded to further government's aims by a process of policy intervention as much as legislative change. In this early stage it is possible to discern an emergence of hybrid regulatory forms (that mix command, consensus and cooperation) from the climate of interdependence between public and private actors that facilitate central oversight. Their adoption will become more apparent in time. The techniques combine cooperation, competition, direction and dependency-enhancing strategies and are adopted to redraw the statutory provisions. The gradual intensification of these techniques enabled their formalization in law. It was the existence of a combination of broadly cultural or environmental factors, however, that was pivotal in defining the cognitive and normative limitations of regulatory activity. These included the responsibility assumed by civil servants and the dependency of local authorities. The most significant factor however was the embryonic stage of the planning system that itself gave rise to a sufficient degree of instability to allow perhaps paradoxically central government to undertake a level of regulatory experimentation. Regulation becomes defined by a mosaic of practices that in combination give central government sufficient purchase to further its instrumental aims.

In this early phase the future regulatory intent of central government with regard to agreements can be identified. The idea of regulation articulated in the archival texts is that of engendering control through fostering a climate of dependency and a willingness to comply. This is achieved in part by central officials providing guidance and assistance on 'best practice', suggesting model drafts and even drafting clauses, as much as the receptivity of planning authorities to accept advice. Without this, the introduction of express oversight requiring all agreements to obtain the Minister's consent before being effective under the Town and Country (Interim Development) Act 1943 may not have been possible. Regulation acquires strongly paternalistic elements which emphasize the capacities of central officials to exercise correct judgement in contrast to the (in)capacities of local authorities. Directive command as a regulatory form follows from encouragement, advice and assistance. This is suggestive of an inversion in temporal terms of the sequence of compliance strategies. Compliance is often viewed as the product of the failings of more prescriptive strategies. The history of the early stages of planning agreements points to command and direction being the product of more flexible techniques that facilitate an introduction of direction rather than as being the result of failing command and control. The historical evidence shows the existence of informal methods that were gradually co-opted into formal law, not because of their inefficacy but the reverse. Effective norms are here being established after being tested informally. Thus, regulation assumes a rather different characteristic; that of effectiveness through flexibility, which then becomes embedded within the formal legal system. Command here is possible only because of the supportive strategies devised by central officials. The structures built provide the foundations for a calibration in regulatory techniques.

Conclusion

In some forms of land-use control, the regulatory discourse finds purchase and its expression through a notion of rights. This is so in the case of planning agreements. Industrialization and its consequences functioned as a catalyst for the creation of a land-use planning system that was state-sponsored and gave a pivotal role to the administration. Organizationally, the result was to diminish a reliance on common law principles, and enable government intervention (whether central or local) through the use of an array of policy and legal mechanisms. In this chapter I have shown how a use of agreements illustrates the transition from a reliance on private law to public principle and its consequent regulatory implications.

Regulation by the government remains premised largely upon the existence of classical command mechanisms. This partly derives from the modern conceptualization of state legitimacy, which continues to be framed according to a potential to wield power over others. This hierarchical view, whilst suited to a specific historical period in the twentieth century, is not necessarily able to accommodate other periods where equally if not more powerful actors challenge the realm of government. This may provide one explanation for a use of contracting practices for regulatory ends. In the post-command and -control world, a use of contracting is seen to compensate for the centre's incapacity to exert direct command in the context where the government remains dependent upon others to execute forms of control. The history of planning agreements indicates that similar strategies may be used where new governance frameworks are introduced. The modes of regulation are not, however, neatly compartmentalized but assume multiple, if hybrid, forms that point to a blurring of distinctions that challenge the oft-accepted taxonomy of regulatory strategies adopted by the government to control behaviour.

This chapter, in concentrating on the early phases of planning agreements, has highlighted how central regulation became effective initially through a use of policy strategies that had no legal foundation but which were enabled by a system characterized by levels of uncertainty. This allowed the government to experiment with its techniques for ordering local activity. In the pre-modern era multiple regulatory strategies emerge and are deployed in a space at the interface of individuated activity and the generation of broad policy goals. Here, regulation must be viewed as a political process where the bargaining strategies of local actors are tempered by central involvement. Contractual rights and interests are moulded by the direction of central government.

The regulation of agreements began with the provision of advice and the exchange of ideas through the collection and dissemination of precedents by central officials. This became more intense through a calibration in the delivery of advice and guidance. The dissemination of the precedents used by authorities gradually became an editorial process with central officials selecting appropriate clauses and then approving whole drafts after 1932. In this way regulation became more systematic and the level of control increased. It ended with the creation of an organized system that documented agreements according to type and subject matter. It gave also central officials the capacity to regulate the practice by defining the parameters of the permissible. It led to the creation of a statutory system, which through legal provision reaffirmed existing practices. The regulation of contracting practices in this context can be seen as being driven by a series of techniques that can be characterized as initially inclusive rather than directive. They involve the participation of the contracting parties and focus upon enhancing the dependency of the local actors. It enabled the subsequent formalization of oversight through legislation. Informality as the precursor to direction facilitated the government's task of regulating agreements and it is debatable whether the effective exercise of formal oversight through a system of ministerial consent could have been achievable without the earlier experimentation. The example of planning agreements might suggest that in a context that encourages prior dependency and inclusive interaction less direct strategies may be potentially as effective as the use of commands.

What can be seen also is the transformation of ostensibly local and lateral rights-based practices that derived their force from the common law principles of land law and contract into a consolidated form of public regulation. It was one that redefined the bilateral and individuated form into a practice that could be regulated by third party actors, especially the government. This cuts across liberal ideas, of agreement being conceptualized in terms of the parties' freedom to bargain and negotiate and instead suggests a role for third parties to regulate the practice by exercising many forms of oversight.

PART 2
Complementarities Between Rights and Regulation

Chapter 5

Taxing Prejudice: Non-Constitutional Approaches to the Problem of Minority Rights

Anders Walker

Introduction

Though notions of democracy and rights often coincide, democratic systems frequently prove hostile to the enforcement of legal rights, particularly those belonging to unpopular, electoral minorities (Tocqueville, 1831; Mill, 1859; Gamble, 1997). This is just as true for nations with strong, individual rights-based political traditions, like for example the USA, as it is for nations with a more complex post-colonial, political heritage (Huntington, 1968; Mamdani, 1996; Oloka-Onyongo, 2001). In fact, precisely because of its strong rights-based tradition, the USA provides a remarkably rich history of creative ways in which constitutional protections for minorities have been circumvented through legal means (Kousser, 1974; Klarman, 2004).

Given that this is the case, what lessons, if any, can the USA provide in terms of creative counter-responses, so to speak, to the inherent problems with rights enforcement that coincide with majority rule? This chapter discusses two examples, both drawn from the 1950s and 1960s, in which policy makers used the democratic process itself to protect minorities. The first strategy, culled from the American South, shows how a southern governor named Luther Hodges set the stage for the racial integration of public schools in North Carolina in 1957 by shifting the cost of maintaining segregation directly onto the shoulders of white voters. Specifically, it shows how Hodges did not try to coerce integration, but rather sought to devolve integration decisions to local majorities, providing them with the option of either tolerating token levels of black students in their schools or embracing their prejudice and losing state funding entirely.

The second example culled from the American North shows how an appointed official named Herbert Wechsler sought to abolish the mandatory death penalty for first degree murder in New York, thereby bolstering the rights of criminal defendants. To accomplish this, Wechsler advocated a re-codification of New York's murder statute, one that promoted reform by erasing the distinction between first and second degree murder and then bifurcating capital trials into a guilt and penalty phase, thereby giving juries the power to convict defendants without necessarily sentencing them to death.

In both cases, state actors turned not to the courts but state legislatures, traditionally bastions of majority will to incorporate moderate reforms into public law. Wechsler, for example, bolstered the rights of capital defendants through the re-codification of New York's criminal code. Meanwhile, Hodges proposed reform by devolving both discretion and financial cost to local officials. Rather than seek to coerce the public, as courts or executive commissions might, Wechsler and Hodges both imposed a type of tax on popular prejudice that made the repression of minority rights possible, but more costly and complicated, for electoral majorities.

How might this be relevant to reformers struggling with the problem of majority prejudice generally, either inside or outside the American context? Both cases illustrate the manner in which policymakers might use the democratic system creatively to enforce minority rights, while escaping reliance on coercive bodies like non-discrimination commissions or courts. Such bodies, though commonly believed to be effective agents of rights-enforcement, often suffer themselves at the hands of electoral majorities who vote to restrict their funding, limit their jurisdiction, or politically influence their membership (Rosenburg, 1991). At best, this results in non-enforcement. At worst, it results in escalating oppression, occasionally even drawing in outside nations to fulfil a regulatory role. To show how architects of reform might minimize the risk of such consequences, a discussion of each example follows.

Putting a Price on Prejudice: Luther Hodges and the Token Desegregation of Public Schools in North Carolina

In May 1954, the United States Supreme Court declared that racially segregated schools deprived African-Americans of their right to equal protection of the law under the Fourteenth Amendment to the United States Constitution (Kluger, 1975). This judicial assertion of a minority right encountered immediate opposition in the American South, where segregated schooling had been a longstanding tradition (Bartley, 1969; Woodward, 1974). Within weeks of the ruling, grassroots opposition began to form in Deep South states like Mississippi (McMillen, 1971). Within a year, political leaders across the South began to capitalize on this grassroots opposition, advocating outright defiance of the Supreme Court (Bartley, 1969).

For leaders who refused to defy the Supreme Court, a variety of problems emerged. Perhaps foremost among such problems was popular outrage. For example, in most states that attempted some type of token integration, mob protest, and occasionally even rioting, resulted (Bartley, 1969; Klarman, 2004). This was true even for traditionally moderate states with relatively low black populations, like Tennessee, Texas and Arkansas. However, in states where leaders made it clear that no integration would even be attempted, like Virginia, South Carolina and Georgia, little or no mob violence emerged (Bartley, 1969). Arguably, voters in these states felt like there was little need to take the law into their own hands.

At least one state proved an exception to this. North Carolina, a traditionally moderate state, integrated two school districts with no mob violence in September 1957, at the very peak of resistance to integration in the South. While some of North

Carolina's success can be attributed to its relatively small black population, at least compared to states like Mississippi, much of it can also be attributed to the creative leadership of its governor at the time, an accomplished businessman named Luther Hodges. Hodges, though born and raised in the South, became deeply concerned that racial extremism would jeopardize the state's economy, particularly attempts to draw northern investment to the region (Hodges, 1962).[1]

As a result, Hodges endorsed an elaborate scheme of formal compliance with the Supreme Court, one that still provided local officials with the opportunity to preserve substantially segregated public schools. This scheme, which amounted to a type of creative compliance, ended segregation formally, by race, but authorized local school boards to assign students to schools based on other factors. These factors included exceedingly vague considerations like 'the best interests' of the child, together with the 'proper administration' of public schools, as well as concerns over 'health' and 'safety' (North Carolina Session Laws, 1955, 310). Voters endorsed such classifications in 1955, particularly after Hodges assured them that it would increase North Carolina's chances of preserving segregation and surviving federal scrutiny (Hodges, 1962).

In 1956, Hodges endorsed an elaborate complement to North Carolina's placement plan, one that devolved almost all decision-making authority to local school boards, not the state. Pursuant to this second 'local option plan' as it came to be known, local officials could decide to admit token numbers of black students to white schools, if they so wished. They could also choose to close their public school systems entirely, rather than integrate. In cases where local boards opted to admit token numbers of black students, and not to close public schools, parents who continued to protest could apply to receive state funds so that they could send their children to private institutions (Morning Herald, 1956a).

While Hodges claimed that this second set of provisions would enable local officials to deal with isolated federal court orders to integrate specific school districts, he acknowledged that this plan would also make opposition to integration more costly for local people. Rather than provide local communities with the luxury of having state officials fight the integration battle for them, his measures placed a considerable amount of responsibility, not to mention cost, on the shoulders of local officials. Not only would local officials confront the administrative costs of dealing with black demands to be placed in white schools, but they would also be forced to fight any federal legal challenge that might ensue from opposition to particular placements. Further, to close a school system, local leaders would need to amass signatures from 15 per cent of the voters in the district, not to mention raise the money needed to build private schools (Durham Morning Herald, 1956c).

When white parents voiced opposition to Hodges's 'local option plan', afraid that it could lead to the closing of public schools, he did little to assure them. Private classes could be held, he told them, in the 'back of a Moose hall', meaning

---

1   '[A] course of defiance would forfeit whatever chance we might have of convincing the rest of the nation that our position in this matter is sincere,' warned Hodges in July 1956, at the height of massive resistance to the Court, 'such a course would get us nowhere' (Durham Morning Herald 1956b).

any given public gathering place, hardly a substitute for a well-equipped school (Durham Morning Herald, 1956c). This type of callousness, though not particularly popular, had its uses. By placing the responsibility on local parents for building private schools, Hodges made political defiance more costly than if the state had promised to keep public schools open and segregated. Similarly, by giving local communities the option to close school systems entirely, he was able to engage in a type of brinksmanship with white parents who might have been only moderately committed to the notion of maintaining white schools – particularly if their children risked attending no school at all.

This brinksmanship worked two ways. While it could be used to intimidate parents who valued education over symbolic affirmations of white supremacy, it also provided 'an outlet valve' as Hodges put it, for extremism. Extremists, rather than feel disempowered by Hodges's local option scheme, suddenly had the opportunity to become the founders, builders, and administrators of entirely segregated private schools. By opening this option to those most prone to engage in defiance, Hodges arguably reduced the moral legitimacy, and perhaps even instrumental appeal, of vigilantism.

The success of Hodges's approach to the desegregation problem, namely a devolution of the burdens of maintaining segregated schools to local communities, became clear in September 1957. That month, school districts in Charlotte and Greensboro both decided to enter token numbers of black students into white schools, rather than fight costly lawsuits in federal court (Durham Morning Herald, 1957a). While a similar action engendered an outburst of popular violence in Little Rock, Arkansas, North Carolina encountered none (Bartley, 1969). Hodges lamented the integration of the public schools, but warned North Carolinians not to engage in violence. He also praised his own work. '[W]e can be thankful that our laws have been designed,' he told North Carolinians on 4 September 1957, 'as to permit an orderly exercise of choice in these matters and our citizens do not have to resort to irresponsible actions to make their wishes felt' (Durham Morning Herald, 1957b).

By devolving discretionary authority, as well as the burden of closing public schools and building private ones onto the shoulders of local communities, Luther Hodges helped create room for moderate reform in North Carolina. Vigilante violence, which emerged in almost every southern state that attempted some type of token integration, did not emerge to the same extent in North Carolina, arguably because Hodges granted local whites a considerable amount of control over the handling of the desegregation crisis in their school districts.[2] Parents who were adamantly opposed to sending their children to school with blacks, for example, did not have to send their children to such schools and could apply for state funds to attend private schools. That few did suggests they might not have wanted to undertake the additional burden of building those schools, even if they ultimately supported the idea of them.

By acknowledging the power of popular prejudice, in other words, Luther Hodges was arguably able to achieve more reform than if he had made a defiant statement in favour of black rights. Though African-American civil rights groups

---

2   But see Tyson (1999).

like the National Association for the Advancement of Colored People, or NAACP, had argued against the institution of segregation on both legal and moral grounds, Hodges did not. In fact, he supported segregation publicly, meanwhile devising legal methods of making the preservation of absolute segregation difficult. Though this was undoubtedly designed to cap integration at a relatively negligible level, the larger lesson is worth noting, namely that acknowledging prejudice can, in some cases, be a positive step towards ameliorating its effects. In this case, Hodges even indulged popular prejudice, making it clear to local majorities that they had absolute discretion over integration in their school districts.

How viable might such a strategy have been in another context? To answer this question it is helpful to compare what Hodges did in North Carolina to what another reformer, Columbia law professor Herbert Wechsler did, at roughly the same time, in New York. There, Wechsler confronted the likelihood of a popular backlash against the reduction of criminal punishment for convicted felons. Felons, not entirely unlike African-Americans in the South, represented a type of unpopular minority that enjoyed little legal protection of their constitutional rights. Consequently, to bolster their rights Wechsler, like Hodges, turned to the democratic process.

Codifying Criminal Law: Herbert Wechsler and the Abolition of the Mandatory Death Penalty in New York

In June 1961, almost four years after Luther Hodges orchestrated the token integration of public schools in North Carolina, Columbia University law professor Herbert Wechsler joined a commission to revise New York's Penal Law (*New York Times* 1961, 39). Wechsler, who had been one of the primary drafters of a substantial model penal code for American Law Institute, agreed to participate on the commission at least in part out of an interest in making the system fairer for criminal defendants. In fact, for the next four years, until New York adopted a new Penal Law in 1965, Wechsler would go from Columbia Law School, downtown, to 155 Leonard Street, to attend meetings and conduct public hearings on reforming the criminal law of the Empire State.

Wechsler's time on the commission forced him to confront a variety of issues: among them a trend on the part of both legislators and judges to impose harsher penalties on criminal defendants, a traditionally unpopular minority. For example, the distinction between first and second degree murder in New York had eroded considerably since the nineteenth century, resulting in increasing convictions for first degree murder. Technically designed to apply to premeditated, planned killings, first degree murder had in fact been expanded to incorporate intentional killings, even if they were neither premeditated nor planned.

This trend towards severity clashed with Wechsler's own views of the appropriate goals of criminal law. Since the 1930s, Wechsler had emphasized the need for rational distinctions in the law, particularly in the realm of homicide.[3] In fact, the

---

3   Wechsler's first definitive statements on criminal law reform emerged in 1937, in two *Columbia Law Review* essays: Michael and Wechsler (1937a) and Michael and Wechsler (1937b).

ultimate purpose of criminal law according to Wechsler was not to expand the scope of punishment but rather to deter harmful behaviour.[4] He advocated rehabilitation, not retribution, and placed a large amount of faith in social science and psychiatry to treat criminals.[5]

While on Leonard Street, however, Wechsler pursued a more strategic agenda. He tempered his desire for rational reform with a concern for what the people of New York would accept, particularly in matters of punishment. The death penalty, at that time still mandatory for anyone convicted of first degree murder in the state, was of particular concern. For Wechsler, the primary obstacle to abolition was popular opinion and in particular the popular demand for revenge.

'[T]he desire for revenge,' wrote Wechsler and his Columbia colleague Jerome Michael in 1940, 'the belief that retributive punishment is just, and the feeling that examples must be made of those guilty of shocking crimes are to a very considerable degree entrenched in the general population' (Michael and Wechsler, 1940, p. 16). So entrenched, in fact, that '[t]oo lenient treatment of offenders,' they continued, 'may therefore lead to lynching, self-help or indifference about prosecution which may be far worse in their social consequences than the utilization of more severe methods of treatment which satisfy the popular desire for severity though they have no reformative capacity.' (Michael and Wechsler, 1940, p. 16.) Wechsler and Michael's mention of the popular desire for severity here was suggestive. According to them, if the law rejected popular demands for harsh punishment, substituting instead goals of rehabilitation or reform, for example, then the public might itself engage in criminal activity or, as they put it, 'lynching' to administer the punishment that they saw fit.

Though Wechsler did not relate conditions in New York to conditions elsewhere, his and Michael's observation that the public might take the law into their own hands resonated with the situation that Luther Hodges had in fact confronted in the American South. There too, popular outrage at the Supreme Court's desegregation order threatened to spill over into vigilantism. To avoid this, Hodges had worked hard to shift decision-making responsibility, as well as some of the cost of maintaining dual schools, to local shoulders. Now, Wechsler sought to perform a similar manoeuvre in New York.

But first, he struggled to convince advocates of abolishing the death penalty that there was a utilitarian rationale for listening to the public's darker inclinations. Evidence of this emerged during a public hearing in 1962, when the committee confronted both proponents and opponents of capital punishment. One opponent, a district attorney named Joseph Ryan, argued that the death penalty did little save incite prurient popular interest. 'The most and worst that the death penalty accomplishes today,' began Ryan, 'is to whip up morbid curiosity in trials, creating

---

    4   Wechsler made this clear early on, in Michael and Wechsler (1937a, 1937b), again in Wechsler (1940), in his preliminary memorandum on the Model Penal Code (Wechsler, 1952), in Wechsler (1956) and, finally, in Wechsler (1968).

    5   This theme emerges in both segments of 'A Rationale of the Law of Homicide,' and constitutes the dominant thesis of Herbert Wechsler's preliminary memoranda for the American Law Institute's Model Penal Code project, published in the *Harvard Law Review* (1952).

a sensationalism that is based on the primal urge to secure an eye for an eye – a tooth for a tooth' (Temporary Commission to Revise the Penal Law of New York, 1962, p. 59). Rejecting such primitive articulations of justice, Ryan counselled the committee to 'remove the criminal courts from the Roman Circus' and to treat murderers just as dispassionately as 'car thieves' (ibid.).

For Wechsler, the Roman Circus, to borrow Ryan's phrase, performed an important, if largely symbolic function. Rather than a source of entertainment, it was in fact a public affirmation of a popularly held belief that retributive punishment was just and that murder deserved, at least in some cases, death. If death was eliminated as a possible sentence, argued Wechsler, then a popular backlash might result. 'Have you had any real cruel murders in the last few years?' Wechsler asked Ryan (Temporary Commission to Revise the Penal Law of New York, 1962, p. 59). 'About five', answered Ryan (ibid.). 'Have you any opinion,' continued Wechsler, 'based on your experience, as to what the effect on the community would have been if you could not have launched a capital prosecution?' (ibid.)

To illustrate his point, Wechsler asked Ryan to consider a hypothetical case in which a criminal defendant confessed to a brutal, shocking murder. Then, he asked Ryan what the popular response might be if the killer did not receive the death penalty. 'Can you imagine what effect on public feeling in your county would be?' asked Wechsler, who then went on to describe a horrible triple-killing that happened in Delaware just after the state voted to abolish the death penalty in 1958, a murder so outrageous that it led to the almost unanimous restoration of capital punishment in 1961. Why did this happen posited Wechsler explained that this happened: '[b]ecause there had been a triple murder and a very, very unforgivable condition so that any mitigation was negated and just a sense of frustration of the community resulted in this sentiment in the legislature' (Temporary Commission to Revise the Penal Law of New York[6] 1962, 59). A practical understanding of popular frustration, felt Wechsler, in other words, should guide reform, preventing it from going beyond what the public might, in a moment of crisis, accept.

Wechsler's comments reflected a certain strategic approach, if you will, to the problem of the mandatory death penalty. Although personally opposed to execution, he recognized the public's desire for revenge, particularly in cases of horrendous crimes. This explains his mention of Delaware, where the state abolished the death penalty in 1958, only to reinstate it after a massive popular backlash, in 1961. Rather than risk a similar fiasco in New York, Wechsler grilled Ryan on retaining the death penalty not as a deterrent, but a means of mollifying public opinion.

'[I]n an abolition situation,' continued Wechsler, 'what you have is an outraged populace turning to the Legislature and denouncing the law and a very real danger that you may end up worse off than you started, which is what happened in Delaware. They have more capital crimes in Delaware today after the 1961 reversal than they had in 1958 before the 1958 abolition' (Public Hearing of RTC, 1962, 66). Ryan had little to say. In fact, none of the proponents of abolishing the death penalty who appeared before the commission seemed to recognize Wechsler's logic. But the commission did. After the public hearing, the commission met informally and

---

6   Hereinafter known as the RTC.

Wechsler alluded again to Delaware, warning that abolition of the penalty could lead to an even more severe backlash in favour of it, particularly in the aftermath of a particularly brutal killing. 'If the Commission induces the Legislature to abolish capital punishment,' noted Wechsler, 'and if thereafter several shocking homicides occur, the Legislature might feel that they were led down the garden path' (Minutes of Informal Meeting of the Temporary Commission, 1962, p. 2). He concluded that the passage of two moderate reforms would constitute a substantial step forward in the direction of improving the law. They were: (1) a redefinition of homicide, specifically a removal of the distinction between first and second degree murder, and (2) a two-stage, bifurcated trial in which the jury decided guilt and punishment separately (ibid.). The commission, although it postponed a formal vote, endorsed Wechsler's suggestions.

Here, as in North Carolina, the careful drafting of statutes created room for enhancing minority rights: in this case the rights of criminal defendants. For example, redefining murder without relying on first and second degrees, a distinction that was traditionally meant to separate planned killings from unplanned ones, did away with the mandatory death penalty, something that had traditionally only applied to defendants convicted of first-degree murder. Further, bifurcating trials in those cases where the death penalty was actively sought by prosecutors, but not mandated by law, had the effect of empowering local juries, granting them the discretion to convict but not necessarily to kill. This, incidentally, paralleled how Hodges took a controversial issue and devolved it to local control in North Carolina. Just like Hodges allowed local authorities to decide whether they wanted to close schools or not, for example, so too did Wechsler allow local juries to decide whether they wanted to impose the death penalty or not, once defendants had already been convicted.

Both strategies imposed a greater burden, or 'tax', on average people, yet by doing so also invested them more closely in the legal process, thereby reducing the chances that they might react against that process in a negative way. For example, Hodges required that local people shoulder the burden of building private schools, but otherwise allowed them to exercise their prejudice. Meanwhile, Wechsler required that local people double the amount of time they spend on juries in capital cases, as well as assume the burden of deciding death once they were there, all the while lobbying to preserve the penalty.

Conclusion

While only snapshots, the efforts that Herbert Wechsler and Luther Hodges took to bolster minority rights in their states arguably provides an example of a democratic model for rights enforcement that did not involve supervisory commissions or courts. The commission to revise New York's Penal Law, for example, was not charged with monitoring the abuses of defendants' rights. Nor were Luther Hodges's efforts to implement local option plans in North Carolina an attempt to police rights abuses. Yet, both Hodges and Wechsler devised legislative measures that, in a sense, taxed the ability of majorities to discriminate.

While such methods certainly had their limitations, perhaps the foremost being a tendency towards moderate rather than full enforcement, they also, arguably, had their place. In fact, if abstracted from their historical context, one might say that they provide analytical models for reform in special cases where judicial enforcement might not be viable, or even possible. Such a situation might arise, for example, where there is a high likelihood of popular resistance to judicial rulings. Why? Because court rulings generally manifest themselves as direct orders that in turn require executive enforcement. While executive enforcement can certainly quell popular dissent, often that enforcement itself requires at least some popular support. This is the case, at least, in democratic states where executive leaders rely on popular votes for re-election, and are consequently reluctant to impose unwanted reforms on an electoral majority.

Here, ultimately, is the crux of the problem with minority enforcement in democratic systems. And here, arguably, is where both Wechsler and Hodges provide the most help. For example, rather than turn away from the people themselves, so to speak, they both devolved decision-making authority to actors at the local level, whether parents of school districts or local prosecutors and criminal juries. Yet, they did not allow such actors complete discretion. For example, both policy makers provided the public with a relatively structured framework from within which they could exercise their prejudice, and also leave room for change. Hodges, for example, allowed local voters to close public school systems but did not, in a manner that is important to remember, allow local majorities to simply continue the operation of segregated schools. Meanwhile, Wechsler devolved decision-making power over the death penalty to local juries, but did away with the distinction between first and second degree murder. This made the death sentence less automatic for defendants found guilty of intentional, but not necessarily premeditated killing.

In addition to devolving power to the local level, both Hodges and Wechsler took popular prejudice seriously, refusing to reject it as morally or politically invalid. In fact, here might be their most remarkable move, at least from the perspective of legal reform. Generally, reformers seek to combat prejudice, not build policy around it. However, both Wechsler and Hodges effectively accepted popular animosity towards certain minorities as a given, and then sought to work together with that prejudice to expand the rights of those minorities.

Driving their desire to accept rather than reject prejudice was a certain baseline fear, namely that if the public were ignored, then certain extreme elements of that public would engage in vigilantism. In North Carolina, the fear was that white parents would do what white parents did in other, similarly situated moderate states, namely threaten harm to black children. In New York, by contrast, the fear was that voters would react against abolition of the death penalty by arguing for an even harsher reinstatement.

Both Herbert Wechsler and Luther Hodges recognized, in other words, that law is fragile. If legal reformers or lawmakers generally do not align the law with majority will, then the majority can in fact disrupt both the legal process, as well as the very existence of the law itself. This is perhaps the second most remarkable similarity that these two leaders shared, namely a decidedly populist view of both the sources of legal power, as well as the parameters of legal change. Rather than an edifice resting on transcendent principles or a coercive set of rules backed by a powerful state, the law was, for both Hodges and Wechsler, a relatively permeable structure that owed its survival to mimicking, if not articulating, popular norms.

Consequently, both men turned to electoral majorities, not judicial bodies or executive or congressional commissions, to begin reform. Neither went directly against the popular will, whether the will to retain the death penalty, or to preserve segregated schools. And, consequently, both reformers proved relatively successful at limiting the vagaries of popular prejudice by imposing subtle taxes on its exercise. In the case of North Carolina, this meant that white voters who opposed integration were left to either construct their own private schools, or to suffer the complete shutdown of public schools in the event that they proved absolutely unwilling to compromise on the segregation question.

Meanwhile, in New York, voters who may have endorsed the death penalty suddenly found the imposition of that penalty harder to attain. Juries, suddenly, had to consider the penalty phases of trials separately. Average citizens, who may have been opposed to limitations on the penalty, found reform buried in the technical redefinition of murder. Though certain segments of the public may have had no problem digesting such a shift, others, arguably, would have needed to a make a considerable investment in time to even comprehend the content and quality of reforms embedded therein. This, arguably, was itself a type of tax on prejudice. It was not a transparent legal opinion, easily attacked by average citizens who knew little of the law. It was, by nature of its sheer scope, harder to grasp. Those who were adamantly in favour of the mandatory death penalty, for example, suddenly had a substantial piece of legislation to study and lobby against.

In conclusion, though toleration of popular prejudice may seem repellent to anyone interested in legal reform, the examples of both Luther Hodges and Herbert Wechsler suggest that accepting prejudice and working around it can, in fact, be critical to policy success. Even if majorities end up doing little more than expressing their prejudice in symbolic ways, that too can be an important part of moving around what might otherwise be a political impasse. Further, the law need not be an instrument of coercion. In fact, in cases where bitter popular resistance exists to a particular reform, it is questionable whether law, by itself, can serve any coercive purpose at all. Both Wechsler and Hodges suggest other, perhaps more productive roles that the law can play. For example, it can structure the manner in which local majorities exercise their prejudice, preventing it from achieving a particularly extreme form. Similarly, the law can also submerge reform within technical legal distinctions, such as the redefinition of the statutory crime of murder. While there are certainly other ways that the law can be used, the two examples presented here provide an alternate mode of thinking about enforcing minority rights in the face of widespread popular prejudice.

Chapter 6

Doing Good Business or Just Doing Good: Competing Human Rights Frameworks at the World Bank

Galit A. Sarfaty[1]

Introduction

Organizational cultures shape how human rights are framed, interpreted and institutionalized. There are often multiple subcultures within an organization, which may correspond to divergent frameworks on human rights and strategies on how they should be implemented. In this paper, I focus on the culture of the World Bank, which is the largest and most influential development agency, and the role of human rights within it.

In the last decade, the World Bank has expressed its recognition and support for the protection of human rights as a prerequisite for poverty reduction. Yet it has no official policy or explicit approach on this issue for guiding staff in their decision making. Why? There have been and continue to be a number of obstacles, particularly, restrictions in the Bank's Articles of Agreement. Given that the Bank's Articles have been recently reinterpreted by the former General Counsel to provide a legal justification for the Bank to work on human rights, a more critical obstacle remains – internal divisions within the organization. I focus here on divisions between staff of different disciplinary backgrounds, which is arguably the central source of disagreement within the Bank. Due to the employees' diverse intellectual backgrounds and methodological approaches to solving problems, there is not a single World Bank approach to human rights. The phrase 'human rights' is interpreted differently depending on whom you ask within the organization.

Employees' disciplinary backgrounds (for example, economics or law) shape how the human rights agenda is framed and whether it will ultimately be internalized

1 This research was generously supported by grants from the National Science Foundation (Grant No. 0513960), the Social Science Research Council-Mellon Mays Program and the University of Chicago's Center for the Study of Race, Politics and Culture. I benefited from discussions at the 2006 Law and Society Association Annual Meeting, where an earlier version of this paper was presented. I would like to thank John Comaroff, Bronwen Morgan and Martha Nussbaum for their invaluable comments, and my colleagues at the World Bank for their cooperation and support. Finally, I am most grateful to Adam Saunders for his unending patience and support. Responsibility for the final draft is entirely mine.

by staff as a whole. Competing interpretive frameworks reflect power dynamics between academic disciplines within the institution. I will focus on two major frameworks – instrumental and intrinsic – which roughly correspond to economic and legal perspectives on human rights. The functionalist framework provides a functionalist rationale for human rights as enhancing development effectiveness and making good business sense. In contrast, the intrinsic framework defines human rights as universal principles that are ends in themselves. This second framework includes two subgroups, which emphasize either the legal or moral dimension. Under the legal subgroup, human rights are defined as legal obligations that derive from the international human rights regime. The moral subgroup, while also adhering to an intrinsic rationale, frames human rights as ethical principles rather than 'rights', based on a conception of human dignity. The second part of this chapter includes a further discussion and a table of these approaches.

Internal divisions in the institutional culture shape the Bank's approach to human rights in at least two different ways, the second of which is the main focus of my paper. The first way I call 'implementation gaps'. Many outside scholars and Non-Governmental Organisations (NGOs), as well as the Bank's own Operations Evaluation Department, have demonstrated failures to effectively implement the Bank's human rights-related programs or safeguard policies (see, for instance, Fox and Brown, 1998; MacKay, 2002; Clark, 2003; Horta, 2003).[2] While domestic political and legal constraints and the level of civil society activism within borrower countries are among the causes of implementation gaps, internal tensions among staff play a significant role as well (Sarfaty, 2005).

The second way in which internal tensions shape the Bank's approach to human rights is what I call 'interpretive gaps'. I argue that interpretive gaps are a critical factor in analysing how human rights get internalized in international institutions and development agencies. Interpretive gaps refer to differences between multiple staff frameworks for articulating, justifying and applying the human rights agenda at the Bank. Competing rights discourses circulate within the institution, and correspond to disparate interpretive communities and subcultures among staff. These discourses represent distinct ways of defining human rights, justifying its relevance with respect to the Bank's mission, and conceptualizing its practical role in Bank operations. Clashes between discourses are more than just debates over language. I contend that these clashes can affect the long-term integration of human rights into the institutional culture. Staff will not internalize human rights norms, and institutional behaviour will not adapt accordingly, if these clashes are not reconciled or at least deliberated over in a meaningful way.[3]

---

2   See also Operations Evaluation Department (2003), World Bank Report No. 25,332; Operations Evaluation Department (2003), World Bank Report No. 25,754.

3   Of course, a reconciliation among competing discourses is only a part of the puzzle of how to internalize human rights in an institution and foster a human rights consciousness among staff. Other ingredients, which I do not discuss in this paper, include an appropriate staff incentive system to motivate behaviour, leadership by senior and middle management, and the investment of sufficient resources to effectively institute policy changes.

This paper is based on observations, document analysis and interviews over more than four years, including one year of full-time ethnographic fieldwork, at the World Bank headquarters in Washington, DC. First, I analyse the various interpretive communities within the Bank's organizational culture, with a focus on the diverse disciplinary communities. After briefly describing how the Bank has evolved in its orientation to human rights, I illustrate how disciplinary communities correspond to distinct frameworks for justifying these issues in Bank activities. I then use a case study of two AIDS projects to reveal competing approaches to the human rights of people living with HIV/AIDS, and their operational implications. In conclusion, I argue that the power of human rights in shaping staff behaviour depends on their discursive fit with an organization's values and culture. Reconciling competing discourses is critical for promoting effective and consistent human rights practice within an institution.

My research seeks to contribute to the theme of the intersection of rights and regulation by focusing on the regulatory, legal, and moral dimensions of human rights in the context of its integration into an international institution. I demonstrate why it is important to analyse competing human rights frameworks among interpretive communities within an organizational culture. Interpretive gaps may lead to under-implementation or inconsistent compliance to human rights norms. Thus, this paper aims to promote further consideration of the regulatory structures that would most effectively bridge different visions of human rights within organizations.

Organizational Dynamics in the World Bank

The organizational culture of the World Bank is characterized by 'interpretative battles', or battles between competing interpretive communities that establish their own meanings based on their respective value systems (Cover, 1983, p. 25, p. 32). These battles have manifested themselves in the Bank's internal debate over human rights over the past decade. They also roughly correspond to competing frameworks on how to approach human rights.

Like other bureaucracies, the Bank contains a range of interpretive communities, whose relative power is based on their level of influence over the overall decision making in the institution. The members of communities share similar characteristics (for example, occupation, age, status within the hierarchy and so on) and may frame problems in a particular way based on their commonalities. Hence, official Bank rhetoric is often contested and negotiated within the institution, despite its commensuration of values into standardized forms (Espeland, 1998, p. 27).

Before describing the most influential interpretive communities within the Bank, I will briefly map out its organizational structure. With over 7,000 staff based in its headquarters in Washington, DC (and another 3,000 in its field offices), the Bank includes a wide range of employees. They come from 160 different countries and include economists, political scientists, lawyers, sociologists, anthropologists, environmentalists, financial analysts and engineers, among others. The basic management structure is a matrix, with overlapping functional and geographic units and parallel reporting relationships.

Employees primarily work in either the operations units or the network units (sometimes referred to as the anchor). Operations is responsible for lending activities and relations with member countries. It is divided into six geographic regions, and then sub-divided into seven thematic areas, such as Environmentally and Socially Sustainable Development, Human Development, and Infrastructure.[4] The network units, which cover the same seven thematic topics and are not sub-divided geographically, offer advisory services to operations staff in the form of reports, best practices, strategies and referrals to experts. Those who work in the network are primarily devoted to conducting research, as opposed to the operations staff who mostly work on project design and implementation.

Based on this brief summary of the Bank's structure, one can already identify a number of competing interpretive communities. For example, there are divisions based on status within the hierarchy (management versus lower-ranked staff), and on age (the older generation versus the newer generation of staff who have a different conception of the Bank's role in a globalized world). Another common division is based on function – operations versus network (research), with operations staff often complaining that those in the network do not understand the day-to-day activities of managing projects and dealing with country governments, and whose research is therefore not always relevant to operational work.

The most significant division that continuously came up in my interviews with staff is a disciplinary one. While the institution should be praised for the breadth of employees' disciplinary backgrounds, there is a clash of expertise that animates much of the Bank's activities and often impedes interdisciplinary work. The most influential community, based on its intellectual leadership and career advancement within the institution, is that of economists.

Economists comprise the large majority of senior management positions and dominate many of the network and operations units. They also have their own research group (the development economics research unit, or DEC), which hires top economists and recent doctorates in economics, and produces high-quality academic papers that influence Bank activities, public policymakers in member countries, and the academic community. Having a separate research unit devoted to development economics research is significant because operations staff do not have enough time to write papers, and network staff often lack an opportunity to research topics of their own choosing. On the rare occasions that they do, their audience is usually development practitioners rather than academia.

In addition, there is no serious career track for non-economists, unlike for economists, and no comparable effort to recruit top lawyers, sociologists, anthropologists and political scientists as there is to recruit economists into DEC.[5] Many lawyers, anthropologists and other professionals are not respected as the best thinkers in their field, and are thus simply seen as technocrats. They often feel that they have to translate their writing and speech into an economist's language

---

4   As of 1 July 2006, the Bank is merging a number of thematic areas so that soon there will be only five thematic areas.

5   One exception is the Young Professionals Program, which recruits 20–40 talented young people from a variety of professional backgrounds, including economics.

and quantify their observations in an effort to gain legitimacy for their ideas. This has discouraged informed debate among different disciplinary perspectives and has created an inferiority complex among some non-economists. Even staff with backgrounds other than economics may call themselves economists in order to gain legitimacy among other staff: I met a public sector specialist with a public policy background who chose the title of political economist for this reason.

As a result of varying technical knowledge and administrative expertise, disciplinary communities may exhibit competing versions of rationality or so-called 'value-spheres' (Weber, 1985). One of the more stark divisions is between lawyers and economists. One Bank lawyer who works in the network discussed how academic discipline affects staff approaches to issues like human rights:

> [With regards to] the two disciplines [of law and economics, there is] a very normative approach to the human rights agenda and a too technocratic approach on the development side. The human rights agenda is dominated by lawyers, and the development agenda is dominated by development specialists, mainly economists. And their way of thinking is totally different. Their training is different, their thinking is different, their tools are different. They might come to the same conclusions or they might share the same opinion of the usefulness of a project, for example, or the soundness of a project. But very often this cross-disciplinary discussion is not fruitful, simply because when I discuss with an economist, for example – and that is something we face every day in this institution, of course – I don't have that economic background and I find it sometimes difficult to judge whether what the other person tells me should be convincing for me or not. Simply because I cannot judge the soundness of his argument because I don't operate in the same scientific set of tools. To me, other arguments may be more convincing because I'm used to that kind of argumentation in a more legal discourse (Interview with Bank staff lawyer A, May 1, 2006).

Thus, disciplinary training can determine how staff frame, interpret and ultimately implement issues like human rights.

Of course, the disciplinary divisions are notional since there is not uniformity within the communities. For instance, there is a range of economists in the Bank, including neoclassical economists who assume rational utility maximization, and new institutional economists who recognize the influence of legal, political and social institutions on human behaviour and the market system. The same is true for lawyers, who come from diverse legal specialities (for example, law and economics or sociology of law) and have practiced in either civil or common law systems. While I recognize the existence of these *intra*-disciplinary differences, I focus on *inter*-disciplinary ones that potentially serve as more significant impediments to staff collaboration.

The Bank's Evolving Relationship with Human Rights

Competing interpretive communities based on discipline roughly correspond to divergent frameworks for human rights, which I describe below. In my comparison of frameworks, I exclude staff who are completely opposed to including human rights in the Bank's activities. There is a sizeable minority of staff who fall into this category, citing legal restrictions in the Bank's Articles of Agreement and noting that human rights are simply beyond the capacity and mandate of the Bank and should instead be handled by organizations like the United Nations (UN).[6] This group of staff has been slowly decreasing, but is certainly still visible.

The recent change in thinking at the institution over human rights is due to a number of factors including outside pressure by advocates and academics, as well as by international organizations like the UN, which has been promoting a human development approach. This approach is a distinct development paradigm exemplified by the Human Development Reports, initially created by Mahbub ul Haq and published annually by the United Nations Development Program since 1990 (Fukuda-Parr, 2002). In opposition to the neoliberal paradigm of the Washington Consensus, it offers an alternative view of development – one that not only generates economic growth but also distributes its benefits equitably and empowers people rather than marginalizing them. This approach broadens the concept of well-being to include factors that go beyond the economic. It is founded on Amartya Sen's theory of human capabilities, which is tied to a concern for sustainable development, gender equality, participation and human rights (Sen, 1999, 1981).

Internal factors that have changed the Bank's overall orientation include the influx of younger staff and more non-economist social scientists who have a more critical perspective on the Bank's work and recognize the role of institutions and governance in economic growth. Another factor is the leadership by former President James Wolfensohn who supported a greater emphasis on non-economic concerns such as civil society participation, the environment and legal and judicial reform. The legal obstacles have also been diminishing, as evidenced by a recent legal opinion by the former General Counsel of the World Bank, who wrote that it is

> consistent with the Articles [of Agreement] that the decision-making processes of the Bank incorporate human rights and any other relevant input which may have an impact on its economic decisions ... [T]here are instances in which the Bank may take human rights into account, and others in which it should. Indeed, there are some activities which the Bank cannot properly undertake without considering human rights (Dañino, 2006).[7]

Divergent Human Rights Frameworks

This section outlines the divergent human rights frameworks held by staff within the Bank and compares their rationales, conceptual foundations and dominating disciplines. While I focus on the disciplinary tensions that correspond to these frameworks, I should emphasize that proponents of each framework are not restricted to a particular discipline. For instance, those that use an instrumental framework are not exclusively economists and do not include all economists within

---

6   The Articles of Agreement mandate that only economic considerations can be relevant to the Bank's decisions, and prohibit interference in the political affairs of Bank members (Article IV, Section 10).

7   This opinion has not yet been presented to or approved by the Board, so it is not considered by many staff as an official Bank legal opinion.

the Bank. An employee's application of an approach may not necessarily reflect his or her discipline, but instead may reflect the controlling way of thinking of his or her department. Another factor is the geographic region where projects or programs are being applied. Certain borrower country governments like China or Russia may be more adverse to the use of human rights language, which they see as too political. Given that these countries are among the largest borrowers from the Bank and a significant source of its revenue, staff working on projects in them are often pressured to avoid explicit references to human rights for fear of angering government officials.

Instrumental Framework

Supporters of an instrumental framework provide a functionalist rationale for protecting human rights – that is, viewing it as a means of achieving developmental objectives. They often understand development as primarily defined by economic growth. Rights are prioritized based on their relative value in achieving poverty reduction. Thus, the 'value-added' by the human rights approach must be demonstrated.

Under this framework, human rights are not universal but are differentiated based on context. Their relative value is determined on a case-by-case basis, in a technocratic fashion. Their application depends on economic arguments that may conclude that certain human rights do not enhance development effectiveness, or that certain rights like civil and political rights should be prioritized over others (for example, economic, social and cultural rights), or the other way around. Or they may assert that human rights may be good for development in certain countries but not in others. Thus, it is common to have discussions of trade-offs within the instrumental framework as staff try to balance competing priorities, often in the face of resource constraints.

Because the most influential discipline in the Bank is economics, this framework holds a lot of weight among staff, and of course among many economists.[8] As a result, even lawyers who adhere to the intrinsic approach still talk about 'economising' human rights in order to appeal to staff (Morgan, 2003). Economising human rights would mean arguing that its promotion enhances development effectiveness and makes good business sense. According to this model, progress is assessed in terms of indicators, rather than compliance to or violation of norms and standards (which is the assessment used by adherents to the intrinsic framework, described below).

---

8   Note that as I mentioned earlier, there are internal debates within the discipline, so you will find some economists who reject this framework and may favour a capabilities approach that resembles the moral dimension of the intrinsic framework. There are other economists who support a strictly economic concept of well-being that does not recognize the value of all human rights to economic growth and may adhere to a trickle-down theory, where promoting economic growth will end up furthering human rights.

The Bank's private sector arm, the International Finance Corporation (IFC), has adopted this framework for human rights in its newly revised Performance Standards.[9] In coordination with the International Business Leaders Forum (IBLF) and the UN Global Compact, the IFC is currently developing a human rights impact assessment tool so that corporations can identify and address human rights challenges in projects based on a model of risk management. As a justification for this work, it makes a business case for human rights by arguing that it i) safeguards reputation and brand image; ii) helps companies gain a competitive advantage; iii) improves recruitment and staff loyalty; iv) fosters greater productivity; v) ensures active stakeholder engagement; and vi) meets investor expectation, among other reasons (IBLF/IFC and UN Global Compact, 2006, pp. 6–7).

Normative Framework

Proponents of the intrinsic framework adopt a normative rationale for human rights – that is, viewing it as an end in itself rather than a means to another goal. Rights are universal legal and moral guarantees against actions or omissions by states. They are indivisible and interdependent. Those who take this approach view development holistically, in that it begins with the proposition that all human beings have certain entitlements by virtue of their status as humans. They measure growth in terms of equitable distribution across socio-economic groups. There are two dimensions of the intrinsic framework, the legal and moral.

Legal dimension The first subgroup within the intrinsic framework is the legal dimension, which presents human rights primarily as a legal imperative and secondarily as a moral imperative. According to this view, human rights impose legal obligations that derive from the international human rights regime, and particularly the Universal Declaration on Human Rights, from which human rights gain their legitimacy. They also imply corresponding legal duties for governments and entail a body of rules and principles (Waldron, 1984), which serve as legal tools that claimants can draw on in courts.

Lawyers in the Bank have, not surprisingly, fallen into this subgroup, as have advocates from human rights NGOs. Unlike other disciplinary communities that are generally interspersed across units in the Bank, lawyers are primarily found within the legal department. Aside from a small number of lawyers in operations who work on legal and judicial reform and other public sector projects, the great majority of lawyers are isolated from the rest of the staff, often working on loan agreements and other technical tasks and having little influence over project design. Perhaps due to their isolation from operations, their strong disciplinary training or the transformative potential of a normative human rights discourse, there are many staff lawyers who express grave concerns about any attempt to dilute the basic legal tenets of human rights and 'water down' corresponding obligations (Interview with Bank staff lawyer B, 4 January 2006; Interview with Bank staff lawyer C, 17 January 2006). They

---

9   This information can be found at http://www.ifc.org/ifcext/enviro.nsf/Content/ PerformanceStandards.

insist that it 'is essential ... that efforts to integrate human rights in development practice not compromise those key characteristics [of legal obligations and duties] in the process, and risk the impoverishment of rights discourse and the undermining of core values and objectives that human rights were conceived to realize' (Decker et al., 2005, p. 49).

Moral dimension A second subgroup within the intrinsic framework is the moral dimension. Members of this subgroup primarily view rights as moral imperatives, founded on a conception of fundamental human dignity and a moral framework of common values. They underemphasize the legal aspect of rights. This view often translates into an implicit promotion of human rights, with its supporters repackaging legal language in alternative terms such as 'empowerment', 'equity', 'participation' and 'accountability'. They often advocate for a principles-based approach that focuses on ethics and social policy goals that are not attached to legal standards.

In the context of the Bank, the group that has most vocally supported this view is the social development unit. There has been a movement among non-economist social scientists in this unit (such as anthropologists and sociologists) to discard the rights language completely, partially in response to what they see as a fear, or even aversion, among staff to the phrase 'human rights'. They think that this 'common sense approach' of avoiding a formal legalistic interpretation accords them greater flexibility and a better chance of convincing the sceptical economists in the Bank and possibly the Bank's Board of Directors to sign on to human rights (Interview with former employee of Social Development Unit, 16 February 2006).

One manifestation of this framework is the Bank's 1999 publication entitled 'Principles and Good Practice in Social Policy: Issues and Areas for Public Action'. Rather than recommending that the Bank assist its members in realizing their international human rights obligations, this paper advises it to 'distill ... lessons of good practice to assist its members to draw upon them in support of their economic and social development goals' (World Bank, 1999, p. 2). It lists a set of 'generally agreed principles', while noting trade-offs that may arise in achieving them. Under an overarching goal of 'the promotion of social development of all the world's peoples',[10] these principles fall within four areas: achieving universal access to basic social services; enabling all men and women to attain secure, sustainable livelihoods and decent working conditions; promoting systems of social protection; and fostering social integration. Thus, in some respects, this view attempts to bridge the instrumental and intrinsic frameworks by recognizing the universality of principles but also the need for member countries to translate these principles 'into practical country-specific results' (World Bank, 1999, p. 12).

Another application of the moral intrinsic framework is the Bank's new Social Development Strategy (2005), which presents the three operational principles of non-discrimination, inclusion, and accountability. According to staff whom I interviewed in the social development unit, there was a debate over the initial use of international human rights language in the strategy and pressure from staff inside and outside of

---

10 This goal explicitly follows from the commitments agreed on at the March 1995 World Summit for Social Development in Copenhagen.

the unit who felt that that language would be 'too political' (Interview with Bank staff member from Social Development Unit, 1 February 2006).

Table 6.1 summarizes the differences between the functionalist and normative frameworks.

Table 6.1 Human Rights Frameworks

	Rationale	Conceptual Foundation	Dominating Discipline
Instrumental Framework	Functionalist	Differentiated Rights based on a growth-based understanding of development	Economics
Intrinsic Framework	1 Legal 2 Moral	Universal Principles primarily based on 1 an international human rights regime 2 human dignity and ethical standards	1 Law 2 Sociology/ Anthropology

Operational Implications: The Rights of People Living with HIV/AIDS

How do these competing human rights frameworks translate into practical effects in World Bank projects? This paper contends that there are operational implications in the way that one interprets human rights. This is particularly true in the context of project loans to borrower countries, which form the bulk of the Bank's activities.[11] How a manager frames human rights-related issues in a project's official documents – by either using an intrinsic or functionalist rationale – can have substantial effects on which populations are targeted and how violations of human rights are addressed.

I take as an example investment projects relating to HIV/AIDS control, prevention and treatment. I compare two such projects: the Tuberculosis and HIV/AIDS Control Project in the Russian Federation (approved on 3 April 2003) and the HIV/AIDS Prevention and Control Project in Saint Lucia in the Caribbean (approved on 6 July 2004). By the time both projects had been approved, human rights thinking had begun to permeate discussions in the Bank on the right to health. However, there is a significant disparity between how, and the extent to which, each project explicitly frames HIV/AIDS as a human rights issue.

---

11 The World Bank lends $15-$20 billion for projects in more than 100 countries. See www.worldbank.org.

The link between HIV/AIDS and human rights is based on the right to health, which is codified in key international human rights documents.[12] The UN Commission for Human Rights' international guidelines on HIV/AIDS and Human Rights recommend 'the need for intensified efforts to ensure universal respect for and observance of human rights and fundamental freedoms for all, to reduce vulnerability to HIV/AIDS and to prevent HIV/AIDS-related discrimination and stigma ...' (International Guidelines on HIV/AIDS and Human Rights UNHCR resolution 1997/33 1997.) Thus, the realization of rights by People Living With HIV/AIDS (PLWHA) requires protection against stigma and discrimination with regard to access to health, education and social services, and the reduction of 'vulnerability'. Vulnerability refers to 'the lack of power of individuals and communities to minimize or modulate their risk of exposure to HIV infection and, once infected, to receive adequate care and support' (Gruskin and Tarantola, 2002).

An analysis of the projects' project appraisal documents reveals two different approaches to the human rights of PLWHA. The project in Saint Lucia exemplifies the intrinsic framework (legal dimension) by addressing the country's human rights legal obligations and aiming to address discrimination, stigma and vulnerability. Its development objective is 'targeting interventions at high risk groups and implementing non-targeted activities for the general population' (World Bank Report Number 29129, 2004). One of its four major goals is to 'reduce the degree of stigma and discrimination associated with the disease.' The report provides no economic justification for pursuing this goal; it is simply presented as intrinsic to protecting the fundamental human rights of PLWHA. The project measures progress towards this goal by measuring 'accepting and non-discriminatory attitudes by the population towards victims of the disease in the workplace and in the community' (2004, 5). A search of the 106-page project document reveals 22 instances of the words 'vulnerable' or 'vulnerability', 20 of 'discrimination', 19 of 'stigma' and five of 'human right(s)'.

In addition, the project explicitly aims to strengthen Saint Lucia's legal and regulatory framework, by '(i) ensuring all citizens the full benefits of the civil, economic and social rights universally recognized as being of important to people living with HIV/AIDS and to other vulnerable groups, and (ii) ensuring the provision of services to all who need them' (2004, 2–3). It promises assistance in the drafting of a new law that will ensure to PLWHA 'full equality and dignity under the law, without stigma or discrimination' (2004, 9). It also includes support for civil society and community initiatives towards effective monitoring and ensuring the right to information.

In contrast, the project in Russia, while implicitly supporting the human rights of PLWHA, takes a more instrumental approach (World Bank Report Number 21239-RU, 2003). Its objectives are to contain the growth of the HIV/AIDS and tuberculosis epidemics in the short term and reverse their growth in the medium-term (2003, 2).

---

12 See, for example, the Universal Declaration of Human Rights (Article 25, Section 1); the International Covenant on Economic, Social and Cultural Rights (Article 12); the Convention on the Rights of the Child (Article 24); and the Convention on the Elimination of All Forms of Discrimination against Women (Article 12).

It explicitly links the objectives to the UN Millennium Development Goals target number seven, which aims to halt and reverse the spread of HIV/AIDS by 2015 (2003, 2). Yet, the project does not target the reduction of stigma or discrimination, which are key requirements of the human rights of PLWHA. A search of its 102-page project document reveals its minimal emphasis on the human rights-related goals of reducing stigma, discrimination and vulnerability. The document includes 16 instances of the word 'vulnerable' or 'vulnerability', but only two of 'stigmatization' (and no references to 'stigma'), one of 'human right(s)', and none of 'discrimination'. There is also no explicit recognition of the need to ensure universal civil, economic, or social rights, as is mentioned in the Saint Lucia project document.

This analysis reveals how divergent interpretive frameworks can shape how different projects on the same topic are designed. It also suggests the variety of factors that may influence which framework is used. Based on its intrinsic framework for addressing HIV/AIDS and human rights, the Saint Lucia project includes components on reducing stigma and discrimination and legal reforms for ensuring civil, economic, and social rights. The Russia project, in contrast, emphasizes prevention and control, while also providing treatment for those infected. The absence of components on stigma and discrimination in this project, and thus the decision not to frame HIV/AIDS in human rights terms, could be due to a number of reasons. One reason may be that the project team was dominated by staff who prefer a cost-benefit analysis to a legal approach, and who concluded that funds would be better spent on other preventative interventions. Another quite likely reason for the disparity between the projects is politics in the borrower country, which has the potential to transcend interpretive gaps. The Russian Government treats the human rights of PLWHA as a sensitive, politically-charged issue that it would prefer to avoid. Even if the Saint Lucian Government took the same view, Russia holds much more influence than Saint Lucia over Bank project design because it is a major borrower and not a country that the Bank wants to upset.

It is thus important to evaluate each project and its human rights framework on its own terms, taking into account multiple factors like the politics in the country involved and the specific views of the staff that designed the project. There is not an optimal approach to human rights that should be taken by all projects. But one should recognize that whichever approach is adopted significantly affects the design and implementation of projects.

Conclusion: Towards Reconciliation

The implementation of human rights in an organisation is based on how it is framed with respect to its culture. Human rights cannot be effectively internalized and consistently applied in day-to-day activities if an institution's staff is not effectively motivated by its relevance. At the same time, we know that institutions are not black boxes, but are composed of a number of subcultures with distinct value systems and skill sets. Corresponding to these subcultures, there are interpretive gaps between staff frameworks on human rights, which may impede their operationalization.

Is reconciliation possible among proponents of competing frameworks, or are the viewpoints incompatible? Are there any areas of compromise between economists, who shun laywers (for instance) for lacking the practical ability to accommodate resource constraints, and lawyers, who criticize economists for diluting the legal and moral power of human rights? These are difficult questions but ones that must be addressed when designing regulations that will be effectively implemented. Some scholars have argued for a convergence or 'powerful synergy' between the instrumental and intrinsic frameworks. According to this view, the frameworks 'can often be usefully understood not as antagonistic or incompatible but as deeply interrelated, as implicated in each other, and indeed as profitably employed by both rights advocates and by economists concerned with growth to achieve common goals' (Steiner, 1998, p. 25).

Reconciliation among frameworks requires that members of communities bridge the interpretive gaps. Perhaps the best opportunity to do so is by seeking individual 'translators' – actors or actor groups who can forge compromises across interpretive communities. These translators can mediate deliberation by recognizing 'the distorting effects of power relationships' (Black, 2001, p. 34). They could seek a common language, rather than a translation of all discourses into one language, which would result in 'discursive hegemony' (Black, 2001, p. 51). For instance, if lawyers were to reframe values in a language of economic productivity and market distortion, this may lead to detrimental 'translation effects' (Morgan, 2003, p. 17). As a result, their approach may be seen as belonging to one disciplinary community and not sufficiently 'owned' by all staff, possibly leading to under-implementation.

In the context of the Bank, translators would likely have to come from within the ranks of the organization in order to win legitimacy among staff, and have significant decision making power in order to influence overall institutional policy. There are at least two potential translator groups. The first group includes proponents of the moral dimension of the intrinsic framework, who promote universal ethical principles (deliberately not framed as 'legal rights') and acknowledge the need to accommodate resource constraints and the institutional capacities of different countries. Yet, their conciliatory efforts have been limited by their small numbers and relative absence in the higher staff ranks of the Bank.

A second potential translator group are employees with interdisciplinary backgrounds who can engage in dialogue with multiple disciplinary communities and launch collaborative programs between them. However, these employees are also small in number and are interspersed throughout the Bank, thus making it difficult for them to join forces and form their own interpretive community. The few individuals who have succeeded in furthering this goal have been responsible for several innovative programs that cross communities. One example is the Social Science and Policy Seminar Series, a bi-weekly series jointly sponsored by the social development unit and development economics unit, aimed at promoting intellectual dialogue among staff by bringing in top scholars in the non-economic social sciences who can influence development policy.

Initiatives like this joint seminar encourage conversations among staff with varying interpretive frameworks who would not otherwise have the opportunity to meet or share ideas. But further efforts must be made to encourage dialogue among competing discourses. They should form part of a regulatory strategy that takes account of power relations among existing interpretive communities. Such efforts are necessary before a human rights agenda can be effectively internalized within organizations.

Chapter 7

Regulatory Rights: Emergent Indigenous Peoples' Rights as a Locus of Global Regulation

Erik Larson[1]

Introduction

How does the growth of international rights regimes influence the activities of nation-states and other actors? World polity theory offers one model of understanding the growth of global processes on national activities. The theory posits that the diffusion of a global culture shapes the behaviour of nation-states and individuals (Meyer, Boli, Thomas and Ramirez, 1997; Meyer and Jepperson, 2000). The growth in global institutions has been particularly dramatic since 1945, which coincides with the growth of the international human rights regime (Hafner-Burton and Tsutsui, 2005). Models of world polity predict some regulation of the actions of states and other actors with the diffusion of legitimate 'scripts' for social action. As such, the theory provides a cultural account of regulation. At first consideration, such a theory may fit well with sociolegal theories of legal consciousness that suggest that institutional orientations shape the impact of law, as actors may embrace or reject certain understandings of law that serve as the basis for legal action (Ewick and Silbey, 1998; Larson, 2004; Silbey, 2005). From this perspective, one may anticipate that the global culture characterizing world polity incorporates a particular orientation toward law that diffuses to shape the impact of law. Analysing these institutionalized orientations toward law and human rights may help to illuminate the transnational dimensions of rights consciousness (Milner and Goldberg-Hiller, 2002).

World polity theory posits a relatively monotonic diffusion and development of global culture, reflecting deep-seated characteristics of western development (Frank

1   Funding for this research was provided by the College of Liberal Arts at the University of Minnesota. This work would not have been possible without the support, encouragement, challenges and feedback of participants in the 2005 Law and Society Summer Institute at Oxford. In particular, Bronwen Morgan offered a number of helpful suggestions after a careful reading of an earlier draft. This work has also benefited from conversations with Ron Aminzade and Liz Boyle. Finally, many thanks go to: Cristina Giordano and Adriano Gonçalves who offered great help at the UN Library; staff, experts and delegates to the Working Group on Indigenous Populations meetings in Geneva; and participants in my Indigenous Peoples' Movements seminar at Macalester College, whose questions and comments provoked me to develop and refine a number of these ideas.

and Meyer, 2002). From this perspective, the emergence of global rights might be understood simply as a further extension of the development of the individual self and diffusion of a particular model of the nation-state. Indeed, most research in the world polity tradition starts with the empirical problem of why states with such divergent social bases have adopted similar structures (Frank, Hironaka, and Schofer, 2000; Drori, Meyer, Ramirez and Schofer, 2003; Schofer and Meyer, 2005). In some sense, these empirical questions may raise issues of a selection bias, as the substantive problems examined are instances of formal compliance with global models.

To overcome this potential issue, I examine what appears to be a divergent case – the growth of indigenous rights – from a different perspective: the level of their emergence internationally. Indigenous rights appear to diverge from the world polity model of the development of particular versions of the nation-state and the individual self, because these rights have a collective nature that is not embodied in the nation-state. In this regard, they lie in a middle ground between individual rights and claims to sovereignty, as collective rights related to the self-determination of a people. Yet, they emerged and are institutionalized within the human rights framework internationally: in June 2006, following the recommendations of the chairperson-rapporteur of a Working Group that had been working for a decade on the declaration, the United Nations Human Rights Council adopted the text for the United Nations Declaration on the Rights of Indigenous Peoples (Human Rights Council, 2006a, 2006b; Schlein, 2006).[2] As such, I examine the emergence and effects of a change within the global polity in order to understand how rights and regulation intersect at a global level, how the content of global culture changes (or does not change), and how institutional processes shape orientations toward law. Given that the newly emergent indigenous rights have, at a minimum, an apparent divergence from extant rights law, these rights pose a question of how to understand their applicability. This indeterminacy of indigenous rights provides the basis for an investigation of the institutional practices that make sense of the law (Silbey, 2005).

My analysis in this article draws on archival research, field research, and interviews I conducted in connection with the meetings of the United Nations Working Group on Indigenous Populations and recent developments related to indigenous rights. I first provide an outline of the relationship between rights and regulation in relation to human rights in a world polity framework. Second, I provide an analysis of indigenous rights in relation to world polity theory, finding that the growth of indigenous rights does indeed represent a departure from the content of the culture of the world polity. My analysis suggests that while world polity theory correctly identifies features of the world polity associated with global diffusion, it underestimates the ways in which these features can be accessed to reshape global culture. Then, I consider the relations between the growth of indigenous rights and their regulatory implications. I find that indigenous rights are associated with the creation of expansive agency and legitimacy that regulate international bodies, states, and the indigenous rights movement itself. By creating the basis for agency,

---

2   This declaration was scheduled to be considered by the General Assembly during the Fall 2006 session but is currently deferred pending further discussion.

indigenous rights enable indigenous peoples and staff affiliated with international bodies to participate in a variety of settings to influence agendas for action. By providing the basis for legitimate action, indigenous rights regulate the activities of international organizations and nation-states to become responsible for and responsive to claims on indigenous rights while at the same time constraining access to the agency associated with emergent indigenous rights.

The Regulatory Force of Human Rights in the World Polity

World polity theory offers a sociological explanation for the developments in the worldwide system of nation-states and the diffusion of universal personhood throughout the world. Premised on the notion that patterns of cultural diffusion externally define nation-states and shape a common element of human experience, world polity theory traces the origins of increasing formal homogeneity to the incorporation of particularly Western models of organization into increasingly autonomous institutions (Meyer, Boli, Thomas and Ramirez, 1997; Meyer and Jepperson, 2000).

The striking uniformity in the diffusion of forms of organization throughout many of the countries of the world poses questions about the origins of these changes. For instance, education (Meyer, Ramirez, and Soysal, 1992; Schofer and Meyer, 2005), science bureaucracies (Drori, Meyer, Ramirez and Schofer, 2003) and environmental protections (Frank, Hironaka, and Schofer, 2000; Schofer and Hironaka, 2005) exhibit a greater degree of empirical regularity across nation-states than one would expect based on the functions that each serves in the variety of nation-states. World polity theory proposes that a global culture produces autonomy in rationalized institutions – such as science – that serves to diffuse models of organization, as nation-states' exclusivity of authority wanes (Meyer and Jepperson, 2000). At the same time, however, world culture defines the characteristics of nation-states as complex organizations, which adopt similar models of organization as legitimate (Meyer, Boli, Thomas and Ramirez, 1997). The content of world culture continues to authorize – perhaps even demand – that nation-states serve as organizers of national society. As a consequence, the scope of activities of nation-states has expanded even in the wake of the development of sources of authority autonomous from traditional state authority.

Despite the pressures to conform to global norms of state structure, these isomorphic structures do not produce uniform effects. World polity theorists refer to the resulting gaps between state rhetoric and state actions and between organizational forms and national needs as decoupling (Meyer, Boli, Thomas and Ramirez, 1997; Schofer and Hironka, 2005). While it might be easy to point to decoupling as mere window-dressing on the parts of states, there may be real consequences to state rhetoric proclaiming support of international norms, particularly as it may encourage individuals to embrace these norms (Meyer, 2004; Schofer and Hironaka, 2005).

Evidence of decoupling is perhaps most striking in the case of human rights protections. Nation-states may ratify treaties or pass laws with the stated purpose of protecting human rights, but act in a manner that nullifies these legal protections (Boyle, Songora, and Foss, 2001; Hafner-Burton and Tsutsui, 2005). Indeed, some evidence points to radical decoupling between ratification of human rights treaties and human rights protection, as governments may *increase* rights violation after ratification (Hafner-Burton and Tsutui, 2005). Due to the weakness of human rights treaties, governments may ratify the treaties merely as means to deflect criticism, offering greater latitude for these governments to violate rights. At the same time, however, the act of ratification provides grounds for legitimate challenges to the government's behaviour, particularly by members of global civil society (Hafner-Burton and Tsutsui, 2005). By mobilizing international networks of experts and activists, a 'politics of shame' (Keck and Sikkink, 1998; Niezen 2003) can serve as a countervailing force to the radically decoupled actions after treaty ratification – or what Hafner-Burton and Tsutsui (2005) label 'the paradox of empty promises'.

This paradox – an increased tendency to violate rights due to radical decoupling combined with enhanced power of international pressures to uphold rights due to the politics of shame – may be better understood as a function of the ways in which formalized legal rights become both a focal point for claims-making and the means through which claims are made. The institution of law itself characterizes the development of world culture, as it emerges in a specialized and semi-autonomous manner (Weber, 1968). Indeed, the universalistic character of law – along with its connection to the nation-state – fits well with world culture (Boyle and Meyer, 1998). While the meaning and applicability of particular legal developments are ambiguous (Edelman, 1992), expression of emergent global norms in treaties or other legalistic statements provides a more formal ground of expression for these norms. Law thereby expresses the content of world culture in a particularly explicit manner, while simultaneously becoming the language and forum in which claims concerning government actions are made (Liu and Boyle, 2001). By combining the explicit expression of the content of global culture and the means of contestation, the institution of international law – much as other types of law – derives its power from its applicability to a large variety of situations, yet its distance from any particular situation (Ewick and Silbey, 1998; Silbey, 2005).

In this light, international human rights can be seen as part of the extension of the culture of a world polity, defining legitimate spheres of activity for nation-states and the limitations on such activity. The cultural characteristics of law serve to shape the behaviour of actors in the global polity. International rights become normative statements and, as a consequence, are regulatory and productive for states and other actors in four ways.

First, by defining the legitimate scope of state activity, rights can create bounded agency for nation-states to be responsible for particular types of issues and problems, but only within particularly prescribed manners of acting. Rights claims are made against states, whether on the actions of the state itself or its indirect actions on regulating its population (Larson, 2005). Particularly in the case of positive rights, rights create agency for the state by defining increasing aspects of social life for which it is responsible. Thus, a right to housing or a right to health care minimally licenses state involvement in these activities.[3]

---

3 If the rights are mere expressions of goals – a case of pure decoupling – then the state is only licensed to act in these spheres. On the other hand, if actors are able to pursue claims

Second, international rights become a set of standards through which state conformity to international norms is measured. International monitoring procedures typically involve reporting by states to international bodies (Weissbrodt, Fitzpatrick and Newman, 2001). This process of monitoring international standards becomes one means to ensure state compliance (Liu and Boyle, 2001; Larson, 2005). Further, concluding recommendations that follow international monitoring procedures may emphasize the development of governmental institutions – such as national human rights commissions or the passage of particular national laws – that produce greater uniformity in states (Larson, 2005).

Third, by providing the means through which claims can be made against particular states, rights produce the potential for agency on the part of domestic actors. In cases in which rights are actionable, this agency is most clear. Even in cases in which rights are not actionable, however, rights embody aspirations of individuals and can serve to direct the goals and activities of individuals (Meyer, 2004).

Finally, by framing the types of legitimate claims that can be made against states, rights serve to limit and direct the types of claims made in domestic contexts. While this impact is most direct in cases in which international law is incorporated into domestic law, the legitimacy and resonance of claims reflect their connection to international norms. A strategy of mobilizing the politics of shame will be ineffective in cases in which the claimant group deviates from international norms.

These four effects represent predictions about the institutional mechanisms through which human rights have regulatory force in the world polity. The first two effects – creating bounded agency for nation-states and monitoring conduct with international standards – represent regulation that happens to and through states. The latter effects – producing domestic actors' agency and aspirations and limiting and directing claims-making – constitute agency and legitimacy that serve as a counterpoint to state power. In the next section, I consider the origins of indigenous rights in relation to world polity theory's characterization of global culture. Then, I consider the extent to which the regulatory effects of emergent indigenous rights support the predictions about the institutional mechanisms through which human rights have regulatory force.

Indigenous Rights

From the perspective of world polity theory, the growth in international rights reflects the increasing prominence of rational actorhood as an organizing principle of world culture. These rights regulate states, but also bind agency to states, licensing them as a source of action and serving as the foundation for articulating responses to issues. The growth of indigenous rights internationally, however, does not fit so well into the characterization of the growth of the world polity as state- and individual-centred. In their content, indigenous rights challenge both premises of global culture. Indigenous rights are collective and challenge a nation-state-centred account of the

---

against the state for not upholding these rights, then a greater sphere of agency exists. In such a case, agency is more diffuse, yet still centered around the state as the primary actor for upholding the rights.

global order. Despite these challenges, indigenous rights have grown within an institutional setting focused around individuals and state action, suggesting that world culture is malleable.

The emergent principles underlying indigenous rights internationally incorporate a collective dimension to the content of indigenous rights (Anaya, 2004). For instance, Articles 12 and 14 of the United Nations Declaration on the Rights of Indigenous Peoples provide for continuing rights to culture and cultural heritage. Both by the nature of a right to culture (which is a collective product) and by the future orientation of the right, such provisions are premised on recognizing collectivities as bearers of rights. Furthermore, the principle of self-determination – which is enjoyed by a people as a collectivity – underlies indigenous rights (Anaya, 2004). This collective orientation embodied in indigenous rights remakes the ontology of rights in international law by creating an intermediate ground between states (long presumed to be the repository of collective rights) and individuals (Anaya, 2004).[4] By providing for a ground on which collective rights are held outside of a nation-state, indigenous rights also challenge the basis of states as the centre of the global order (Niezen, 2003). In this regard, indigenous rights appear to run contrary to the dominant global culture.

Given the characterization of world culture in world polity theory, it is puzzling that indigenous rights emerged at the global level itself. World polity theorists may offer two explanations that address the paradox of the emergence of indigenous rights. First, it could be that these anomalous rights developed at the periphery of the world polity. Diffusion of the cultural content of the world to particular countries and actors correlates strongly with the membership in international bodies. World polity theorists interpret this correlation as evidence that such points of connection serve as 'receptor sites' for global norms (Meyer, Boli, Thomas and Ramirez, 1997; Frank, Hironaka, and Shofer, 2000; Hafner-Burton and Tsutsui, 2005). From this perspective, one would expect that the origins of international efforts to establish indigenous rights occurred with fewer connections to the global polity, accounting for how these rights run counter to the dominant features of world culture.

A second potential explanation consistent with findings by world polity theorists is that these rights may by an instance of the emergence of a 'specializing identity claim' that serves not to move away from the content of global culture, but to integrate an excluded group within global culture. Individual personhood has become the fundamental basis of actorhood, as universal standards (human rights) have displaced particular standards (citizenship rights). Specializing identity claims,

---

4   The contrast with world polity theory is evident:

[T]he rise of democratic, political, capitalist economic, and scientific cultural institutions reshaped this older system, promoting the legitimation of (a) the individual person, developing into the citizen, and (b) the corporate collective community, developing into the nation state … Between individuals and states, each with identities legitimating action, other former or potential loci of human identity weakened. Occupations, organizations, and family systems all lost most of their direct ties to spiritual or natural forces. The whole process leaves individuals and nation-states as the primordial entities (Frank and Meyer, 2002, 87).

from this perspective, are 'dramatic assertions of the general needs and rights of individual personhood ... organized under individual (rather than corporate) rights' (Frank and Meyer, 2002, 90). These specialized claims become roles that individuals can take on and their growth serves as an index of role differentiation, rather than a particularistic deviation from individual personhood. Specializing identity claims occur as individualism expands to break down older corporate orders and to delegitimate stigmatization or exclusion. 'Specializing identities displace difference to realms *outside* society (in natural, spiritual, and historical domains) in order to clear the way for equal access to roles and personhood' (Frank and Meyer, 2002, 96, emphasis in original). From this perspective, the growth of indigenous rights reflects the declining legitimacy of exclusion of indigenous peoples. Specializing identity claims remove the differences that mark indigenous peoples based on history, spirituality and/or nature.

Examination of the history of international indigenous rights can help determine if either of the above explanations is persuasive. While indigenous peoples' movements have a long history, these movements began to have a greater impact in the wake of national civil rights policies and international attention to human rights in the 1960s and 1970s (Coates, 2004). National policies concerning civil rights, particularly in the USA, served as a model to mobilize concerns of indigenous peoples. Early mobilization efforts, largely drawing on an educated elite of indigenous peoples, grew into organized movements, such as the National Indian Youth Council in the USA (Anaya, 2004, p. 77). At the same time, international attention concerned the elimination of racial discrimination. In 1971, a group of anthropologists organized a conference concerning ethnic conflict in Latin America, which culminated in the release of the Barbados Declaration, holding that indigenous peoples had to be involved in their own liberation (Martínez Cobo, 1981; Declaration of Barbados 1971). Also in 1971, in the wake of increasing international attention to large-scale human rights violations in Latin America, the United Nations Economic and Social Council authorized the Sub-Commission on Prevention of Discrimination and Protection of Minorities to commission a study of discrimination against indigenous peoples. Early international efforts to raise awareness of these issues came from Non-Governmental Organisations(NGOs) founded by anthropologists (Brysk, 2000).

While national indigenous rights movements were organized in a number of countries, the main impetus to develop international indigenous organizations came from North America (Burger, 1987; Maiguashca, 1994; Coates, 2004). In 1975, the World Council of Indigenous Peoples was formed in British Columbia, drawing together representatives of peoples in the Americas, northern Europe, Australia, and New Zealand (Burger, 1987; Coates, 2004). In 1977, there was a host of international indigenous meetings: the World Council of Indigenous Peoples held a second General Assembly; the academics reconvened the Barbados group with indigenous representatives who passed a resolution to unite indigenous peoples; the Inuit Circumpolar Conference formed uniting peoples from Greenland, northern North America and north-eastern Eurasia, and a subcommittee on ending discrimination of the Special NGO Committee on Human Rights held an international conference in Geneva concerning discrimination against indigenous peoples. Representatives of 60 indigenous peoples attended the NGO conference in Geneva, which issued a final resolution, including a call for the establishment of a United Nations Working Group under the authority of the Sub-Commission on Prevention of Discrimination and Protection of Minorities and a call to revise international law on indigenous peoples (in particular, International Labour Organization Convention 107) to move away from an emphasis on integration (Martínez Cobo, 1981). Subsequent international meetings of indigenous peoples focused attention on topical issues, such as the relation between indigenous peoples and land (Special NGO Committee on Human Rights, 1981).

In response to pressure resulting from the international meetings, the United Nations created the Working Group on Indigenous Populations as a subsidiary body of the Sub-Commission on the Promotion and Protection of Human Rights.[5] The Working Group established guidelines for participation that enabled a number of indigenous peoples' organizations to contribute to general debate at each year's meetings, forgoing the requirement that NGOs had to have consultative status to participate (Office of the High Commissioner for Human Rights). Over time, the number of participating indigenous groups expanded (Burger, 1987; Coates, 2004). From early in its activities, the Working Group noted the inadequacies of existing human rights provisions for indigenous peoples. Its first report noted:

> The members of the Working Group took as their starting point the fact that the general provisions on human rights ... were applicable equally to members of indigenous populations and to other groups. In practice, however, it was not advisable to rely solely on principles ... for in their passive form, they would not give protection but could have adverse effects on indigenous populations, who for historical reasons were disadvantaged in society (Working Group on Indigenous Populations, 1982, 14).

From this basis – and the contributions of indigenous delegates – the Working Group developed a Draft Declaration on the Rights of Indigenous Peoples. In addition to these principles that formed the basis of negotiations that led to the Declaration on the Rights of Indigenous Peoples, the Working Group and indigenous delegates encouraged the Economic and Social Council of the United Nations to create a Permanent Forum on Indigenous Issues, whose members consist equally of experts selected by states and experts selected by UN staff in consultation with indigenous peoples.

The history of the international indigenous rights movement includes some of the main elements predicted by world polity theory, but the nature of the connections of these elements diverges from the theory's postulates. The movement became more active internationally after the United Nations and anthropology made indigenous issues part of the international agenda. While the movement was unevenly distributed based on the connections to the world polity, the leaders of the indigenous rights movement were located in those nation-states most closely integrated into the global polity, rather than emerging from more peripheral sites. This fact, however, may seem to offer support for the idea that indigenous rights are a specializing identity claim. Indeed, the movement was institutionalized within international bodies designed to combat discrimination. Consequently, one could anticipate that those people in

---

5   The Sub-Commission is the same that authorized the study on the problem of discrimination, but was renamed in the interim period.

countries more closely bound to the world polity would more likely push for indigenous rights. While this pattern did indeed hold, a gap in the theoretical explanation comes about because the claims were made for collective rights of a corporate non-state body. Further, the displacement that occurred was not of individual difference outside of society, but as a self-determining collective that should renegotiate its relation with the nation-state (Anaya, 2004). Finally, the transnational indigenous peoples' movement's rejection of an integrationist stance (embodied in pre-existing international law, such as International Labour Organization Convention 107 with its emphasis on the development of the capacity of indigenous peoples as individuals), in favour of approaches based on the promotion of self-determination of indigenous communities as peoples, demonstrates a commitment to forms of social life that challenges the dominant features of world culture.

While world polity theory correctly identifies features of the international system that played an important part in the indigenous rights movements, the theory does not provide a convincing account of the relation between the movement and content of world culture. Rather than the world polity exercising influence by diffusing cultural scripts, the indigenous rights movement used access to the structures of the world polity to reshape global culture. The global indigenous rights movement, therefore, should be understood as an instance of institutional entrepreneurship, with leaders employing a strategy of position (Steinman, 2005). Institutional entrepreneurship – an attempt to change how decision-makers understand law – serves to remake decision-making. By claiming access to international bodies that considered issues about indigenous peoples, the transnational movement used its status to engage in this institutional entrepreneurship.

The nature of global culture enabled this institutional entrepreneurship. The culture of the global polity includes its own oppositional culture, as acceptance of the tenets of modern individualism is not universal, even in societies in which there are deep connections to world society. In this regard, the status of indigenous peoples carries meaning within global culture that gives it some resonance.

> What indigenous people do have is what migrants and the children of migrants (i.e., most of the rest of us) feel they lack: a sense of belonging, a sense of rootedness in place. It is this longing to belong that has become one of the most valued ideological commodities in the era of late capitalism (Lee, 2003, 84).

While the framing of grievances as non-discrimination explains an important means through which claims could fit within existing global institutions (Morgan, 2004), the transnational indigenous movement has gained a great deal of its international support from international NGOs whose work involves other issues, such as environmental concerns. The presumption that indigenous peoples enjoy special relations with the environment, including traditional knowledge, mobilized support from these organizations and movements. 'Eco-indigenism' became a manner in which to articulate claims for indigenous rights, albeit one which carries with it the distinct possibility of undermining self determination (Niezen, 2003; Sissons, 2004). The international indigenous rights movement thus carried some broader resonance within the world polity by expressing 'popular misgivings about the impacts of technology and the pace of life and the corresponding eclectic search for spiritual expression, in modern society' (Niezen, 2003, 52).

Paradoxically, those indigenous peoples more closely connected and integrated into global institutions were better able to frame claims in opposition to global culture (Li, 2000; Niezen, 2003). The movement grew out of the developed countries and had leaders who were more assimilated into global civil society through education. Rather than inequality in world polity producing a culture that merely reflects the interests of dominant states (Beckfield, 2003), access to the world polity produced an opportunity to challenge – and change – the institutions of the world polity.

Two implications follow from the above discussion. First, global culture has to be politically activated. The institutions of the world polity are, at least partially, autonomous from the nation-state system (Hagan, 2003). Given the history of the transnational indigenous rights movement, the ability to mobilize these institutions varies based on the connections with the global polity. Second, global culture involves ambiguity that must be worked out or institutionalized, suggesting that the content of this culture can be remade. International law serves as a means to express these sentiments. Indigenous rights are expressed in legalistic terms as part of the global human rights infrastructure (Niezen, 2003). The human rights framework does not completely determine the character of indigenous rights, but the incorporation of indigenous rights into international human rights serves to remake the notion of rights (Anaya, 2004). As such, the institutionalization of these rights reorders global decision-making. The next section of paper explains how there are regulatory impacts of the institutionalization of these rights.

The Regulatory Impacts of Emergent Rights

Even before the Human Rights Council adopted the Declaration, and indigenous rights advocates faced on-going negotiation about what the precise content of these rights should include (Working Group Established in Accordance with Commission on Human Rights Resolution, 1995/32 of 3 March 1995 2006), their emergence and partial recognition illustrates the impact of such rights on regulatory activity. The image of greater malleability of the world polity that emerges from the discussion of the history of indigenous rights suggests that these rights have impact in a variety of spheres. In this section, I focus first on international bodies, then on states, and finally on the indigenous rights movement itself.

International Bodies

The trajectory of the emergence of indigenous rights demonstrates the importance of access to international organizations. After holding international conferences and building on the momentum of international attention, indigenous peoples were able to push for the establishment of the Working Group. The Working Group became an important site of international focus on indigenous peoples and also served to encourage the development of a formal document in support of indigenous rights. Even when these rights remained in draft form, there was agreement on a number of underlying principles for these rights (Working Group Established in Accordance with Commission on Human Rights Resolution, 1995/32 of 3 March 1995 2006). In this sense, the basis for indigenous rights was at least somewhat institutionalized within the world polity. This institutionalization in turn shapes international developments by legitimating attention to indigenous issues and by licensing participation of indigenous peoples in international forums. These findings highlight the ways in which the regulatory impact of international human rights in relation to the creation of bounded agency and the direction of claims-making is broader than hypothesized. Agency is bound and standards apply not only to states, but also to global actors, as the content of global culture is remade.

With the development of international law and norms on indigenous rights, the principles underlying these norms became an important aspect of world culture. Prior to the global indigenous rights movement, the primary source of international law on indigenous peoples was International Labour Organization (ILO) Convention 107. Drawing largely on experiences in Latin America, the premise of ILO Convention 107 was that indigenous peoples' labour was under-utilized, posing a developmental problem to both the indigenous populations and to the countries (Martínez Cobo, 1981). Consequently, the convention called for measures to protect indigenous peoples and for 'their progressive integration into the life of their respective countries' (ILO Convention 107). Based on the preliminary standard setting activities of the Working Group and indigenous peoples' dissatisfaction with the assimilationist approach of Convention 107, the ILO revised this convention during the late 1980s. Despite formal limitations on the participation of indigenous peoples in the ILO (which allows governments, employer representatives and union representatives to participate), the norms emergent in international discussions shaped the development of a revised ILO Convention (Anaya, 2004). In 1989, the general conference of the ILO adopted Convention 169 to revise Convention 107. Convention 169 recognized 'social, cultural, religious, and spiritual values and practices' at a collective level (Article 5) and noted that indigenous peoples 'shall have the right to decide their own priorities for the process of developments' (Article 7). Convention 169 represented a shift in codified international law about indigenous peoples.

> Convention No. 169 can be seen as a manifestation of the movement toward responsiveness to indigenous peoples' demands through international law .... Indigenous peoples have demanded recognition of rights that are of a collective character, rights among whose beneficiaries are historically grounded communities rather than simply individuals or (inchoate) states ... [T]he normative concept underlying indigenous peoples' self-determination rhetoric took hold to a substantial degree in Convention No. 169. Even the qualified usage of the term *peoples* implies a certain affirmation of indigenous group identity and corresponding attributes of community (Anaya, 2003, 59–60, emphasis in the original).

The formal principles of international law, therefore, changed subsequent to the institutionalization of principles of emerging norms in world culture.

While Convention 169 has been ratified by only 17 countries, its status and the principles underlying the emerging international norms serve as the basis for international bodies' approach to issues involving indigenous peoples. For instance, in 1991, the World Bank issued Operational Directive 4.20 that required informed participation of indigenous peoples in development projects that affected them. Informed participation fit with the newly emerging principles of indigenous peoples' participation and self-determination. 'The World Bank adopted Operational Directive 4.20 after a period of expert study that helped reshape attitudes within the bank toward greater programmatic action concerning indigenous peoples ... in line with contemporary trends in thinking about their rights' (Anaya, 2003, 67). From the late 1990s, the Bank undertook a review of the policy, issuing a revision with Operational Policy and Bank Procedure 4.10 in 2005 (World Bank, 2005c, 2005d). The review process included, for the first time, direct consultation with indigenous peoples about the policy itself (World Bank, 2005b). While the revised policy and procedure have been criticized for potential shortcomings in relation to emerging international law on indigenous peoples,[6] they incorporate direct reference to indigenous rights: 'The Bank policy on Indigenous Peoples recognizes Indigenous Peoples having distinct social, cultural and economic rights' (World Bank, 2005b, 4). Formally, the Bank held that there are no legally binding obligations for promoting indigenous rights, but that the emerging principles and practices created a basis for the policy.[7] As such, these emergent rights serve to regulate the activities of the international body (Sarfaty, 2005).

---

6   In particular, indigenous experts and representatives expressed two primary concerns with the new World Bank Policy and Procedure. First, they worried about the potential use of domestic institutions (rather than World Bank procedures) to determine the impact of projects, since the standards could end up being poorly and inconsistenly enforced. Second, they criticized the revision for requiring only consultation, rather than consent, of the indigenous peoples affected by proposed projects (World Bank, 2005c; MacKay, 2005). The latter concern relates to the interpretation of international law, as ILO Convention 169 calls for consent in the instance of relocation. The Bank has held that Convention 169 is not clear international law (World Bank, 2005a), but in its public reply to concerns seemed to acknowledge that there is some level of indigenous consent required: 'Should a borrower ultimately decide to proceed with a project in the absence of broad community support by affected Indigenous Peoples, the Bank would not provide support for the project in question' (World Bank, 2005b, 14). Both issues will be further addressed in a forthcoming Indigenous Peoples Guidebook. The recent passage by the Human Rights Council of the Declaration on the Rights of Indigenous Peoples suggests that The World Bank's Guidebook may be more explicit in calls for consent, as Article 30, Section 2 calls for indigenous peoples to give 'their free and informed consent prior to the approval of any project affecting their lands or territories and other resources' (Human Rights Council, 2006b, 15).

7   '[T]here is no universally accepted convention or treaty which comprehensively addresses the rights of indigenous peoples. However, there are emerging international principles and practices relating to Indigenous Peoples. Those principles and practices are not universally binding in nature, but nevertheless, the proposed Policy is consistent with them .... Nevertheless, the international instruments and practices surveyed above, including the General Assembly Resolutions, indicate the emergence of international principles and practices, particularly with regard to (i) consultation with, and participation of indigenous peoples on decisions affecting them, and (ii) recognition and protection of the rights of indigenous peoples, including land rights and rights to natural and cultural resources.' (World Bank, 2005a, 7–8.)

As indigenous rights become a more prominent feature in global culture, there are also increasing efforts to monitor the status of the ways in which these rights are incorporated into international organizations. While this monitoring had an ad hoc status in earlier times, the Economic and Social Council of the United Nations established the Permanent Forum on Indigenous Issues to serve as the primary source of expertise, awareness and information on indigenous issues. With such a structure in place, the concepts of indigenous rights and participation became easier to diffuse throughout international bodies. In its work, the Permanent Forum can issue recommendations to international bodies, actors, and indigenous representatives. For instance, the Permanent Forum noted that indigenous issues receive scant attention in the Millennium Development Goals and issued a series of recommendations to integrate indigenous issues into the implementation of the Goals (Permanent Forum, 2005). In such recommendations, the content of the emergent rights may also be expanded by connecting them to a broader set of institutional processes, such as reporting.

Institutionalization of principles of indigenous rights globally also has influence on and is influenced by staff of international bodies. The structure of international bodies affords staff the opportunity to mobilize agency (Hagan, 2003). Given the nature of work in international meetings, members of the secretariat serve as a key point of contact. The members of the secretariat that support the Working Group serve under the United Nations Office of the High Commissioner for Human Rights. Most of the individuals have a background in human rights work and, as a result, some commitment to the promotion of indigenous rights. Beyond this background, however, the exposure and nature of the work may further shape this commitment, as illustrated by the exchange between a secretariat member and me in an interview:

Q: What, if anything, has changed your understanding of indigenous issues?
A: I think, like other people who are listening in to the meetings and hear the different statements. After a while – there are always fresh insights and ways of looking at things.

This member of the secretariat, in particular, noted that reports of human rights violations were 'shocking' and that discussion of different relations to land were 'enriching', suggesting that the participation of the indigenous delegates may reinforce the commitment of the secretariat staff. Other research with workers for global institutions concerned with human rights found that being 'on mission' produced a high degree of commitment to the ideals of the institution (Hagan, 2003). The experience of the Working Group secretariat suggests that even more mundane tasks (such as working with a group of indigenous people holding Human Rights Commission fellowships each summer or even interacting with indigenous delegates at Working Group meetings) may similarly increase commitment. This commitment may, in turn, influence the actions of the secretariat:

We're seen [by the indigenous delegates] a bit as the good guys, which is good. You can sense that in the atmosphere of the room. We try to answer their questions honestly and send back e-mails to demystify the UN – we break down the formalities and try to be easy-going and as welcoming as possible. The idea is to try to convey the message, 'this is your meeting'.

Indeed, the secretariat has produced a series of documents that encourage indigenous peoples' participation in international forums.[8] The work for the secretariat's staff and patterns of interaction with indigenous people, therefore, may reinforce each other in a manner that creates an in-built constituency for the promotion of the ideals underlying the emergent rights, binding agency to these international bodies.

Finally, the emergent principles of indigenous rights include the principle of indigenous participation. Recognition of the importance of (at a minimum) consulting indigenous peoples encourages greater participation by indigenous peoples in a variety of international meetings. For instance, indigenous peoples participated in the World Conference on Women in 1995 and the Social Summit in 1996. This participation can lead to rights being incorporated into additional legal instruments. Indigenous delegates participated in the 1992 Earth Summit, which produced the Convention on Biological Diversity. Article 8(j) of the Convention (on conservation) holds that parties:

> Respect, preserve and maintain knowledge, innovations and practices of indigenous and local communities embodying traditional lifestyles relevant for the conservation and sustainable use of biological diversity and promote their wider application with the approval and involvement of the holders of such knowledge, innovations and practices and encourage the equitable sharing of the benefits arising from the utilization of such knowledge, innovations and practices.

The incorporation of indigenous rights into the convention expands on the foundation of non-discrimination in which international indigenous rights first took hold.

Even prior to a completed declaration of indigenous rights, the emergence of a general level of commitment to indigenous participation as part of world culture has had a series of regulatory effects on international bodies. These bodies face pressure to adapt to the changes in the global norms by both organizational processes and change in formal policies. Monitoring of action and staffing patterns create means through which these principles diffuse, while the principles become expressed more formally through changes in policy and law. Together these features point to the expansive nature of agency and legitimacy. As actors are authorized to participate in a forum, they may gain power by influencing agenda-setting activities (Bachrach and Baratz, 1963). Legitimacy remakes global culture as an issue becomes a concern which actors must consider. While this process of articulation fits world polity models of the rationalization of world culture, it happens in a manner that remakes the content of the culture to lead to the diffusion of new cultural content. The participation of indigenous peoples in the world polity underlies this diffusion. Of particular importance was the establishment of the Working Group with its open-door policy on indigenous participation. While formal decisions of the Working

---

8   One particularly helpful bit of advice is to participate in the meetings of the Sub-Commission on the Promotion and Protection of Human Rights, even though the participation for NGOs is limited to those with consultative status with the Economic and Social Council (Office of the High Commissioner for Human Rights). The document then goes on to suggest particular organizations that may be helpful in locating an NGO that would share a speaking slot.

Group are with its expert members, the indigenous delegates and secretariat staff share information that can shape the agenda of the Working Group. One member of the Secretariat reflected on the Working Group:

> It is a big forum where [indigenous delegates] lobby for their concerns ... A lot of topics and initiatives raised in the Working Group – the Permanent Forum, the Special Rapporteur [on the Situation of Human Rights and Fundamental Freedoms of Indigenous People] have come from the Working Group. Ideas come out of the discussion of the Working Group.

The participation has led to the diffusion of the ideas about indigenous rights – including the right to participate – in a manner that regulates the activities of other international bodies.

States

Despite a lack of fully operational rights of indigenous peoples, the principles underlying indigenous rights serve to regulate the actions of states. First, the norm of participation and the operation of an international forum such as the Working Group provide indigenous people with an opportunity to engage states in dialogue in a manner that may not be available domestically. Second, while the Declaration took over a decade of negotiation and while only a limited number of countries have acceded to ILO Convention 169, the emerging principles and laws have been incorporated into international law beyond their formal application, as international justice institutions look to them to interpret the meaning of indigenous rights law. Finally, with the development of indigenous rights as collective rights, the scope for making claims against states has also expanded. These findings show how the regulatory effects of international human rights are more robust than hypothesized, as emerging ideals of international law are used to set standards and monitor states and as these ideals also shape domestic actors' agency, aspirations and claims-making activities.

The development of a semi-autonomous system of global governance has provided aggrieved groups the opportunity to mobilize support for frustrated domestic causes (Keck and Sikkink, 1998). When movements are unable to induce a government response domestically, they may seek additional support from international non-governmental organizations or social movements who may then activate international pressure on the otherwise non-responsive government. Given that activity moves from the domestic to the global and back to the domestic sphere, Keck and Sikkink label this process as the 'boomerang effect'. Clearly, the development of a transnational indigenous peoples' movement and the development of specialized governance bodies expands the opportunities for such effects. Indeed, the materials prepared to brief indigenous delegates about participation in the Working Group suggest that delegates prepare local and national media for their statements so that they have the greatest domestic impact (Office of the High Commissioner for Human Rights).

These international bodies, however, also have impacts greater than a source of appeal to wrest a response out of an intransigent government. The Working Group serves as a meeting place for more cordial, if not entirely cooperative, relations between government and indigenous delegates. In many cases, the lack of a domestic institutional means of participation and the more visible nature of meetings in a domestic environment (with the subsequent political meanings that may be attached and disseminated for such meetings) mean that the international meetings provide an opportunity to meet within a more neutral environment. A member of the Working Group secretariat explained that there are 'positive reactions' to the participation in the Working Group of indigenous delegates and governments:

> [Some governments have] taken our suggestions as a Working Group, such as having a quota system in Parliament, as a basis for discussion. They discussed the ideas with the indigenous representatives that have been at the Working Group. Many indigenous people can meet the government representative here.

While the impact of these meetings may be limited due to government representatives having limited authority, the possibility for discussion provides a means through which to shape domestic agendas without having direct access to domestic political institutions.

Similarly, the principles of emerging international law and norms serve to shape the behaviour of nation-states (Meyer, Boli, Thomas and Ramirez, 1997). In some cases, there are clear instances in which the content of global culture is incorporated into national law, even though such content is not fully articulated. A member of the secretariat explained that '[s]ome legislations – like the Philippines' legislation on indigenous issues – is based on the ILO [Convention] and Draft Declaration.' In addition to the potential influence of the norms themselves, the secretariat becomes a resource to interpret the ambiguous rights:

> Through the UN system on the country level, the OHCHR gives input. Through our seminars and activities, we bring indigenous peoples and governments together to negotiate. We present recommendations. We get telephone calls from indigenous peoples and governments to get advice on the state of indigenous rights.

The ambiguities of legal meaning are frequently worked out in the field that is regulated (Edelman, 1992; Suchman and Edelman, 1997). In this instance, however, the meanings are filtered through the expertise of the secretariat, which also serves as the bridge between groups on rights claims. The effects of the international bodies on states as both meeting places and interpreters of global norms again highlights the expansive nature of agency at the global level, particularly as it relates to the participation of indigenous people in the global polity.

The development of international norms about indigenous peoples has been occurring in law via court decisions even before the Human Rights Council passed the Declaration. The Inter-American Court of Human Rights has adopted an 'evolutionary' interpretation of human rights. In the *Mayagna (Sumo) Awas Tigni* case, the court upheld the finding of the Inter-American Commission on Human Rights, that in granting a logging concession, the Nicaraguan Government violated the Mayanga Awas Tingni community's indigenous communal property rights. A concurring decision of the court made specific reference to ILO Convention

169 (which Nicaragua had not ratified) and the Draft Declaration (Anaya, 2003). These concurring references were reinforced in the Inter-American Commission on Human Rights decision in the Dann (2002) case. The Commission, in holding that the United States violated the indigenous property rights of members of the Dann tribe of the Western Shoshone, interpreted the Inter-American Declaration on the Rights and Duties of Man in light of emerging international norms: 'Consistent with this approach, in determining the claims currently before it, the Commission considers that this broader corpus of international law includes the developing norms and principles governing the human rights of indigenous peoples' (Dann, 2002, paragraph 124). The court's decision specifically referenced ILO Convention 169 (which the USA has not ratified) and upheld the collective nature of indigenous rights. These decisions formalize the principles that have been institutionalized into the world polity, reflecting a process similar to the manners in which the meaning of compliance with government regulation of business becomes institutionalized (Edelman, 1992; Bridges and Nelson, 1999).

With indigenous rights serving to introduce a collective right not embodied in state sovereignty, the scope for acting on the basis of rights has also expanded, with a concomitant impact on the regulation of state activities. Building on the success of the *Awas Tingni* and *Dann* cases, the Inuit Circumpolar Conference has filed a suit against the United States for its failure to limit greenhouse gas emissions (Inuit Circumpolar Conference, 2005). While the claim is based largely on a model of cultural integrity rather than self determination (Metcalf, 2003), the petition reflects the greater prominence of cultural protections in existing law, the ability to claim harm to rights based on culture, and the difficulty of incorporating a remedy based on self-determination in the circumstances. The filing, however, does request as part of its remedies for the USA to take the Inuit into account in its decision-making about climate change. Relying on narrative evidence, the petition details a number of consequences of global warming on the Inuit (travel on the ice has become less safe; traditional knowledge about weather has been undermined; a greater number of people have fallen through the ice; igloos are not able to be built due to changes in snow; and the ability to hunt for traditional sources of food has been undermined) and connects these consequences to harm to rights (for example, undermining the ability to use and enjoy traditional lands; undermining the ability to use and enjoy tangible and intellectual property; harming health, life, physical integrity, and security; harming subsistence; and forcing residential relocation). Together, these rights claims are connected with the underlying claim that indigenous rights are bound to their environment, which is the basis of indigenous cultural and physical survival. The primary petitioner[9] − Sheila Watt-Cloutier, elected chair of the Inuit Circumpolar Conference − resides in Canada. The petition itself is filed on behalf of all Inuit in Canada and the USA. The claim in this case, therefore, represents an attempt to regulate state behaviour as it impacts indigenous people as a collective that exists (at least partially) outside of the state. While no declaration about the case has been issued by the court yet, the case is notable for its basis for action, as it rests, in part, on the duty of the USA to avoid trans-boundary environmental

---

9   There are also 63 individuals named in support on the petition.

harm. The supporting material in the petition, however, refers only to states' duties to avoid trans-boundary harm to other states. To the extent that the court upholds any claim in the petition, it would formalize the manner in which the collective nature of indigenous rights has remade the ontology of international rights. Even if the court rejects the petition, the ability to use indigenous rights in this case serves minimally to mobilize a 'politics of shame' in a new manner, as it challenges recent United States' claims about upholding human rights (Canadian Broadcasting Corporation, 2005).

Indigenous Movement

In addition to international organizations and nation-states, the indigenous peoples' movement itself is regulated, particularly in regard to who may claim status as indigenous and what types of claims can be made. Formally, articulated rights and law delimit who has access to rights and to what these rights may apply. Given the emergent nature of indigenous rights, however, such formal criteria do not exist. The process through which indigenous rights access and claims are regulated, however, suggest that the movement is regulated by institutionalizing agency and legitimacy, which serves to authorize various actors to reject certain claimants or claims. Beyond directing claims, international human rights also regulate access to these claims.

Indigenous rights, although institutionalized within the broader framework of human rights, are non-universal: that is, they apply only to indigenous peoples. As such, these rights have an inherent regulatory edge, as only certain peoples have claims to such rights. Within law, the typical way of regulating such access is through definition, with criteria for identifying beneficiaries established in the law itself. The difficulty in defining indigenous peoples in international law is the varied experiences and the subsequent difficulty of either excluding some indigenous peoples or including some non-indigenous peoples (Daes, 1996; Neizen, 2003; Coates, 2004; Sissons, 2005). In practice, the Working Group has adopted a subjective non-definition definition of indigenous peoples, allowing indigenous peoples to identify themselves. This practice reflects the preference of indigenous peoples, who have a history of being subject to governments' declarations that they do not exist and who prefer a means to identify indigenous peoples that is consistent with self-determination. Despite the formal procedure of subjective self-identification, there are informal practices identifying indigenous peoples, which largely are based on a set of enumerative criteria that are frequently part of the indigenous experience (Martínez Cobo, 1987). In addition, the meaning of indigenous people identifying themselves applies in a collective manner, with the broader indigenous movement responding to improper assertions of indigeneity. Indeed, the United Nations bodies rely 'upon organizations of indigenous peoples themselves to draw attention to any improper assertions of the right to participate as "indigenous" peoples' (Daes, 1996, 21). Or, in the words of a member of the Working Group secretariat:

> People who represent nobody – they are indigenous and are living in Europe, but with no connection to the community – often give the most radical statements that are nonsensical. These people don't have any influence. They have no community support ... [Other

indigenous delegates] go up and ask, "Where are you from? We don't know who you represent.' They give them a grilling.

At the level of a people, other indigenous peoples could engage in activity to regulate access to legitimate access to agency. At the 1994 and 1995 meetings of the Working Group, representatives of the Afrikaner-Volksfront prepared and made statements claiming status as an indigenous people. During the presentation, other indigenous representatives walked out of the hall as a sign of rejection. A secretariat member explained the events in light of Working Group procedures:

> [W]e have a position on participation for the Working Group which ... means that we do not deny the participation of any organization that claims to be an indigenous organization. We did not want to deny [the Afrikaner-Volksfront] – as soon as you deny, you have to explain why. It leads to definitions and marginalization, exclusion .... What happened at that point and on that occasion – it was all very friendly – indigenous organizations who knew they were going to speak decided to leave the room as they spoke. Many or most of the indigenous delegates left the room and when they were done speaking, they returned. They explained to the Boers that they did not consider South African Boers as indigenous.

After the meetings, a petition was signed by 82 indigenous participants expressing concern at this participation (Working Group on Indigenous Populations, 1994, 12). In the official reports of the Working Group, the Afrikaner-Volksfront was not identified as an indigenous people's organization. The process through which agency has been institutionalized for indigenous peoples has authorized indigenous peoples and relevant staff of international bodies (who, in practice, follow the lead of indigenous peoples) to regulate access to indigenous status.

Outside the context of international meetings, the meaning of 'indigenous' has been incorporated into procedures used by international bodies as part of the process of institutionalizing legitimacy. This meaning reflects a particular range of historical construction that relies on the people having some level of exclusion from the nation-state, reinforcing the notion that indigenous rights represent a reworking of the ontology of rights. Assertions of indigenous rights in Fiji and Tanzania that run counter to accepted uses of the term simply do not figure into the decisions made by international financial and justice institutions (Larson, 2005; Larson and Aminzade, forthcoming).

The institutionalization of agency and legitimacy and identification of indigenous peoples relates to regulating the legitimacy of claims and the cultural continuity of the indigenous rights movement. The global indigenous rights movement incorporates a range of cultural content that influences the ways in which claims about indigenous rights violations are framed (Morgan, 2004; Sissons, 2005). In addition to the positive content of the types of arguments that are made in favour of indigenous rights, the cultural content of indigenous rights excludes some claims. In particular, the claims should be non-sovereignist and non-violent (Niezen, 2003; Anaya, 2004). Claims by Bougainvillian rebels to have indigenous rights in their struggle for secession from Papua New Guinea simply lacked resonance with global culture (Gillin, 2006). This aspect of the cultural content may also have the perverse effect of making use of indigenous rights more difficult for indigenous peoples who are more isolated from the world polity (and hence less familiar with the cultural content of indigenous rights) and who appear less 'authentically' indigenous (Li, 2000; Tilley, 2002).

Despite a lack of articulated indigenous rights in the form of an operative international declaration, the premises underlying indigenous rights have become embodied in agency and legitimacy in manners that serve to regulate international bodies and nation-states as these principles diffuse and become formally institutionalized in international law. Expansive agency and legitimacy, however, are not limitless, as the applications of indigenous rights must fit within the larger constructions of indigenous rights in the world polity. Indigenous peoples and staff of global governance institutions who work most closely with indigenous peoples serve to regulate access to agency and legitimacy, reproducing the grounds on which orientations to law are institutionalized (Ewick and Silbey, 1998).

Implications for the Intersection of Rights and Regulation

Law is an important component of world culture and international rights. By embodying and elaborating the norms of world culture, law and rights becomes a focal point for international claims making. As such, the rights attached to international law are regulative and productive. Traditionally, application of international law and rights have regulated states, creating responsibility by binding agency to states, serving as a source to articulate polity, and shaping actors' ability and desire to make claims.

Considering the content and history of indigenous rights, however, suggests a greater dynamism to the development of institutions in the world polity. Earlier, I suggested four ways in which international rights are regulatory. In light of the discussion of the history of indigenous rights and their regulatory effects, I want to reconsider these four regulatory mechanisms. First, while international rights do create bounded agency for states as the primary responsible party for upholding rights, the development of indigenous rights suggests that international rights also underlie the development of agency for a somewhat autonomous international sphere. Second, the direct reporting and measurement of conformity to international norms certainly applies to states when rights are embodied in treaties to which states have acceded. These norms, however, can also be applied to states prior to formal accession and also can serve to measure the adequacy of international institutions. For instance, a special rapporteur's review of the status of indigenous peoples provided recommendations to international financial institutions about improving their treatment of indigenous peoples (Stavenhagen, 2003). Third, while rights can serve as the basis for actors' agency, such bases have a cultural content that may regulate the access to this agency. Finally, rights may limit or direct claims, but the institutionalized understanding of these rights is subject to remaking and expansion.

As a whole, these observations point to the importance of the expansive nature of agency and legitimacy in the international system. Both agency and legitimacy can be used by a variety of actors dynamically to develop the particular content

– and, indeed structures – of the world polity. Rights are not solely bound up with states, but enable a degree of autonomy on the part of experts, secretariats, and rights holders, particularly in relation to the interpretation and deployment of these rights.

These rights are expansive both in form and substance even though the particular content of these rights is still contested. Formally, the establishment of the principles underlying indigenous rights – including the principles of self-determination and participatory consultation – has created space for agency for indigenous peoples and for international bodies that specialize in indigenous issues. This agency particularly takes the form of agenda-setting activities. Given the semi-autonomous nature of the international system, this agenda-setting can have a good deal of impact. Substantively, the development of indigenous rights has changed the content of global culture to incorporate collective rights that are not invested into the nation-state via sovereignty. These rights are collective in nature both as rights and to those entitled to those rights, as witnessed by the authority granted to indigenous peoples to identify and regulate access to these rights. Further, even though indigenous rights are institutionalized within the human rights framework, they provide a foundation for expanding other collective rights beyond the sovereign nation-state. For instance, an expert member of the Working Group made an intervention at the 2003 session about the human rights status of peoples whose states were threatened with extinction due to rising sea levels, suggesting that such peoples should still have access to self-determination (Hampson, 2003).

The expansive nature of rights is not unlimited due to the institutionalized nature of orientation toward law. The applicability and actionability of rights is enmeshed with legal consciousness, which emerges in an institutionalized manner through which certain actions and actors become accepted as legitimate. Political processes of clarifying and settling meaning establish particular orientations toward law which subsequently shape future invocations of law (Larson, 2004; Steinman, 2005). These institutionalized orientations toward law regulate which actors invoke rights, how these invocations proceed, and the responses to these invocations. Such orientations, of course, can change. Such transformations to the orientations toward law are likely when the nature of agency changes, such that new actors are enabled to have influence on agendas or particular actors have an enhanced basis for effective action. These orientations toward law may also be altered with changes to the nature of legitimacy, as particular ideas or orientations take on greater relevance within a variety of social contexts.

PART 3
Politics and Ideologies: Hybrid Dialectics of Rights and Regulation

Dancing in New York City: The Cabaret Law, Alternative Cultures and Neoliberal Urbanism

Laam Hae[1]

Introduction

Frank, a graduate student at Syracuse University, has a strange anecdote about clubbing in New York City bars (Interview, Frank Bryan Ellis, 3 March 2006). In summer 2005, Frank was hanging out in an Upper East Side bar, Mustangs, with a couple of his friends. The throbbing music made Frank and his friends swing their bodies to the rhythm of the music, until they were stopped by the bouncer of the bar. To this bewildered crew, the bouncer pointed to a sign hanging on the wall which announced 'No Dancing.' When Frank and his friends protested, the bouncer threw them out of the bar.

This seemingly nonsensical act – the bouncer's interruption of Frank and his friends' dancing – was, in reality, a perfectly reasonable one, given that the cabaret law in New York City has rendered it illegal for more than three patrons to move together rhythmically in an unlicensed place – an average New York City bar, like Mustangs. The cabaret law requires that an establishment that has social dancing in bar or restaurant businesses – legally called 'cabarets' – be located in a proper building in an appropriate zone, and be licensed and equipped with proper safety and soundproofing measures. While these requirements appear straightforward, in actuality, over the last two decades dance clubs[2] in Manhattan have faced increasing

1   I would like to thank my adviser Dr Don Mitchell at Syracuse University for his insightful comments on this paper, his 5-year supervision of my dissertation and his immense support and guidance in other aspects of my academic life. I also thank my colleagues at Syracuse University, Reecia Orzeck and Cyril Ghosh, for carefully reading this paper and for providing incisive comments and editorial advice. Also many thanks to Dr Bronwen Morgan – without her time and effort, this publication would not have been possible. My final thanks go to Dr Bronwen Morgan again and to the other authors of this book for sharing their opinions on my paper and for providing valuable insights, all of which have improved the paper immeasurably. Any remaining errors are mine.

2   Here, I operationally define 'dance clubs' as including both 1) bars whose businesses are not entirely focused on dancing, or which are not located in a proper zone that legally allows social dancing among customers, but where social dancing can occasionally happen due to occasional dance parties or incidental social dancing among patrons to the canned

difficulties in acquiring cabaret licenses, not least because the planning zones where social dancing – even social dancing among three people – is permitted have been drastically reduced in size. The process of applying for a cabaret license has also become more expensive, complicated and unpredictable. Furthermore, an accelerating outcry from communities against nightspots and their political mobilization to reclaim the 'quality of life' in their neighbourhoods has led to the city's increased crackdown on dance clubs by implementing a new institution that strictly polices the compliance of the provisions of the cabaret law by dance clubs.[3]

The increased surveillance of dance clubs according to meticulous legal dictates regarding where and under what conditions even the most modest dance activities can take place has sparked off a city-wide controversy over the legitimacy of the cabaret law. Those who have been engaged in anti-cabaret law activism have argued that dancing is a fundamental human right, one intimately linked to freedom of expression, and that this freedom is impaired by the enforcement of the cabaret law. Meanwhile, mayors, city government officials, the planning commission members, local politicians and community board members have endorsed the legitimacy of the cabaret law's regulations on dance clubs on the grounds that dance clubs are a community nuisance, and the freedom of expression they may enable should be trumped by local residents' rights to a high 'quality of life'.

This chapter analyzes this divisive urban phenomenon revolving around the regulations of dance clubs. In particular, it attends to the role and meaning of the cabaret law and other governmental regulations on dance clubs in New York City, in relation to the drastic transformation of urban space in recent decades particularly since the city government broadly adopted a neoliberal approach in its urban policy. The constant invocation of the cabaret law and other associated regulations by the city government does not only aim to protect citizens and further promote public well-being (in other words, quality of life) by curbing problems of safety and noise associated with dance clubs. The city's regulatory drive against dance clubs is, I argue, implicated in the government's efforts to find solutions to the conflicts and contradictions that have appeared as a consequence of intensive urban restructuring such as gentrification. The direction that the government has taken in its search for solutions has been skewed toward creating everyday spaces of social norms and cultural life that are consistent with the directives of a newly emerging neoliberal urbanism that has been the main source of urban spatial restructuring, rather than, for instance, being geared toward protecting spaces of alternative cultures that have historically contributed to such urban restructuring but are considered a nuisance in the restructured environment. This direction has yielded numerous regulatory

---

music, the DJ's music or live band performances, and 2) clubs that are located in a zone that legally allows social dancing, have dance floors, usually have more than a 200 person capacity and whose businesses are mostly concerned with dancing.

3   Communities' oppositions have not been limited to premises that offer social dancing. As a matter of fact, they have primarily targeted any nightlife businesses that brought serious nuisances – such as noise, patron vandalisms, heavy traffic and so on – to residential neighbourhoods. Nevertheless, the city has routinely depicted only social dancing as a nuisance crime duly subject to governmental regulations. The reason for this is one of the issues covered in this chapter later.

arrangements by the municipality to safeguard the social and spatial rights of a certain class – in other words, its rights to a high quality of life – that is at the centre of the neoliberal urbanism.

This research is situated within a body of literature on the political economy and the social relations of neoliberal urbanism and on the emergence of punitive urbanism under neoliberal urbanism. Following Mitchell (2003) I use the concept of 'modes of regulation' developed by the regulationist school in order to explain what my research demonstrates as the significance of laws and regulations in both reflecting and reorganizing the conflict-ridden nature of 'creative destruction' – one of the primary processes of capitalist restructuring. I will also draw attention to the importance of geography in this process, by revealing how the act of displacing certain spaces can mediate and realize renewed power relations in urban capitalism. In this way, I want to demonstrate how and why a new capitalism requires a spatialized 'institutional fix' (Peck and Tickell, 1994) to overcome its contradictions and to continue its survival.

Political Economy and Landscapes of Neoliberal Urbanism

In recent urban studies scholarship, there has been a surge in research that demonstrates what Davis (1990, p. 223) calls 'the militarization of city life'. This body of literature has demonstrated that certain sectors of city populations have been more and more militarily policed and displaced from revitalized urban spaces through architectural designs, surveillance technologies, 'zero tolerance' by the (public or private) police and laws and regulations that criminalize the behaviours or presence of these populations (MacLeod, 2002, p. 605; see also Davis, 1990; Christopherson, 1994; Fyfe and Bannister, 1998; Flusty, 2001; McArdle and Erzen, 2001; MacLeod, 2002). This type of militarization has found widespread support from civil society because it has championed such well-intentioned purposes as safeguarding urban residents from threats, social ills and nuisances traditionally associated with cities. A closer look at this rhetoric, however, reveals that it is not the protection of the city's public per se that the militarization purports to, but only that of a certain class of people, their property rights and their quality of life. Consequently affluent communities are often legitimately 'gated' (McKenzie, 1994) and 'walled' (Judd, 1995) against those deemed to be threats and urban ills, thus creating a contemporary version of 'urban apartheid' (Davis, 1990, 226).

What accounts for the rise in this militarized urbanization in contemporary cities? If 'urbanization is a spatially grounded *social* process' as Harvey (1989a, p. 5, emphasis added) rightly puts it, we may have to seek an explanation for the unfolding of this military urbanization in its relation to certain social processes at work in contemporary cities – in particular, the (changes in) social relations, the political economy of the capitalism hegemonic at this time, and the contradictions that inhere in it.[4] In this vein, I stand in line with urbanists who have argued that the distinctive historical landscape of militarized and punitive urbanism, described above, has been

---

4   While the ways in which cities are managed and experienced are overdetermined by numerous forces, it has been persuasively demonstrated that urbanization and social relations involved in it have been primarily shaped (if not exclusively determined) by the directives of

deeply connected to the advent and development of neoliberal urbanism. In other words, the punitive urbanization has much to do with the emerging need of the neoliberal cities to find a spatialized 'institutional fix' to the continuously emerging contradictions that occur in the process of creative destruction. Then, what is it about neoliberal urbanization that necessitates these punitive regulatory arrangements as a 'fix'?

Since the late 1970s, many North American and Western European cities have gone through dramatic changes in their landscapes. Urban landscape is installed with post-industrial symbols – such as upscale condos, corporate offices, chic shopping centres, leisure complexes full of corporate commercial businesses, museums, art galleries, sports events, cultural festivals and so forth (Zukin, 1991; Sorkin, 1992; Knox, 1998). The formerly derelict residential or commercial neighbourhoods (the dereliction caused by the white flight or by the fiscal crisis of city governments during the 1970s), or manufacturing districts abandoned in the sweeping process of deindustrialization in North America and Europe were the ones that have felt this transformation most dramatically. Such transformations have been extolled both as the sign and the facilitator of restoration of urban vitality and economic health.

Most urbanists have generally interpreted this new urban phenomenon as the urban materialization of transition from a Keynesian welfare regime to a neoliberal regime in Western society, coupled with the changes in the dominant regime of accumulation from Fordism to post-Fordism (Lipietz, 1986; Harvey, 1989a, 1989b; Dicken, 1992; Peck and Tickell, 1994; Brenner and Theodore, 2002). In order to overcome financial crises and worldwide economic stagnation that set in during the 1970s, the US and British governments moved away from the managerial role that they had so far taken in steering their national economies and adopted the neoliberal approach, in which governmental intervention was denounced and market autonomy was upheld as the principal organizing mechanism of economy and society (Harvey, 2005). These macroeconomic and political shifts since the 1970s have had conspicuous imprints on the direction of urban politics (Brenner and Theodore, 2002, 367). White flight had already shrunk municipalities' coffers in many cities by the end of the 1960s, and the fiscal crisis in the 1970s and subsequent drastic cuts in federal fiscal support, and the accelerating deindustrialization added more difficulties to the management of cities in those countries.

Devoid of the main financial sources of revenue, cities now needed to turn to the private sector to garner financial resources. This explains why municipal governments have mobilized an assortment of policies to facilitate wholesale private participation in the local economy and urban redevelopment. These developments indicate that the nature of urban governance is no longer managerial, but *entrepreneurial* (Harvey, 1989a; Hubbard and Hall, 1998), which means that urban governance is more structurally friendly to and allied with private interests, and more prone to endorsing market-oriented pro-growth and capital accumulation rather than to prioritizing public services or welfare redistribution. The capital accumulation in the city is no longer realized through traditional manufacturing employment, housing provisions

---

a specific capitalist system dominant at the time that cities are operating (see, for example, Knox, 1993, 8–14).

for the working class or through the Fordist method of production and consumption. City governments in alliance with private interests seek to entice into their territories those businesses that can grant cities with global competitiveness in the post-Fordist era – such as businesses related to high-tech or biochemistry industries, financial services, high-end office businesses, entertainment, media, advertising, tourism and sports. Cities' desire to attract this type of businesses and the relevant labour forces has been realized through a competitive drive of urban redevelopment to build a physical infrastructure favourable to desired industries, and housing provisions and a quality of life friendly to the social and cultural values of the desired workforce.

To attract footloose global capital to these projects, the pro-growth urban coalitions (including city governments themselves) offer tax incentives and other inducements. Now, urban space and the built environment in it is one of the essential resources left in municipalities' hands, on the basis of which cities can seek their economic revitalization according to changed macro-scale political economic environments. And, certainly, urban governance has not only become more concerned with market calculus and financial efficiency, but also sought to incorporate the concerns and interests of new businesses and newly transplanted residents.

Laws, Regulations and Institutions for Punitive Policing

In *Production of Space* (1991), Lefebvre details how space has been so produced as to constitute and serve the dominant modern capitalist system. According to Derek Gregory's reading of *production of space*, 'abstract space' – the space emblematic of the modern capitalism in which exchange value is predominant and capital accumulation is the main goal – requires two principal processes for it to be effectively produced and reproduced. The first process entails commodification – 'an intensified *commodification of* and *'through space'* (Gregory, 1994, 401, emphasis added). Neoliberal urbanization, for example, has a particular kind of commodification of space as its aim – such as redeveloping urban space into profitable office/commercial/ housing districts for state-of-the-art post-industrial businesses and labour forces that work for these businesses, and representing this type of commodification of derelict neighbourhoods as legitimate (as if the economic profit will trickle down to everyone) and even necessary for the restoration of the urban economy. However, space does more than this. Urban space, commodified as such, becomes one of the key units and conditions through which the particular combination of a mode of production, consumption and reproduction of a specific capitalism can be realized – hence 'commodification through space'. Transformed urban space, landscapes and built environments in neoliberal cities provide a proper (if fraught with struggles) grounding on which qualities of neoliberal economy – such as flexible accumulation – can be embedded into the local economy. Without the upscale housing and cultural spaces for lifestyle consumption that can accommodate the social and cultural tastes of the labour force that cities seek to ensure within its boundaries, it may be hard to realize neoliberal capitalism within cities. The mechanism is dialectical and circular. A new capitalism is one of the main forces that trigger the transformation of urban space, so the features of transformed urban space mirror the kind of the exchange and use value that chracterize the new capitalism. But this new capitalism, in turn, cannot be realized without being fixed, and mediated, through the transformed urban space.

Lefebvre further points to another equally important process. In addition to an intensified 'commodification of and through space', abstract space also needs 'a heightened *bureaucratization of* and '*through space*' (Gregory, 1994, p. 401, emphasis in original). Space should be divided, categorized, bureaucratized and thus subject to controls for effective state management (especially of the capital accumulation process). Once bureaucratized and under control, space becomes one of the key units and conditions of surveillance and disciplinary control, through which the broader economic, political, social and cultural life is regulated and made stable in cities.[5] The two processes – 'commodification of and through space' and 'bureaucratization of and through space' – dovetail and reinforce each other to better (re)produce abstract space in harmony with the directives of the political economy of capitalism.

Regulation theory further explains why commodification goes hand in hand with bureaucratization in order to make space more integral to the operation of capitalism. Regulation theory points out that the ongoing survival and (re)production of a specific regime of capital accumulation is achieved through its corresponding 'mode of regulation' – which is defined as 'a set of state and private institutional forms, social practices, habits, and norms (such as those governing wage determination), which induce private individuals to act in the interests of achieving overall economic stability' (Johnston et al., 2000). Capitalism, due to its volatile, contradictory and conflict-ridden nature in the process of creative destruction and uneven development, necessitates the regulatory mechanism that can put its operation in order and stability. The regulatory mechanism is practiced through institutions, law, regulations and rules, and/or it can be embodied in social norms, practices and habits that are at work either in the state apparatus or in civil society. When such stability cannot be maintained any more, a new regime of accumulation emerges accompanied by a new mode of regulation, which would help a new regime to be successfully created and reproduced. In these processes, 'creative destruction' becomes the main work of the new mode of regulation, which tries to replace existing regulatory and institutional arrangements that stand in the way of creating the new regime with those that can better serve the newly emerging capitalist conditions of production and consumption (Brenner and Theodore, 2002).

The importance of the mode of regulation in sustaining or revolutionizing the existing regime of accumulation underlines the fact that market equilibrium alone cannot move a capitalist system along. The presence of the state in the market – its intervention into the market in the form of providing and assisting certain modes of regulation – has been integral in, and constituent of, market operations, even under neoliberalism whose proponents have constantly insisted on the necessity of granting the market an autonomy away from non-market agencies (such as the state). On the urban scale, numerous private projects and other market operations would

---

5   Derek Gregory points to pages 341 and 387 in *Production of Space* (Lefebvre, 1991) for this discussion (Gregory, 1994, 401n).

not have existed without the municipalities' policies which facilitate a favourable business climate – for example, tax incentives and subsidy programs inaugurated by urban governments to abet the workings of private capital. Such policies can also be identified as a mode of regulation deployed in order to attract to and retain in cities global capital and businesses that can otherwise be hypermobile. Neoliberalism is ideological in this sense, since it seeks to inculcate the notion that the economy and social life under it is a product of a free play of market instead of being carefully calculated and strategically produced by non-market actors (Harvey, 2005, 5–38).

The emergence of punitive urban policies has also had an impact on an emerging need for a new mode of regulation. The proliferation of anti-homeless laws in the USA is a case in point. According to Mitchell (2003a, p. 166), anxious local interests 'seek to stabilize their relationship with peripatetic capital' that can otherwise leave the locality whenever chances look better in other places. Besides proffering alluring inducements to global capital, local actors seek to tackle the increasing problem of homelessness, whose presence can defile the image of the city in the eyes of the credit-rating financial institutions. However, the latter is not an easy task; the economic policies that favour certain sectors of employment have resulted in escalating economic polarization that has become more and more salient in neoliberal cities, and produced an army of urban underclass (such as homeless people, squatters, pan-handlers and so on). This underclass is not only an unavoidable result of capital accumulation, but more importantly is a necessary part of it as 'the industrial reserve army,' whose presence helps employers to depress wages (quoted in Mitchell, 2003a, 173):

> The contradiction, then, is that the homeless and poor are desperately *needed*, but not at all *wanted*, and so the solution becomes a geographical one: regulating space so that homeless people have no room to be *here* (Mitchell, 2003a, p. 174, emphasis in original).

Therefore, for Mitchell, the anti-homeless laws are implemented as the 'mode of regulation' (Mitchell, 2003a, pp. 175–176), through which local coalitions try to solve the contradiction of homelessness in a spatialized way. This means nothing other than that the laws are not intended to eliminate homelessness, but just to eliminate homeless people from public space, which, in the absence of these unwanted people, now presents a sanitized, ordered and stabilized view. The ban on homelessness from public space is implemented by criminalizing the use value of urban public space closely associated with homeless people's survival – that is, by outlawing all the activities that '[homeless people] must do [in public space] in order to survive' (Mitchell, 2003a, 163), such as sleeping or begging in public.

Creative destruction and the resultant uneven development in neoliberal urbanization have led to the criminalization of certain values of, and certain rights claims to, urban space, which conflict with neoliberal urbanism's notions of private property value, or claims to a high quality of life (which is none other than a collectivized and spatially extended rights claim of property value), and so on.[6] The values and rights claims opposed to neoliberal urbanism may be the legacy

---

6   I owe this insight to the discussion in the meeting that the authors of this publication had in Baltimore, 2006.

of a previous period – such as Keynesian ideas of government and welfare, or 1960s and 1970s liberalism and counter-culture. They may also be the use value essential to the livelihood and the culture of those who represent the 'deleterious social consequence' of 'an increase in economic and social polarization' (MacLeod, 2002, p. 603) – such as homeless people. Condemned as symbols of urban decline, they can be deemed to be disadvantageous and even hostile to the exchange value that neoliberals seek to realize in urban space. However, ironically, these symbols are sometimes the necessary conditions on which neoliberal urbanism can flourish; homelessness (or, the existence of urban underclass) is necessary for the workings of neoliberalism, as Mitchell has contended; in another example, counter-cultures that previously characterized certain urban spaces are often repackaged in real-estate marketing to induce yuppies to move into the areas. To resolve the contradictions of such unavoidable but unwanted co-existence between conflicting values and, subsequently, to re-code urban space with rules, norms, values and rights claims that can better assist neoliberal directives, the mode of regulation, in the spatialized forms of punitive laws, regulations and institutions, has been constantly evoked.

Urbanists have pointed out that those laws, regulations and institutions established and implemented by city governments to manage conflicts have been likely to champion rights claims for urban life and urban space made by new businesses and residents, rather than other values and claims.[7] Saturated with the revanchist sentiments[8] (Smith, 1996) and hypothetically premised upon the 'Broken Window' thesis (Wilson and Kelling, 1982),[9] these laws, regulations and institutions blame the so-called undesirables for bringing with them an urban decline to the city. Even political speech opposed to neoliberal values has been restricted in public spaces in the newly vitalized neighbourhoods through local ordinances (Mitchell,

---

7   The work of resolving contradictions by laws, regulations and institutions requires (further) creative destruction and has produced as many contradictions as solutions.

8   According to Smith (1996, p. 45), revanchism was 'a right-wing movement built on populist nationalism and devoted to a vengeful and reactionary retaking of country' in France in the late nineteenth century – retaking the country from the increased liberalism in the Second Republic. Smith (1996, 45) makes a parallel between fin-de-siècle French revanchism and the revanchism that he observed in the 1990s New York City – the latter as 'a broad, vengeful right-wing reaction against both the "liberalism" of the 1960s and 1970s and the predations of capital.'

9   James Q. Wilson and George Kelling argued that the signs of disorder in communities, such as broken windows, would invite more serious crimes, if left negligent and untended: 'One unrepaired window is a signal that no one cares, so breaking more windows costs nothing .... Untended property becomes fair game for people out for fun and plunder' (1982, 31). Wilson and Kelling imply that 'disreputable or obstreperous or unpredictable people,' such as 'panhandlers, drunks, addicts, rowdy teenagers, prostitutes, loiterers, the mentally disturbed' – not violent people, nor, necessarily, criminals – can be 'broken windows' that will invite real crimes into neighbourhoods (1982, 102). Many city governments have adopted this thesis as a philosophy of their 'quality of life'-type initiatives, and legitimated the police violently cracking down on quality of life offences like aggressive panhandling, homelessness or graffiti (for a critique of the 'broken window' thesis and its appalling implication for homeless people, see Mitchell, 2001).

2003b). Zoning regulations have been so rewritten as to divide urban space between land-uses proper for a new quality of life and the ones that defile them; New York City's efforts to zone out pornography shops, despite their intimate relationship with freedom of expression, is one such instance (Papayanis, 2000). Thus public streets have been legally privatized with the effect that private interest can effectively disallow undesirables on the (now) privatized streets with property right claims (Mitchell, 2005). Building gated communities and installing surveillance cameras in public space have been authorized by laws and ordinances (McKenzie, 1994; Fyfe and Bannister, 1998). All these regulations have been enforced with a glut of endorsements from neoliberal interests – despite their pronounced insistence of the retreat of regulatory commands out of market operations. This phenomenon simply repeats the old axiom that well summarizes the nature of capitalism: 'the hidden hand of the market will never work without a hidden fist' as *New York Times* columnist, Thomas Friedman, once commented (Ali, 2003, pp. 260–261).

New York City's effort to regulate and zone out dance clubs is, I contend, another example of the mode of regulation deployed to solve neoliberal contradictions in the manner of punitive spatial policing. The historical geography of dance clubs in New York City from the 1980s onwards demonstrates how laws, regulations and institutions have been at the centre of creative destruction of urban space, economy and culture in the city. An analysis of the nature and the process of creative destruction in urban space, as it has involved New York City's club landscape, throws light upon struggles between conflicting groups over urban space and urban culture and the contradictions that inhere in such struggles and, therefore, why it was necessary for the municipality and other neoliberal social formations to attempt to displace dance clubs from urban space through laws, regulations and institutions.

Rezoning of the Cabaret Law in the 1980s in New York City

From the late 1980s through to the early 1990s, a change in the zoning regulation in New York City went into effect that would affect the locations of the city's dance clubs. From then on, the city's zoning regulation of dance clubs, conditioned by the cabaret law, would require special permits for a new club to open, particularly in the commercial and manufacturing zones in Manhattan, formerly as-of-right for dance clubs. The rewriting of the cabaret law in such a way was one of the municipality's strategic moves to settle a decade-long struggle between the city administration and community coalitions on the one hand, and the city's club and bar industry on the other, over the neoliberalization of urban space in the city. In other words, it was a spatialized institutional fix to resolve the contradictions that the neoliberalization of urban space had brought into the city neighbourhoods.

The cabaret law was originally created during the Prohibition era to control speakeasies, and later developed into a tool to impose zoning and licensing regulations on live music venues that sold to the public food or drink (places that were legally named 'cabarets'). Cabarets could only be located in certain neighbourhoods, and outside of these neighbourhoods only background music was allowed, with a restricted number of players (a maximum of three) and with a limit on the types of instruments (the exclusion of horns and percussion) (Chevigny, 1991, p. 1). The limitations imposed on live music, especially the limitation of horns and percussion, was unquestionably intended to prevent the 'wild' and 'Bohemian' elements of black jazz music (especially those developed in Harlem) from encroaching to the rest of the city.[10] Since this racist inception, the cabaret law has been used to control the whereabouts of the city's entertainment businesses that have been deemed deviant and obscene by the city's authority.

However, by the 1970s when the city's fiscal crisis had devastated the city's economic, political and social bases, clubs and small bars that had live music and/or dancing ironically enjoyed a fairly permissive regulatory atmosphere (Horsley, 1978, p. R4). This was partly due to a cutback in the budget of the enforcement agencies (Chevigny, 1991, p. 78). It seems that the regulations were also relaxed because of the mixed signals given to illegal parties and clubs. At the same time as dance clubs were vilified as tax dodging enterprises and sanctuaries for prostitutes, drug dealers and other petty criminals, and unsafe environments prone to the breakout of fire and violence (Narvaez, 1976, p. 1, 46), there seemed to be some awareness among government agencies and business sectors that big discos were one of the few remaining economic resources that could resuscitate abandoned buildings in the city (Horsley, 1978, p. R1), and that small social clubs could function as 'a social necessity and a means of keeping roots in shaky communities' (Narvaez, 1976, p. 1). Unless a given establishment committed a serious nuisance, what was going on inside its premises was ignored by the enforcement agencies.

This period was, therefore, characterized by a thriving nightlife and dance subcultures developed through parties and clubs that legally or illegally occupied buildings in downtown and uptown neighbourhoods left deserted in the midst of a devastating economic decline. Downtown lofts were the places where experimental jazz was played (Chevigny, 1991, p. 79) and David Mancuso created a new type of dance culture in his loft party that was going to shape the next three decades of club cultures. According to Lawrence (2004, pp. xi–xv), the city's clubs and parties in this period gave birth to 'a new mode of DJing,' 'dance floor design,' and music and dancing aesthetics that are still backbone qualities of the contemporary club scene. Others also pointed out that dance clubs were important sites of identity politics; they were places in which, 'away from the scrutinizing eye of society, a vision of an alternative and more egalitarian society [was] pursued, tested, revised, experimented' by the city's marginalized contingents, such as African-Americans or homosexuals (or both) – a vision that was 'expressed in the ongoing quest for new ways to combine music with music, music with dancing, and at times, music with dancing, drugs, and sex' (Fikentscher, 2000, pp. 6–7). For these contingents, urban

---

10 According to Chevigny, during this era live jazz music was supposedly associated with social dancing 'because at that time the music was always played for dancing' (1991, 56), and Chevigny surmises that this was one of the reasons why live jazz music was heavily policed by authorities (1991, 78). By the 1950s, jazz music and dancing had largely been bifurcated into two separate genres, but in the language of cabaret law, live jazz music clubs were still treated as serving dancers (1991, 69).

space was a playground for politics in which identities were proclaimed through music, social dancing and other forms of bodily expression.

However, from the late 1970s onwards, the situation reversed rapidly. As a means to recover from the fiscal crisis, the Koch administration chose to open the door wide for private developers to redevelop formerly derelict neighbourhoods, so the developers could upgrade those neighbourhoods into either upscale residential areas (such as the East Village), or corporate commercial districts or office centres (such as Times Square). The courtship from the city administration toward private developers was embodied in various pro-development incentive programs (Fainstein, 1994; Mele, 2000) and the generous granting of zoning variances to private renewal projects (Sleeper, 1987; Zukin, 1989; Smith, 1996; Bagli, 2005, p. 53). Indeed, from 1981 onwards, the city enjoyed a real-estate market boom (which was going to culminate in a steep downturn at the end of the decade).

It became obvious to the coalition of the city administration and the private development sector that urban space would be one of the most promising sources of the city's otherwise plummeting economy. This explains why the Koch administration started to take a hard-line approach on 'quality of life' issues – that is, in order to keep urban space appealing to the well-heeled class that had settled into the city through extensive gentrification. The administration had also taken seriously the newcomers' increasingly vigorous opposition to the 'carnival atmosphere' that the city's alternative lifestyles and spaces, such as live music and dance clubs, had created in areas that were now being redeveloped as gentrified (Horsley, 1978, p. R1; see also Horsley, 1979; Gross, 1985).

The commodification of urban space mainly targeting middle-upper class yuppies now necessitated the bureaucratization of the space, in order to safeguard the rights claim of the new residents to the space and its quality of life against cultural institutions valued by the other groups that inhabited the same space. The city's search for a legitimate tool to accommodate this rights claim ended with the move to tighten the enforcement of the cabaret law, a law that could effectively be put to use monitoring the boundaries of entertainments that would be allowed in different neighbourhoods. In 1982, the Department of Consumer Affairs (DCA), the administrative body in charge of granting cabaret licenses, was given the power to shut down establishments without mediation by courts (Chevigny, 1991, p. 81).[11] In 1984, as the City comptroller's office asked for increased investigations into unlicensed businesses, the city administration allocated increased budget and personnel to the DCA in order to strengthen the enforcement of the cabaret law (Freedman, 1986, p. A1). Bills requiring clubs to be equipped with heavy safety and soundproofing measures were proposed or passed (Dunlap, 1983). The punctilio of applying for the cabaret license got much stricter, which seriously delayed the opening of cabarets (Chevigny, 1991, 76-77; Gross 1985).

---

11 To acquire a cabaret license, clubs should get approval from a handful of municipal departments, such as the Department of Buildings, the City Planning Commission (CPC), the Fire Department and the Police Department (together with recommendations from the relevant community board), and submit all the approvals to the DCA which would then decide whether or not to grant the license.

The increased regulation of dance clubs was ironic and contradictory considering the history of gentrification. The image of counter-cultures and Bohemianism (cultures and styles that dance clubs had incubated and nurtured), had been significantly repackaged in the marketing of such areas as East Village or SoHo by the real-estate developers. These areas' image which was sanitized in the process of marketing was deployed in order to tap into the aesthetic sensibility of the yuppie class, and to heighten the appeal of these places to them. Once the real estate capital symbolically appropriated and commercialized the Bohemian image into the 'form of the newly fashionable lofts, or Bohemian ambience of the restaurants, bars, galleries and shops' (O'Connor, 1998, p. 227), the 'productive community' (ibid.) that had produced the Bohemian cultures in these areas was forced to move out, due to such factors as skyrocketing rents, new resident communities' protests, municipality's authorized eviction, or landlords' refusal to renew the lease – the process of what Mele (2000) refers as 'symbolic inclusion'. The fate of dance clubs located in these neighbourhoods was similar to that of other counter-cultural institutions. For example, in SoHo, the legendary house music club, Paradise Garage, eventually had to shut its doors because the landlord did not renew the lease, due to the neighbouring community's protests and also in expectation of the redevelopment of the building. Having fulfilled their role as one of the pioneers of revitalization of the neighbourhoods, clubs were now considered anathema to neighbourhood revitalization rather than an honourable part of it.

In order to pay the increased rents, and make ends meet, clubs in these areas needed to have entertainment. However, the stricter enforcement of the cabaret law by the municipality made this almost impossible. For example, live music clubs that wanted to stage more than three musicians and/or include horns and/or percussions in the live music performance, or any small dance clubs were as limited in location and operation as big discos, whereas the live music venues that played music by not more than three musicians or not including percussions and/or horns were subject to much fewer regulatory rules in terms of location and other measures.[12] Needless to

---

12 In Sections 32–15 of the Zoning Resolution, Use Group 6 A was defined as follows: 'Eating or drinking places, including those which provide outdoor table service or incidental musical entertainment either by mechanical device or by *not more than three persons* playing piano, organ, accordion, guitar, or any string instrument [to the exclusion of percussions and horns], and those which have accessory drive-through facilities' (emphasis added). Such places were allowed as-of-right in C1, C2, C4, C5, C6, C8, M1, M2 and M3 Districts and a special permit was required in C3 Districts (CPC, 1989, 2). However, if the eating or drinking businesses wished to have more than three musicians playing in the premises and/or to have musicians play percussions and horns, the locations that those businesses could choose were, to a considerable degree, restricted. These businesses were categorized as Use Group 12 A in Sections 32–21 of the Zoning Resolution, defined as 'Eating or drinking places, without restrictions on entertainment or dancing.' Such uses were permitted as-of-right in C4, C6, C7, C8, and most manufacturing districts and by special permit in C2, C3, M1-5A and M1-5B. Such businesses were only permitted in hotels in C5 districts and were not at all allowed in C1 districts. Use Group 12A also included businesses that accommodated social dancing, whether it was small bars or clubs, or big discos. This meant that the live music venue that had more than three musicians and/or had percussions or horns played were basically subject

say, the brunt of these stricter requirements was felt most severely by small and more creative venues, due to the budgetary demands that these requirements imposed. In the Lower East Side, the controversial closure of 8 B.C., a club that had brought vibrancy to the long-deserted Alphabet City testified to this ironic fate of dance clubs.

By the mid-1980s, the media pronounced that 'the party seems to be over for Lower Manhattan clubs' (Gross, 1985). Clubs in other places, such as Gramercy, Flatiron District, the places where the abandoned residential or manufacturing buildings had been subjected to the vehement force of gentrification shared a comparable fate. It was the musician's union that first burst into the scene with counter-actions against this increasingly dire situation for clubs. The union took the municipality's regulation through the cabaret law to the State Supreme Court, and it made the Court rule two provisions unconstitutional under the constitutional guarantee of freedom of expression – first, in 1986, the provision of the zoning resolution in the cabaret law that regulated incidental musical entertainment by distinguishing types of musical instruments, and subsequently, in 1988, the provision that regulated eating or drinking establishments by the number of musicians (CPC, 1989, p. 2). The musician's union successfully argued that it was noise level or crowd, but not the type of instruments or the number of musicians performing in clubs that caused serious problems in the surrounding residential neighbourhoods.

This defeat pushed the municipal government to rewrite the cabaret law in 1989, distinguishing 'between two types of eating or drinking establishments with entertainments' – 'those with no dancing and a capacity of up to 200 persons, and those with dancing [regardless of their size] and/or a capacity exceeding 200 persons' (CPC 1989, 6). The CPC stated that the purpose of the zoning changes according to these two distinguished uses was to impose 'more restrictive regulations' (CPC, 1989, p. 1; McHugh, 1989, p. 23) on the second use, while drastically loosening zoning restrictions formerly imposed on some type of the former.

This new proposal had dance club owners unite with each other to form a union-like organization, called the New York Cabaret Association (renamed the New York Nightlife Association in the 1990s). By mobilizing club owners to voice their opposition to the proposal, the association could succeed in having the CPC drop the proposed curfew regulations.[13] However, it was impossible for the association to make the CPC drop the plan to drastically limit the locations where any establishment

---

to the same zoning and licensing rules as the big discos. As the enforcement of the compliance of the cabaret was tightened, musicians who could play in unlicensed clubs in neighbourhoods not zoned for cabarets in a more relaxed regulatory climate in the 1970s found it hard to find places to play.

13 The Commission's decision to drop the early closing proposal was also made, due to an unrelated suit brought by Limelight (a discotheque in Manhattan) at that time, in which the New York Court of Appeals decided in July 1989 that any local regulation could not preempt state regulations on hours of operation of the businesses licensed by the State Liquor Authority (CPC, p 5; McHugh, 1989, p. 23). Those businesses were allowed to stay open until 4:30 A.M. by the State law.

with social dancing might exist without having to get a special permit.[14] Thus, under the new proposal, sizable commercial areas formerly zoned as-of-right for dance clubs, such as neighbourhoods in NoHo, Lower East Side, TriBeCa, the Flatiron District, and some parts of the East Village, Murray Hill and Gramercy would now require a special permit for new dance establishments, in addition to 'the existing three dozen other licenses necessary to open a club' (McHugh, 1989, p. 23).[15]

The terms of special permits[16] not only became too costly and time-consuming, as a representative of the New York Cabaret Association stated in the public hearing for the new proposal (CPC, 1989, p. 17). How could small venues that have occasional

———————————

14 Under the modified zoning resolution, eating or drinking establishments with entertainments but not dancing and a capacity of up to 200 persons, which was newly categorized as Use Group 6C, were permitted as-of-right in C1-5, C1-6, C1-7, C1-8, C1-9, C2-5, C2-6, C2-7, C2-8, C4, C6, C8 and most manufacturing districts. Special permits should be acquired for Use Group 6C in C1-1, C1-2, C1-3, C1-4, C2-1, C2-2, C2-3, C2-4, C3, C5, M1-5A and M1-5B districts. On the other hand, eating or drinking establishments with entertainment and a capacity of more than 200 persons, or any capacity with dancing, which was categorized as Use Group 12A, would be allowed as-of-right in C6, C7, C8 and most manufacturing districts. Special permits should be granted for new businesses to open in such areas as C2, C3, C4, M1-5A, M1-5B, M1-5M, M1-6M and the Lower Manhattan Mixed Use Districts. On the surface, it were only C4, M1-5M, M1-6M and the Lower Manhattan Mixed Use Districts that were added to the existing special permit requirement areas for this kind of use.

15 In these neighbourhoods, existing nightclub locations would be grandfathered under the new proposal.

16 The Board of Standards and Appeals may grant the Special Permit to this use group 'for a term not to exceed three years, provided that the following findings are made' (CPC 42–3):

1. That a minimum of four square feet of enclosed waiting area within the zoning lot shall be provided for each person permitted under the occupant capacity as determined by the New York City Building Code. The required waiting area shall be in an enclosed lobby and shall not include space occupied by stairs, corridors or restrooms. A plan shall be provided to the Board to insure that the operation of the establishment will not result in the gathering of crowds or the formation of lines on the street.
2. That the entrance to such use shall be a minimum of 100 feet from the nearest residential district boundary.
3. That such use will not cause undue vehicular or pedestrian congestion in local streets.
4. That such use will not impair the character or the future use or development of the surrounding residential or mixed-use neighbourhoods.
5. That such use will not cause the sound level in any affected conforming residential use, joint-living work quarters for artists or loft dwelling to exceed the limits set forth in any applicable provision of the New York City Noise Control Code.
6. That the application is made jointly by the owner of the building and the operators of such eating or drinking establishment.

However, the restrictive move did not end there. Businesses in Use Group 12A that were going to open in C6-1, -2, -3 and -4 districts had to provide a minimum of four square feet of waiting area within the zoning lot for each person permitted under the occupant capacity as determined by the New York City Building Code. 'The required waiting area shall be in an enclosed lobby and shall not include space occupied by stairs, corridors or restrooms. In these districts the entrance to such use shall be a minimum of 100 feet from the nearest residential district boundary' (CPC, 1989, 33).

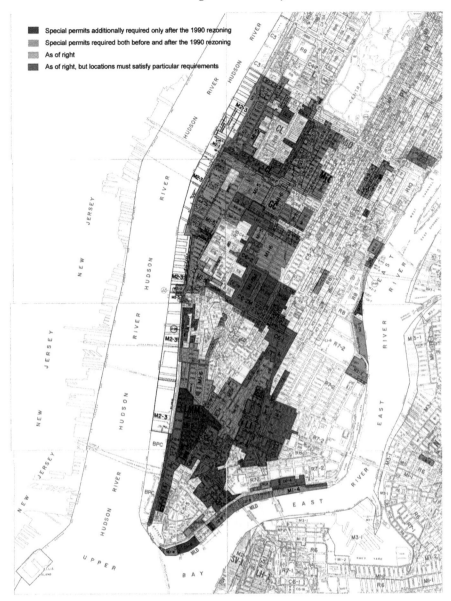

**Figure 8.1 Location of Dance Clubs in Lower and Midtown Manhattan after
the 1990 Revision of the Zoning Laws**
Source: Department of City Planning, New York City.

small dance parties afford such requirements?) In addition, granting special permits
would also be subject to the unpredictable discretion of the Board of Standards and
Appeals and Community Boards that could impact the (dis)approving of the granting

of special permits. Needless to say, the views of these two agents had not been at all friendly to dance clubs and the subcultures affiliated with dance clubs. In particular, the fact that the law was re-written to enforce more restrictive regulations on premises that allow *any size* of social dancing, whereas spaces for other entertainments were to be regulated according to the size of the venue capacity, seems to imply the degree to which any possibility of spaces for social dancing – even the spaces that allowed a minimal degree of social dancing – were dissaproved of by residential communities than spaces for other entertainments, perhaps due to the association of those dance spaces with more noises, violence, vandalism and hedonism.

While some (especially large) clubs were responsible for these nuisance effects which seriously affected nearby residential neighbourhoods, the municipality's wholesale regulation of any size of dance clubs meant that the municipality was more concerned with responding to residents' complaints over dance clubs, and therefore did not feel obliged to make an effort to create regulations more sensitive to the fact that dance clubs had been invaluable cultural institutions. It seems that the municipality needed to find every possible regulatory tool, through which it could manage and control the counter-cultural spaces that had once dominated the city's downtown, but were now nothing other than neighbourhood nuisances. Other entertainments were protected by the First Amendment and therefore should have been regulated by the size of patrons and the level of noises that these entertainments created, rather than by themselves. However, for social dancing, which had not been granted the First Amendment entitlement in the Supreme Court,[17] the municipality did not have to be vigilant of its regulations being subject to the strict scrutiny of the First Amendment. Hence, it was relatively safe to regulate social dancing itself as a violation, instead of regulating the size of capacity, or the level of noise that the businesses that had social dancing would cause.

The disregard toward the number of social dancers in the language and enforcement of the cabaret law was to have a devastating impact on the city's nightlife and subcultural scene in the 1990s, during which former mayor, Giuliani, took advantage of the law's blindness.

Increased Crackdown on Nightlife in the 1990s

In the 1990s, Manhattan was still a battlefield. More accurately, the battle had become so intensified that, by the time that the present mayor Michael Bloomberg succeeded the former Mayor Giuliani in 2002, commentators started to declare that New York's club scene was no longer on the map (Romano, 2004). With the 1989 revision of the zoning resolution of the cabaret law, the municipality had managed to create a legal tool through which they could restrict the location of dance clubs. However, even with this revision, neighbourhood conflicts associated with nightlife businesses did persist, and demanded more of an institutional fix. In the mid-1990s,

---

17 In 1989, exactly the same year that the Planning Commission rewrote the cabaret zoning resolution for dance clubs, the Supreme Court disqualified social dancing from First Amendment protection (in its decision of *City of Dallas v Stanglin*), because the Court did not recognize any expressive interest in social dancing (Chevigny, 1991).

therefore, the cabaret law was resurrected by the city administration to cope with these conflicts, but this time not only to regulate how dance clubs were operated, but also to break the morale of nightlife cultures in gentrified neighbourhoods, by abusing the meticulous provisions of the cabaret law.

In the early to mid-1990s, dance clubs in the city did not leave a particularly beneficial impression in the public's mind. A few remaining neighbourhoods where clubs were legally allowed to open after the 1989 revision – such as Chelsea – started to be gentrified from the early 1990s onwards (Howe, 1992, 1993; Snyder, 2005). In these neighbourhoods, land-use for dance clubs started to rejuvenate the same old conflicts with residential use that had increasingly encroached into those neighbourhoods. In addition to the chronic disturbance that dance clubs had posed for residential neighbourhoods – street noise, patrons' vandalism, congested traffic – the scandals associated with frequent drug trafficking and the disreputable saturnalia among clubbers inside a few of the city's megaclubs in the early 1990s astounded newly migrated residents, to say nothing of Mayor Giuliani, who used to prosecute drug dons, as United States Attorney in the late 1980s. *Inter alia*, Limelight, perhaps the biggest megaclub in the city in the early- and mid-1990s, was an incessant source of scandals of decadence for New York tabloids. The parties arranged and provided by the spookiest 'club kids' of Limelight acquired, according to Owen (2003, 59), 'a reputation as the most outrageous in town,' and it became an open secret that Limelight was a 'drug supermarket' for young kids, as Assistant US Attorney Eric Friedberg later called it (Owen, 2003, 254). Probably, the public's moral panic toward Limelight and other megaclubs in the city must have reached its apogee with the conviction of the owner of Limelight, who had been charged with drug trafficking (and whose network, it turned out, spanned from Brooklyn and Staten Island to Israel and Russia) and the murder committed by the leading club kid in Limelight, Michael Alig, in the mid-1990s. In line with the fire in 1991 that killed 87 people in an illegal social club called Happy Land, the Limelight fiasco has become an unpleasantly recurrent image of the New York nightlife, ascribing to it extremely dishonourable stereotypes, which, many surmise, have provided a rationale and justification for the governmental crackdown (Owen, 1997b).

It is fairly easy to foresee that dance clubs, with all these troubles, could hardly be tolerated by the neoliberal hegemonic bloc in the Giuliani administration,[18] also famous for its puritanical and authoritarian reign over urban life. 'Giuliani time' (Smith, 1998) is often characterized with wholesale city policies devoted to raising the bar of 'quality of life' in the city by pitching the militarization of public space against urban undesirables. Indeed, reminiscent of the language of the 'Broken

---

18 Giuliani was perhaps more neoliberal in his economic policies, and more neoconservative in his social and cultural policies than Koch. Under the Giuliani administration, policies were initiated and implemented in order to benefit big corporations and their workforce, which, while under the pretext of bringing back the fiscal health of the city, took welfare benefits away from those who needed them more urgently than ever, converted welfare systems to work fare program and made a radical budget cut for public spending (Gotham Gazette, 2005).

Windows' theory,[19] such populations as homeless people, panhandlers, prostitutes, squeegee cleaners, street artists, graffiti artists, jaywalkers, 'reckless bicyclists', unruly youth and street protesters were blamed as the 'visible signs of a city out of control' (Smith, 1998, p. 3), and were subjected to the enforcement of various ordinances and rules to control and displace them. Such punitive policing brought about city-wide controversies over its legitimacy, since most of this population was better affiliated with nuisances that *may or may not* invite more serious crimes, rather than with serious crimes themselves. Whether this pre-emptive nuisance policing indeed contributed to reducing crime rates, as the city administration has contended, is still a point of dispute, but commentators point to the reality that this type of policing certainly enhanced the sense of safety and security (if not real safety and security) that has long been lost among middle-upper class residents. Some even extol Giuliani as the mayor who restored the paradigm of cities as livable places (Jackson, 2005).

In any case, in this political climate under the Giuliani administration, clubs could not avoid being one of the main targets of a 'quality of life' campaign, especially when the club industry would not make the so called "good neighbourly" efforts to appease and accommodate angry community residents. Community coalitions, such as 'Save Chelsea', or 'The Save Avenue A Society', which opposed nightlife businesses in their neighbourhoods, were increasingly looked upon as 'activist' crusaders who fought against social ills and endeavoured to preserve a wholesome community against 'sloshy club and party nights' (Farber, 1995, n. p.). Community anti-nightlife campaigns got support from local politicians who, according to Bastone (1997), would always work for those community members who would promise voting constituents, as opposed to nightclubs that would vote against them. The community boards' unremitting petition to governmental agencies ushered in a law in 1994 that enabled community boards to challenge the state liquor authority (SLA)'s granting of a liquor serving license to a business in their neighbourhoods if there were already three licensed businesses within a 500 foot area – the so-called '500 foot rule'. This 500 foot rule has been a useful institutional fix to the problems that residential communities had with their neighbouring nightlife businesses, but communities boards have also complained that the SLA has not always incorporated communities' challenges into its decision (Owen, 1997b).

Further appeals by communities to disempower and even displace raucous nightlife businesses in their neighbourhoods were well-received at the municipal administrative level in the mid-1990s. The *Daily News* reported that such dance clubs as Sound Factory and Webster Hall, and even the formative site of the American punk movement, CBGB, started to have problems with the city agencies, as well as with their residential neighbours (Farber, 1995). In the same *Daily News* article, it was reported that the city now felt at heart the need to have a task force comprised of agents from all relevant city departments that 'could all go in at the same time [to the club] if the club is breaking the law and possibly padlock the club' (Farber, 1995, n.p.). The municipality's wish soon came true. The Giuliani administration

---

19 As a matter of fact, George Kelling, one of the inventors of the Broken Windows thesis, came to NYC to advise the high-ranking personnel in the New York Police Department (Gotham Gazette, 2005).

reinforced the power of the Social Club Task Force that was originally created by the former mayor Dinkins to then monitor illegal social clubs after the Happy Land fire. The Task Force was put under the direct oversight of the Deputy Mayor, and renamed as the Multi-agency Nightclubs Task Force – or MARCH (Multi-Agency Response to Community Hotspots) – in 1997, but this time for the purpose of monitoring the violations of the cabaret law both in illegal and legal clubs. An institution now emerged as a mode of regulation in order to stabilize the contradictory and volatile process of urban restructuring, reflect in the neighbourhood conflicts over the operation of dance clubs. The professed rationale for this reinforced regulation was to curb the 'secondary effects' of dance clubs which were, according to the authorities, 'a magnet for drug sales, underage drinking, loud music and other conditions which create an atmosphere *conducive* to crime' (Owen, 1997a, emphasis added; see also Buckland, 2002, p. 130).[20] Again, like other 'Broken Windows' that had been the focus of governmental crackdown, clubs were culprits that defiled the quality of life because they might foster a criminal environment. However, an accusation such as this could not be applied to every one of the numerous bars and clubs that were going to be fined and padlocked by the Task Force.

Visits by the Task Force, comprising officers from each department involved in the cabaret licensing were quite spectacular. The owner of Crossroads, a rock club[21] located in the Upper East Side, recollected his experience of one such spectacular visit to his club by governmental officers in his interview with the *Village Voice* (Rothman, 1999).

> There was one real bad experience ... It was late [19] 97, early [19] 98. They had about 40 officers come in a citywide raid, representing the police department, the fire department, the health department, the vice squad, the consumer affairs department and a legal team. You'd think they were making a Mafia bust. No crime had been committed. Not even a violation had been committed ... But they make you shut the music off, turn the lights up. If you were a customer, would you stay? All that city found during the raid was an ice scoop illegally touching an ice cube and an obstructed window view ('an unrepealed prohibition-era law'). The window, he explains, was merely obstructed by a good neighbour policy sign and a photograph of the Upper East Side rapist. Charges were dropped, but the stress was too much.

While many instances of what was called 'creative ticketing' (Bastone, 1997) that the Task Force issued to the establishments – such as the one above regarding an ice scoop – were far from reasonable, the summons issued by the Task Force that brought about most of the controversies concerned social dancing. Giuliani revived the three people provision that until then had been lying dormant in the cabaret law,

---

20 It seems that the government's enforcement of the cabaret law has not been discriminating against the club's patron's sexual orientation or ethnic composition. However, also see Buckland (2002, pp. 128–158) for an argument that the governmental crackdown was more crippling to homosexual venues.

21 While the enforcement of the cabaret law was concerned with regulating dance clubs, it seems that the task force's visits were not discriminatory to the types of night spots (such as rock music club), if they were causing problems to the neighbouring residents. The reason of this indiscrimination will be suggested later in this section.

and started to have the Task Force police the strict compliance of the provision. Therefore, if more than three people were detected to move rhythmically together, it now constituted a violation and was subject to the issuance of a ticket by the Task Force. Since a fairly large portion of the commercial area where people could drink was not zoned for social dancing (due to the rewriting of the cabaret law in 1989, as was described above), and since the Task Force took very seriously the literal definition of social dancing as more than three people dancing rhythmically together, any incidental dancing by more than three people that could happen in any clubs not licensed for social dancing became a legal violation, and vulnerable to receiving citations (recall here Frank's experiences described in the introduction). The real problems with nightclubs might be noise, congestion or drug transactions, but now the target of the policing and regulation also included an expressive activity like social dancing itself, as if social dancing – however minimal – was responsible for all these problems.

The task force shut down 50–60 establishments (legal and illegal) between August 1996 and 1998 (Rohde, 1998, p. B3). Jim Chu, the owner of Den of Thieves, 'a progressive music bar on the Lower East Side', got a ticket in 1996 for customers dancing in his bar, which was not licensed for a cabaret. Chu changed his bar in a way that the bar's structure could discourage customers from dancing (Owen, 1997b). Until 2001, Coney Island High, Baby Jupiter, Hogs & Heifers, Lakeside Lounge and many other clubs were all either fined or padlocked by the Task Force.[22] Hogs & Heifers had to spend almost one hundred and fifty thousand dollars to pay for fines, legal fees and the renovations required to get a cabaret license (Span, 1998) after it was padlocked by the Task Force. Such crackdown on dancing created a locally unique landscape that had a sign saying 'No Dancing' inside bars, and workers inside clubs started keeping a watchful eye over any rhythmic movements by customers which could be construed as dancing. This meant that to reorganize the cultural life in line with the changed social and economic demography of renewed urban spaces, social dancing, no matter what fundamental right it may express, became an excuse through which clubs and bars could be controlled or displaced.

That is, the cabaret law was used to crack down on any nightlife establishments beyond simply dance clubs. Residents' complaints increasingly extended to any ordinary nightlife businesses that caused nuisances inimical to the character of residential neighbourhoods, as well as any performance clubs (like live rock music clubs) and dance clubs. Commentators suspected that the creative reinterpretation of the social dancing provision of the cabaret law – the provision of three people dancing together – was used as a 'catch-all' tool (Romano, 2002, n.p.) in order to clamp down on the 'anything-goes' spirit that persisted in some New York nightlife businesses, whether in dance clubs, rock band clubs, or even ordinary bars. Social dancing is one of the basic elements of these nightlife establishments: can one imagine a rock club without head-banging patrons? Thus, prohibiting social dancing in these establishments was tantamount to sounding a death-knell for them. In other

---

22 This information is retrieved from the website of an anti-cabaret law activism, *Legalize Dancing New York City* (LDNYC) (http://www. legalizedancingNew York City.com/ whoweare.html).

words, prohibiting social dancing could be interpreted as a governmental tactic to 'creatively destroy' urban cultural life – that is, it was a method of inducing into the gentrified neighbourhoods the type of commercial businesses that could bring about a gentler cultural atmosphere and sense of security and order, by eliminating the existing establishments mostly associated with wild crowds.

There is another repercussion that the prohibition of social dancing has had in the transformation of urban cultural life. Accelerating gentrification made it more necessary for clubs and bars to have entertainments that require patrons' social dancing in order to make enough profits to pay the bill and rent (Rothman, 1999). In case of small and alternative venues in which music, performance and patrons' dancing were important, this was the only option for making profits. Otherwise, they would have to convert themselves to cocktail bars or trendy lounges that would invite a wholly different set of patrons who prefer expensive bottle service over music and dancing. As a matter of fact, the costly process of getting the cabaret license in addition to extremely inflated rents led to the reality that only moneyed entrepreneurs could open clubs and who, it has been reported, may only be concerned with catering to upscale patrons (Romano, 2002).

Confronting the reality that good, old and alternative clubs have been rendered out of sight, the local media has several times questioned whether the New York club scene would be decimated by 'skyrocketing real estate, extreme Quality of Life enforcement and neighbourhood anti-nightlife sentiment' (Rothman, 1999, n.p.).

Conclusion

Laws, regulatory policies and institutions, as a 'mode of regulation', have been deployed to resolve contradictions generated in the creative destruction of built environments or social life induced by urban neoliberalism. The resolution is, often, a spatialized one, because geography is an essential factor and mediator in the workings of a specific capitalism and thus reorganizing geography is one of the constituent parts of reorganizing conditions on the basis of which a new capitalism can proceed. I have tried to argue that the revival of the cabaret law in New York City during the '90s and the law's strategic use in reordering the cultural components of urban spaces by being employed to regulate cultural spaces such as dance clubs, is an instantiation of this process. Despite the fact that the clubs themselves were partly responsible for inviting increased municipal regulations, the spate of hyper-regulation by the municipality makes us rethink how urgent it was for the municipality to secure, by any means, a sense of security among new and affluent residents. It seems that the rights claims of new residents to urban space and urban culture have been getting more policy legitimacy than any other cultural claims.

However, a spatialized resolution has also had an effect of suspending, displacing or aggravating contradictions, instead of resolving them. Clubs that were displaced from other areas (due to such spatialized resolutions) and relocated in such areas as West Chelsea – one of the few remaining areas where clubs could legally locate – started to have similar neighbourhood problems as gentrification in these areas picked up. The municipality also has had to deal with the increasing anti-cabaret law activism and public awareness of the illegitimacy of the cabaret law.[23] In 2005, activists and lawyers filed a complaint against the city administration challenging the social dancing provision of the cabaret law. While the judge has dismissed the case,[24] the anti-cabaret law group has been preparing another lawsuit.

In the midst of these conflicts, it has been reported that musicians have had difficulties in finding places for their performance and have moved to other countries where dance clubs are more favourably accommodated (Romano, 2004). In the New York club scene, the predominant species are now business orientated venues, whereas clubs that consider music first have become more rare. Anti-cabaret law groups have argued that the municipality's regulations on social dancing and dance clubs have negatively affected the once-prosperous cultural landscapes which have now been replaced by high-class or corporate ones, and, therefore, New Yorkers are left with very limited (and more expensive) choices of accessible culture. Disappearance of subcultural spaces, such as dance clubs and other important nightlife spots, can eventually make it natural for people to think that such nightlife institutions are not a proper use of land in Manhattan anymore. For, the institutional logic of laws and spaces ensures that once established, they have the effect of gradually and secretly universalizing and naturalizing the norms that they try to establish (Blomley, 2003, 122). And, such transformation in the popular notion of legitimate cultural activities in regenerated urban spaces may be the ultimate goal of the neoliberal mode of regulation, because such transformation is indeed integral to the very condition of survival and reproduction of neoliberal urbanism.

---

23 The anti-cabaret law activism, advanced by the two organizations, LDNYC and *Dance Liberation Front* (DLF), has been raising public awareness with regard to the problems of the cabaret law in the city and has also produced significant political responses (if not real changes) from the municipality. Given the restrictions on space here I cannot go into details of this anti-cabaret law activism. For more information on LDNYC, consult http://www. legalizedancingNew York City.com/.

24 The judge dismissed the case based upon his assessment that social dancing is not entitled for protection under the First Amendment.

Chapter 9

Rights and Regulation in Bush's America; or, How the New Right Learned to Stop Worrying and Love Equal Rights

Jeffrey R. Dudas[1]

Introduction

The policies and, especially, the figure of George W. Bush call forth contrasting assessments. Asked by the Pew Research Centre in March 2006 to use one word to describe Bush, a random sample of Americans produced the following list: 'incompetent', 'good', 'liar', 'Christian', 'honest', 'arrogant', 'strong', 'integrity' and 'ass' (Pew Research Centre, 2006). For all of its diversity, there was yet another plausible description of Bush that did not make the list. What would it mean to treat Bush administration policies, and Bush himself, according to this alternative image? What would it mean, that is, to depict George W. Bush as a champion of equal rights?

Consider, for example, President Bush's July 2006 reauthorization of the 1965 Voting Rights Act. Passed without amendment by the House of Representatives and the Senate, Bush immediately signed it into law. The previous reauthorization of the Voting Rights Act, in 1982, did not go so smoothly. Although two southern members of the House of Representatives succeeded in delaying the 2006 reauthorization for a short period, there was no repeat of the acrimony that occasioned the 1982 reauthorization, in which a substantial number of southern Congressional representatives loudly protested the act's infringement on state's rights. Nor did Bush repeat Ronald Reagan's equivocal support of the Voting Rights Act,[2] in spite of the vigorous opposition to reauthorization of Abigail Thernstrom, Bush's own nominee to the United States Commission on Civil Rights (Thernstrom and Blum, 2005).

1 I am grateful to Erik Larson, Anders Walker and, especially, Bronwen Morgan for comments on an earlier version of this essay. I also benefited from the trenchant comments of Lennie Feldman and Claire Rasmussen at the 2006 Law and Society Association meetings in Baltimore, Maryland. Mary Dudas has consistently guided me through the matters presented here and elsewhere.

2 Prior to signing the reauthorization, the Reagan administration had voiced doubts about the continuing need of the federal government to oversee elections in the deep south.

Instead, Bush argued that the Voting Rights Act was a crucial part of the nation's commitment to guarantee as a matter of right that citizens will have equal opportunities to succeed through individual self-exertion. Indeed, reauthorization of the act was a way to:

> ensure that every person enjoys the opportunity that this great land of liberty offers. And that means a decent education and a good school for every child, a chance to own their own home or business, and the hope that comes from knowing that you can rise in our society by hard work and God-given talents (Bush, 2006).

Or consider Bush's consistent support of 1991's Americans with Disabilities Act (ADA). Again tying equal rights to the pursuit of individual opportunity and self-sufficiency, Bush noted:

> I am proud that [we] saw the need for a comprehensive law to liberate the energies and talents of people with disabilities .... Employers now provide a range of "accommodations" to ensure that employees with disabilities can keep their place in the wage-earning world, resulting in unprecedented economic opportunities. And, outside of the workplace, the promise of the ADA, coupled with the entrepreneurial spirit of the private sector, has enabled people with disabilities to enjoy much greater access to a wide range of affordable travel, recreational opportunities, and life-enriching services (Bush, 2001).

Consider a final, especially revealing, example. As a presidential candidate during the 2000 election, Bush explained his opposition to a pending congressional bill that would have prohibited job discrimination against gays and lesbians. Juxtaposing the 'special rights' that would give preferential treatment to gays and lesbians to the equal rights that allow, for example, racial minorities and people with disabilities to compete in the marketplace on a level footing with their peers, Bush explained: 'I support equal rights but not special rights for people. [Nobody] should be given special protective status. Everyone ought to have the same rights' (*New York Times* 10/12/00, A22).

While it may be tempting to dismiss such defences of equal rights as little more than the platitudes of a professional politician, we will do well to take them seriously. For taking Mr Bush's rights talk seriously allows for the examination of a series of linkages. Bush's rights talk, that is, tethers his presidency: first, to the conservative intellectuals who articulate the New Right's political vision; second, to the middle-class and working-poor Americans that that vision champions; and, third, to the conduct of the American 'Culture Wars'. Animating each is, on one hand, an aggrieved, resentful figure conventional to American political culture and, on the other hand, a particular vision of equality. Treating the Bush administration as iconic reveals at once the ubiquity and flexibility of American rights-discourse; it reveals also a disciplinary, regulatory regime that is, paradoxically, internal to the practice of rights themselves.

I will here explore how the Bush administration, New Right intellectuals and ordinary, resentful Americans all embrace a particular conception of equal rights. I will argue, moreover, that their celebrations of equal rights champion a traditional figure in the American imagination: the 'forgotten Americans'. Although they are hard-working and virtuous, their efforts are consistently mocked and their equal rights are denigrated. The culprits are, on one hand, the excessive and deviant rights-claims of socially-marginal Americans (racial minorities, women, gays and lesbians) and, on the other hand, witless governmental officials who, wracked with guilt, support the interests of the marginalized at the expense of the virtuous.

Indeed, this simultaneous embrace of the equal rights of forgotten Americans and rejection of the illegitimate, irresponsible rights-claims of socially-marginal Americans is at the core of New Right political critique. A halting embrace of rights, New Right critique forwards a particular vision of America – one that portrays the nation as under siege from the irresponsible activism of formerly-powerless Americans. In so doing, it pursues a theme of grievance and decline that is central to the culture wars that dominate contemporary American politics.

Culturally evocative, this conservative rights-talk also does concrete political work. First, it constitutes the identities of the middle-class and working-poor Americans in whose name it is employed and who themselves employ it. Interpreting their interests as consonant with national prerogatives, they become 'counter-subversives', their own activism a zealous defence of the American way of life. Second, conservative rights-discourse enacts a disciplinary, regulatory logic that radiates in two directions at once. On one hand, it stigmatizes the activism of socially-marginal Americans, declaring their attempts at redistributive social change to be unfair and un-American. On the other hand, conservative rights-talk regulates the aspirations and activism of forgotten Americans themselves. Their condemnations of supposedly deviant rights-claims, that is, insulate from critique the forces that actually threaten their material interests. Expressing a regulatory political vision that opposes attempts to create a fairer and more just society, I shall conclude, conservative rights-discourse is a major force in the contemporary retrenchment of American politics.

Rights and the Politics of Nationalism

The conservative embrace of equal rights is, perhaps, one of the most surprising aspects of contemporary American politics. A rights discourse that relentlessly pursued equality was, after all, one of the primary rhetorical weapons used by the egalitarian social-movements of a generation ago. Putting conservatives on the defensive, the rights talk employed by, for example, the Civil Rights, women's rights, disability rights and pay-equity movements helped to erect a moral high ground for redistributive politics. Moreover, in so far as rights provide 'standards of legitimacy' for the nation's politics, it was normative terrain that was animated by the spirit of Americana (Scheingold, 1974, ix). Opposition to the 'rights revolution' (Epp, 1998) could thus be accosted not simply as morally dubious but as actually un-American (Passavant, 2002, pp. 114–124).

From another perspective, though, there is nothing unusual about conservative rights-discourse. Indeed, conservatives were mobilizing their own conceptions of equal rights all along. As I will discuss in the following section, prominent conservatives (such as Barry Goldwater and William F. Buckley, Jr) championed a contrary version of equal rights beginning, at least, in the early 1960s. At no time, then, was the American discourse of equal rights the sole property of progressive activists.

Yet that conservative rights-discourse is now more prominent and persuasive than it was a generation ago. Dependent for its specific meanings and effects on prevailing cultural and institutional standards, which have turned Right, conservative rights-talk now arguably dominates the American rights lexicon. Indeed, 'contemporary America [is] both more hostile to most familiar types of progressive democratic rights movements and more supportive of neoconservative or reactionary movements' (McCann and Dudas, 2006, 38).

So too is the work that conservative rights-discourse accomplishes now more noticeable. That work is at once cultural and political. On one hand, rights discourse is partially constitutive of the identities of those who employ it. Rights discourse thus works as a conceptual resource – empirically to help its users make sense of their interests and normatively to help them evaluate the legitimacy of the world in which they live (Dudas, 2005; McCann and Dudas, 2006). Frequently this leads to the activation of a specifically political consciousness of one's situation, such that that situation is understood not as a natural product of one's abilities but rather as the outcome of conditions that are, in principle, changeable (Crenshaw, 1988). Engel and Munger make the point:

> Rights may influence identity by altering how individuals perceive themselves ... bringing about a new perspective on who one is and what one expects. The self, so constituted, acquires an identity that can, under certain circumstances, lend itself to the perception that he or she is being treated unfairly – that rights are being violated (2003, 242).

On the other hand, rights discourse has strategic currency. This is because most Americans share the values traditionally associated with rights: equality, fairness, due process and the like. Formulating one's interests according to these values, consequently, increases the chances that the claims will be intelligible to a wider audience. In this sense-making role, rights talk can sometimes generate the support of otherwise-indifferent populations for the goals of the speaker (Scheingold, 1974; McCann, 1994).

Rights discourse thus does cultural and political work. It frequently initiates a nascent political consciousness and provides the instrumental mechanisms by which politics is conducted. Simultaneously 'appealing to everyone's sense of fairness' and functioning as a 'medium of self-expression, a rite which helps the individual to reflect in action [their] own [identity],' rights discourse exhorts audiences to action even as it affirms and constitutes the moral worth of the speakers themselves (Edelman, 1964, p. 137; see also Dudas, 2005).

Moreover, rights discourse harbours an inevitably nationalistic dimension. This dimension is central both to the impacts of conservative rights-discourse and, especially, to the way that rights discourse expresses an often submerged, but deeply disempowering and exclusionary, regulatory regime. 'Liberal rights', notes Passavant, 'are haunted by the spectre of nationalism' (Passavant, 2002, p. 12). Because 'the possibility of having one's ... rights protected is contingent upon being recognized as an American,' right talk is 'inextricably linked to the normalizing and exclusive patterns of national identity politics' (Passavant, 2002, p. 8). Rights-claims, accordingly, initiate a rhetorical process according to which people are identified either as internal or external to the national polity. A claim on the nation itself, a rights claim associates the interests that it expresses with national virtue and so, conversely, identifies opposing interests with un-American activities. Rights discourse, that is, turns those who employ it into counter-subversives, defenders of the American way of life. In so doing, it converts opponents into subversive enemies of the nation itself (Rogin, 1987; Dudas, 2008).

The nationalistic, regulatory dimension of contemporary conservative rights-discourse is even more paradoxical. Not only are the liberating promises of rights tethered to an exclusionary, disempowering logic; those promises also lead those who employ conservative forms of rights talk away from actual liberation itself. The perceptions of unfairness – the resentments – that initiate the rights consciousness of many middle-class and working-poor Americans are themselves tied to an accurate recognition of increasing economic uncertainty and anxiety. Their response to this anxiety – their rights discourse – places blame for it on the unfair and un-American rights-claims of socially-marginal Americans. There is, though, little evidence to substantiate this placement of blame. Moreover, their rights discourse distracts middle-class and working-poor Americans from interrogating the structural processes that are responsible for imperilling their material fortunes.

Though it amounts to a sort of self-regulation and disempowerment, the conservative rights-discourse employed by a growing number of resentful Americans is not altogether unproductive. Fostering a counter-subversive persuasion, it turns its users into patriotic opponents of redistributive social-change. In so doing, the nationalistic, regulatory dimensions of rights discourse express the 'culture wars' that define contemporary American politics.

Rights and Regulation in the Theatre of Culture War[3]

Conservative rights-talk conjures a recurring figure in American political thought: the 'forgotten American'. This figure – the forgotten American whose equal rights are neglected, whose successes are denigrated, and whose voice in public affairs is marginalized – is central to the self-identifications of many resentful Americans. It is, moreover, both conventional to American political thought and, I will argue, the hero of New Right political and cultural critique. The forgotten American appears prominently, for example, in William Graham Sumner's classical liberal manifesto *What the Social Classes Owe to Each Other* (1883). Dubbed the 'forgotten man' by Sumner, he is an industrious and successful citizen who is nevertheless victimized by 'social doctors' and misguided politicians who elevate the interests of the underprivileged both at his and society's expense (Sumner [1883] 1995, 107–131).

Rechristened 'forgotten Americans' by presidential candidate Barry Goldwater's speechwriter in 1961, and described by commentator Peter Schrag in 1969 as

---

3   This section is adapted from Dudas (2008).

'perhaps the most alienated [people] in America' (Schrag [1969] 1995, 396), this appellation stands in contemporary times for predominately blue-collar, working and middle-class whites who were once the backbone of the Democratic Party's New Deal coalition. A population to whom Richard Nixon referred to as 'the silent majority', they are distressed, on one hand, by the protests of socially-marginal Americans and, on the other hand, by a government that rewards the lazy and indolent with 'excessive government programs' that are funded with their tax dollars (McGirr, 2001, p. 214). Convinced, in Nixon's words, that 'they have a legitimate grievance that should be rectified and a just cause that should prevail,' an increasing number of middle-class Americans accepted Nixon's invitation to join the ranks of the Republican Party (Wills, 1970, p. 311).[4] As Keck notes, the 'appeal to "Middle America" – to the "forgotten man" and the "silent majority"' was a critical part of the Republican Party's allure; it amounted, according to Kazin, to the Party's 'identity of choice' (Kazin, 1995, p. 253). 'To appeal to these voters,' Keck writes, national Republican candidates 'repeatedly denounced both the liberal elites who were running the welfare state ... and the unruly ... masses who were threatening [their] peace and quiet' (Keck, 2004, p. 111; see also McGirr, 2001, pp. 214–215).

Indeed, the resentment of 'Reagan Democrats'[5] initiated a sea change in the American political landscape. The product of what Goldwater described as the 'revolt of the Middle American', American politics has become dominated by a dual resentment: of entrenched federal officials who waste taxpayer money on unpopular programs, and of the traditionally-disadvantaged Americans who are the beneficiaries of these programs (Goldwater, 1970, p. 45). Resentment, that is,

> Over the continuous insistence that society must shoulder a mass responsibility and a mass guilt for everything which is not perfect in the human condition. It's pretty hard to convince a man who has worked hard all of his life, lived according to his own moral precepts, and paid ever-increasing taxes to support the social engineering and paternalism of the liberals in government that he is today responsible for slums, ghettos, poverty, discrimination and crime in the streets. [Such] collective guilt ... [should never have been applied to] responsible citizens who performed their work, fulfilled their civic responsibilities, and added to the forces which add up to good in our society (Goldwater, 1970, p. 66).

This aggrieved, resentful figure is, in fact, at the centre of New Right critique. Consider Samuel Francis' sympathetic (1993) portrait. Made up primarily of 'middle American radicals', Francis depicts the New Right as both 'an electoral coalition concerned with winning elections and roll calls' and as the 'political expression of

---

4   Wills writes that 'Nixon did not invent "the Forgotten American" – neither the phrase nor the concept; but he used it perfectly' (Wills 1970, 312; see also Goldwater 1970, 49–53). The success of Nixon's appeal to white, middle-class resentment was prefigured in the previous presidential election cycle. The disaffection and grievance that characterizes these former New Deal Democrats, in fact, was first revealed in their surprisingly strong support of George Wallace's 1964 presidential campaign (Carter 1995).

5   As Ronald Reagan himself told audiences in the late 1960s: 'We all started out as Democrats but somehow the Democratic Party left us. It left us when it switched to so many philosophies that we could not accept' (Reagan 1968, 135).

a relatively new social movement that regards itself as the depository of traditional American values and as the exploited victim of the alliance between an entrenched elite and a ravenous proletariat.' Locating grievance at its core, Francis notes that resentment propels New Right politics. 'The New Right', he contends, 'is not a conservative force but a radical or revolutionary one [that] seeks the displacement of the entrenched elite, the discarding of its ideology of liberalism and cosmopolitanism, and its own victory as a new governing class' (Francis [1993] 2003, p. 314).

Moreover, New Right politics is an explicitly cultural politics. Indeed, it aims, first, to 'radicalize Middle American consciousness [so as to] perceive the ways in which exploitation of the middle class is institutionalized and understand how it can be resisted.' Second, New Right critique aims to cultivate the resentment of those middle-class and working-poor Americans by expressing salient concerns over 'crime, educational collapse, the erosion of their economic status, and the calculated subversion of their social, cultural, and national identity by forces that serve the interests of the elite above them and the elite's underclass ally.' Operating at the level of perception, New Right critique seeks to construct a new political vision, one that will elaborate an 'infrastructure of cultural hegemony' on which political action is based (Francis [1993] 2003, p. 422). Or, as commentator and sometime presidential candidate Patrick Buchanan exhorted the delegates at the 1992 Republican National Convention:

> My friends, this election is about much more than who gets what. It is about who we are. It is about what we believe. It is about what we stand for as Americans. There is a religious war going on in our country for the soul of America. It is a cultural war, as critical to the kind of nation we will one day be as was the Cold War itself (Buchanan, 1992).

Explained by Hunter (1991) as the struggle to determine 'how we as Americans will order our lives together,' the American 'culture wars' to which Buchanan alluded loosely emulate the German *Kulturkampf* of the late nineteenth century (Hunter, 1991, p. 34). Hunter argues, however, that, unlike the *Kulturkampf*, America's culture wars are fought on largely secular ground.[6] A battle of competing 'moral understandings', the culture wars express disagreements over 'different and opposing bases of moral authority and the world views that derive from them' (Hunter, 1991, pp. 42–43).[7] Accordingly, political debate over issues as varied as 'abortion, child

---

6 Wills, though, disagrees. He argues, in fact, that the American culture wars amount to a 'conflict of one religious vision with another', where the 'religion of the [New Right] is judgmental, punitive, and individualistic' (Wills, 1992).

7 Hunter argues that the culture wars are driven by the competition of two particular world views. The 'orthodox' world view enacts a 'commitment on the part of adherents to an external, definable, and transcendent authority' that 'tells us what is good, what is true, how we should live, and who we are.' Its competitor, the 'progressive' world view 'resymbolize [s] historic faith according to the prevailing assumptions of contemporary life' such that the 'truth tends to be viewed as a process, as a reality that is ever unfolding' (Hunter, 1991, 44). Unsurprisingly, the orthodox world view tends to be favoured by cultural conservatives and the progressive world view is preferred by 'liberals or cultural progressives' (Hunter, 1991, 46).

care, funding for the arts, affirmative action, gay rights, values in public education [and] multi-culturalism' is dominated by normative judgement. 'It is precisely this reason', Hunter argues, 'that political action ... tends to be so passionate' (Hunter, 1991, p. 42).

Moreover, much of this passion is expressed according to nationalistic prerogatives. 'The contemporary culture war is ultimately a struggle over national identity – over the meaning of America, who we have been in the past, who we are now, and perhaps most important, who we, as a nation, aspire to become' (Hunter, 1991, p. 50). Presidential elections, for example, are thus less about who gains authority over the executive branch of the national government and more about, as in Buchanan's formulation, the 'soul of America'. Similarly, debates over affirmative action policies focus not only on whether such policies are appropriate recompense for past mistreatment. They focus also, as United States Senator Joseph Lieberman implied during debate over California's anti-affirmative action Proposition 209, on whether those policies are 'un-American' (Lieberman, 1995).

To argue that debates over rights take place in a theatre of culture war is thus to argue that they take place in a cultural environment that elevates normative and nationalistic anxieties over concerns of practicality or expediency. It is also to acknowledge, accordingly, that contemporary conflicts over rights are 'often intensified and aggravated by the way they are presented in public' (Hunter, 1991, p. 34). Rights are understood either as tools of subversion or counter-subversion – for use either to defend, or undermine, the sources of American character and success. Contemporary debates over rights intersect with debates over the meaning of America; they contribute to the cultural conflict that permeates 'the lives of most Americans, even those who are or would like to be totally indifferent' (Hunter, 1991, p. 50).

It is thus unsurprising that the use of nationalistic rhetoric to defend and attack rights is a key part of the New Right's push for cultural hegemony. Barry Goldwater's attacks on the 'extravagant and shameless misuse' of civil rights by 1960s liberals offered an early intellectual blueprint. On one hand, the rights-claims for redistribution of resources that were fashionable in the early 1960s (which Goldwater dismissed as 'human rights' and 'natural rights' unhinged from legislative or constitutional moorings) infringed upon the states' rights as located in the 10th Amendment of the US Constitution. On the other hand, those rights, such as the one to an integrated public education that was established by the US Supreme Court in *Brown v Board of Education*, were themselves mockeries of true, legally-defined civil rights (Goldwater [1960] 2003, pp. 222–225).

Yet Goldwater was also a champion of individual rights properly defined, particularly those of 'whole men' (in other words, forgotten Americans). The rights of these whole men[8] were particularly important for protecting individual initiative, and so individual freedom, from the overbearing influence of government.

---

8 The 'whole man' was a central motif of Goldwater's acceptance speech at the 1964 Republican National Convention. It was a reference to how Goldwater's brand of conservatism supposedly acknowledged both the economic and spiritual aspects of individual life. Liberalism, in contrast, was allegedly consumed by the issue of economic inequality, focusing only on the material well-being of Americans (Goldwater [1964] 2003).

We seek only to secure his rights, guarantee him opportunity, guarantee him opportunity to strive with government performing only those needed and constitutionally sanctioned tasks which cannot otherwise be performed (Goldwater [1964] 2003, p. 244).

At once dismissive of contemporary misuses of rights and effusive about what rights supposedly once meant, Goldwater's nostalgia was a template for New Right critique.

Indeed, prominent conservative intellectuals frequently lament that dubious rights-claims have corrupted the original meaning of individual rights. Consider, for example, William F. Buckley, Jr's long-standing formulation. The dean of modern American conservatism, and founder and editor-in-chief of the *National Review*, Buckley has consistently objected to the 'mutation' of the meaning of rights in contemporary times (Buckley, 1994, p. 79). It is, in fact, a favourite theme of Buckley's to note how modern usages of civil rights go far beyond what their early advocates claimed, such that now 'everything goes under "civil rights"' (Buckley, 1988a, p. 69; see also Buckley, 1996, 1994).

The expansion of the meaning of rights, Buckley alleges, yields a variety of undesirable consequences. It, first, converts public policy into exercises of 'reverse discrimination' against whites, whose own rights are denigrated (Buckley, 1998, 1996, 1988b, 1985). Second, it gives the 'civil rights lobby' a potent weapon with which to attack as racist and otherwise insensitive all principled arguments against such preferential treatment (Buckley, 2003, 1998, 1996, 1994, 1988a). Third, it intimidates public officials and popular audiences alike, who must acquiesce to unfair and un-American activism or risk being cast outside of the prevailing, though perverted, standards of justice and equality (Buckley, 2003, 1996, 1994, 1988b). 'Someone, somewhere, somehow', pleads Buckley, 'has got to stop the civil-rights thing. It is making a joke out of one or another of our Bill of Rights' (Buckley, 1988a, p. 69).

Similarly illustrative are the multiple formulations of Thomas Sowell. A staunch opponent of affirmative action policies, Sowell argues that those policies are animated by a logic of equal results that is at war with the initial goal of civil rights. According to Sowell,

> The very meaning of the phrase "civil rights" has changed greatly since the *Brown* decision in 1954, or since the Civil Rights Act of 1964. Originally, civil rights meant, quite simply, that all individuals should be treated the same under the law. Many Americans who supported the initial thrust of civil rights ... later felt betrayed as the original concept of equal individual *opportunity* evolved toward the concept of equal group *results* (Sowell [1984] 1988, 310, original emphasis).

Declaring any consciousness of race and gender in public policy morally noxious and socially destructive, Sowell argues that the affirmative action policies enabled by the new meaning of rights: 1) reward already well-off members of traditionally-disadvantaged groups; 2) fuel resentment and jealousy amongst non-preferred populations, and 3) lead to fraudulent 'claims of belonging to the designated beneficiary groups' (Sowell [1989] 1996, 237). All told, the corrupted rights-claims that underlie affirmative action policies threaten 'social disaster' (Sowell [1989] 1996, 282).

Consider, finally, Mary Ann Glendon's *Rights Talk* (1991), which traces the same perversion of rights and also links it to destructive social impulses. Having colonized both American political discourse and our own private discussions with one another, Glendon argues that rights talk is the 'carrier of the few values that are widely shared in our society: liberty, equality, and justice under the law' (Glendon, 1991, p. 3). Yet the social understanding facilitated by rights talk resembles something closer to miscommunication.

Indeed, because contemporary rights-talk has become unmoored from its original civil rights vision (with Americans applying it to an ever-expanding group of interest-based claims), it now generates a series of unintended and destructive consequences. First, rights talk is 'hyper-individualist'; it discourages us from recognizing communal duties and responsibilities and, so, encourages us to act licentiously. Second, rights talk now works as the 'language of no compromise' (Glendon, 1991, 3). Our 'strident' rights talk, that is, makes our conflicts absolute and all-encompassing, turning otherwise negotiable disputes into all-or-nothing affairs. Defeating the ancient, deliberative goal of politics, rights talk locks us into fruitless combat with one another. Glendon makes the point:

> Our rights talk ... promotes unrealistic expectations, heightens conflict, and inhibits dialogue that might lead toward consensus. Its silence concerning responsibilities ... seems to condone the benefits of living in a [democracy] without accepting the corresponding obligations. [Rights talk] corrodes our fabric of beliefs, attitudes, and habits (Glendon, 1991, pp. 14–15).

Rights talk has thus become a scourge on the polity, at once miseducating us about the requirements of American citizenship and amplifying interpersonal conflict to dangerous levels.

Accordingly, contemporary American conservatism is not uniformly hostile to civil rights. Instead, it is hostile to the supposed abuses of rights, either consciously by greedy and unprincipled hucksters or unconsciously by otherwise well-meaning citizens who lack alternative vocabularies for pursuing their interests. Moreover, the culprit of this alleged perversion of rights is a faulty logic of equal results. Assaulting both the body politic and the rights of forgotten Americans, rights themselves have become subversive.

Anxiety and equivocation over rights is not limited to the intellectual wings of modern American conservatism. Instead, as Hunter prophesied, it is a culture wars' trope that infiltrates popular American thought and practice, influencing the understandings of a growing number of Americans. The collected (1994) essays of Greenhouse, Yngvesson, and Engel are illustrative.

Their essays make three particularly relevant points. Detailing how long-time community elites ('insiders') attribute negative changes in their 'ways of life' to the irresponsible legal activity of 'outsiders', they first note that the insider/outsider distinction marks identity and, so, is a conceptual resource for long-time residents to make sense of changes that they find threatening. Stigmatizing already socially-marginal outsiders as greedy and litigious (out 'for a fast buck', in the words of one of Engel's interviewees), the distinction affirms the moral worth of insiders, who understand themselves as responsible and esteemed community members. Insiders' anxiety over litigiousness thus reaffirms the community's pre-existing distinctions in status and power, even as it dresses up those inequalities in the reassuring, facially-neutral language of community harmony (Greenhouse et al., 1994).

Second, the essays note that insiders' condemnations of the legal activity of outsiders are not condemnations of legal activity writ large. Instead, insiders frequently engage in legalistic behaviour of their own. Moreover, insiders interpret their own law-use as consistent with the community values (hard work, keeping promises, being a good neighbour and so on) that are thought to be assaulted by the law-use of outsiders. Law-use is thus at the centre of community, both as a conceptual resource for justifying the prevailing insider/outsider dynamic and as an engine of the virtues that insiders ascribe to their communities.

Third, impugning the law-use of outsiders obscures the large-scale and impersonal economic processes (such as the loss of an agricultural base or the rise of a service-orientated economy) that are driving the changes that the three communities in the study are undergoing. To the extent that these changes disempower insiders, they are far more responsible for altering the community's way of life than is the litigious behaviour of outsiders. Insiders, that is, mistakenly place blame for challenges to their material self-interests onto the relatively benign presence of the community's socially-marginal members. In so doing, they displace blame and critical engagement away from the actual processes that harm them.

And so too does the New Right's qualified embrace of equal rights work. First, obsession with how rights have lost their association with an individualism that emphasizes self-sufficiency and equal opportunity – obsession, that is, with how rights lost their allegedly traditional meaning – works as a conceptual resource for understanding how contemporary American society has become a grotesque inversion of its former self. The loss of traditional meaning explains how formerly-powerless Americans have seized control of the nation's cultural and intellectual institutions. It explains, that is, the gullibility of well-meaning whites, who, lacking stable vocabularies and fixed moral and ethical principles, are easy targets for the crafty machinations of traditionally-disadvantaged Americans. And it explains how the people who the nation once valued have become the victims of an upside-down society; the loss of traditional meaning, that is, explains how forgotten Americans became simultaneously ignored and despised.

Indeed, the obsession with rights marks the identities both of forgotten Americans and of the traditionally-disadvantaged Americans whose activism is so threatening. Needing only their equal rights to succeed, self-sufficient and hard-working Americans are nevertheless 'forgotten, unrespected, mocked' (Wills, 1970, p. 312). Worse, they are denigrated as the historical recipients of unfair advantages. Their brand of individualism is surpassed by an individualism of license and greed, by a philosophy that holds that aberrant rights-claims are the keys to success. In the exhaustion of the traditional meaning of rights we see also the decline of individual merit and self-sufficiency (of equal opportunity) and the rise of entitlement and preferential treatment (of equal results).

Second, the New Right's stilting embrace of rights encourages attempts to reclaim the allegedly original meaning of rights. It authorizes, that is, a series of legal mobilizations that are explicitly geared towards opposing the extravagant rights-claims of the traditionally disadvantaged in the name of rights themselves. As much national service as self-interested activism, the New Right's counter-uses of rights talk seek to purify rights, and to thereby make them once again safe for use by the self-sufficient individuals who were the original heroes of American democracy (Goldberg-Hiller and Milner, 2003).

Third, New Right critique consistently evades the major causes of the resentment that consumes forgotten Americans. To be sure, the New Right political vision does offer an economic analysis, one that purports to free Americans of the overbearing governmental influence that supposedly hampers self-sufficiency. Conservative intellectuals and public officials consistently tout the importance, in fact, of tax reform. As Edsall and Edsall (1992) detail, cultivating resentment over allegedly unfair tax burdens (in particular, the graduated or progressive tax scheme) has been a constant feature of modern conservative politics. Economist and Reagan Administration official Bruce Bartlett recently made the same point: 'tax cuts are the glue that holds the Republican coalition together' (Bartlett, 2006, p. 193).

Yet there is little evidence that the obsessive focus on tax cuts has improved the lives of middle-class and working-poor Americans. Consider, for example, the GOP's consistent failure to address the nation's worsening health care problems. Its problems, according to Sered and Fernandopulle (2005), are the result of converging structural factors (such as decentralization, the dominance of employment-based health care plans, and the political influence wielded by the health care industry) that deny high-quality and affordable health care to many middle-class and working-poor Americans. These are exactly the people that the New Right champions and whose resentment provides the raw material for GOP prominence. And yet the Republican Party has made little effort to create a more inclusive health care system. In fact, it led opposition to the Clinton Administration's proposed overhaul (Skocpol, 1996). Not the result of sinister motives, the GOP's disinterest in the material interests of middle-class Americans instead reflects the difficulties involved in maintaining a governing coalition that pursues as many often-contradictory goals as does the Republican coalition (e.g., running a limited government, deregulating the economy and protecting traditional social arrangements: Keck, 2004).

But the loud championing of middle-class Americans insulates the New Right from their criticism, even though such Americans have little to show in return for their fidelity to the GOP (Frank, 2004). Instead, middle-class and working-poor Americans are encouraged to blame their economic hard times on witless federal officials and the duplicitous minorities who manipulate those officials. Accordingly, the New Right's electoral and governing successes, as well as its political vision itself, is premised on middle-class and working-poor Americans misidentifying the causes of their resentment.[9]

9	There is, though, little reason to presume (as does political commentator Thomas Frank, for example) that a simple change in voting behaviour – shifting back to supporting the Democratic Party, for example – would result in significantly more responsive policies.

And rights talk is a central medium through which such misidentification proceeds. Indeed, conservative-rights talk blames federal officials and socially-marginal Americans for threatening economic livelihoods, wrecking local ways of life, and undermining America itself. Yet it does this in the absence of persuasive evidence, and in the face of compelling data that locates the sources of their hard times elsewhere.

The resentment of middle-class and working-poor Americans over perceived slights to their rights is the raw material that propels the New Right's participation in the culture wars. It is the denigration and dismissal of their rights that makes so many otherwise laudable Americans forgotten. Similarly, the rights talk employed both by forgotten Americans and the New Right intellectuals who champion them has assumed a prominent place in public discourse, making rights-claims on behalf of traditionally-disadvantaged Americans increasingly unfashionable (McCann and Dudas, 2006). The abuse of rights, moreover, is consistently identified as the root cause of the difficulties that underlie middle-class and working-poor resentment; deviant rights-claims, not structural causes, are thus to blame for personal and national decline.

The rights discourse employed by President Bush, New Right intellectuals, and an increasing number of American citizens enacts a morality tale. In expressing the resentment that pervades American culture, it identifies heroes and villains. And how they practice rights is what distinguishes good, productive (yet denigrated) citizens from bad, parasitic (yet esteemed) citizens.

Conclusion

The counter-subversive persuasion that conservative rights-discourse fosters in those who employ it initiates a two-sided regulatory logic. On one hand, it stigmatizes the rights-claims of relatively-powerless Americans as threats, in part, to national interests. Conservative rights-discourse seeks to discipline already socially-marginal Americans, to entrench their powerlessness by labelling attempts to overcome it as violations of the equal rights of all Americans. To the extent that this stigmatization is persuasive and this disciplining effective, it makes the liberation promised by rights all the more difficult to attain.

On the other hand, conservative rights-discourse regulates the behaviour of those in whose name it is offered. It has the effect of discouraging middle-class and working-poor Americans from recognizing the actual causes of their discontent, satiating them instead with the psychic rewards of participation in a nationalistic crusade – a culture war in which opponents fight not with guns and bombs but with competing visions of America. A discourse meant to silence un-American attacks on their material interests, their rights-talk is instead a spectacular exercise in self-regulation.

The centrist drift of the Democratic Party in recent years, manifest in the disinterest of 'new Democrats' in combating race and class-based inequalities, makes the emergence of an economic justice agenda unlikely (Roedinger, 1997, pp. 48–60).

And so as we approach the intersection of rights and regulation a familiar figure emerges. An icon of conservative rights-talk and the forgotten Americans that it champions, he exemplifies the current American equivocation over rights. At this intersection, peddling equal rights and the twin regulations that they enact, stands none other than George W. Bush himself.

Chapter 10

Rights as Regulation: The Integration of Development and Human Rights

Sundhya Pahuja[1]

Introduction

Recent attempts to integrate human rights and development have come from several quarters. Not only human rights organizations, but international institutions of all stripes are increasingly asserting that 'human rights have become a more important aspect of development policy and programming since the end of the Cold War' (Piron and O'Neil, 2005, ii). The suite of millennial and post-millennial documents, including the 2000 Millennium Declaration (2000) and the 2005 World Summit[2] all recognize 'that development and human rights are interdependent and mutually reinforcing.' And the 2005 report of UN Secretary-General Kofi Annan, *In Larger Freedom*, extends even further, suggesting that the notion of 'larger freedom ... encapsulates the idea that development, security and human rights go hand in hand' (Annan, 2005, p. 5).

This convergence between human rights and development is part of a wider trend in international law, and one which has been almost uniformly welcomed. Cassese, for example, has recently observed with approval the increasing 'interpenetration ... of previously somewhat compartmentalized areas of international law' such as development and human rights, which 'shows that at least at the normative level the international community is becoming more integrated' (Cassese, 2001, p. 45). Such welcome has also been offered from more unexpected quarters, including those otherwise critical of the development project.[3] And even those who question the

---

1   I wish to thank Bronwen Morgan for her encouragement and assistance in the creation of this chapter, as well as participants at the joint Law and Society Association / Socio-Legal Studies Association Summer Institute held at Oxford in the summer of 2005 for their engaging and thought-provoking comments on my project. I also wish to thank Susan Mathews for her close reading and insightful comments, and Jeremy Baskin for his critical interlocutions.

2   Documentation from the World Summit is available at http://www.un.org/ga/59/hl60_plenarymeeting.html.

3   Adam Gearey, for example, otherwise critical of development and attentive to its aporetic quality, suggests, if tentatively, that 'there are clearly exciting developments within this body of work [development] not the least the attention ... [to] human rights obligations ...' (Gearey, 2005, p. 109.) And in a similarly surprising vein given her critique of development,

extent of the convergence between human rights and development to date, arguing it to be 'weak' at best, generally make that argument in the context of advocating more, not less of it. Alston, for example, argues that 'the [Millennium Development Goals] initiative is of major relevance to human rights ... If human rights are not seen to be part of that agenda, the rhetoric of the past couple of decades about the integration or mainstreaming of human rights into development efforts will have come to little' (Alston, 2005, p. 757). And although he is critical of the so far limited and partial 'extent to which the international development and human rights communities have taken one another's priority concerns on board in their own work' (Alston, 2005, p. 758), his goal is to find 'ways in which the strengths, resources, and support of the international human rights and development communities can be mobilized in order to reinforce one another in their efforts to achieve shared goals' (Alston and Robinson, 2005, p. 1).

However, in contrast with this ascendant orthodoxy and the increasingly 'commonsensical' understanding that human rights and development should be integrated as deeply and as quickly as possible, I will argue that their integration should be understood as the creeping transformation of a promised sphere of 'rights' into a domain which may aptly be called 'regulatory'. This transformation results in a contraction of the sphere of politics in the 'global' arena. Neither development nor international human rights (law) tends particularly to be conceived of, nor to conceive of itself, by reference to the bodies of literature outlined in the introduction to this Volume as representing the respective traditions of 'rights' and 'regulation' scholarship. However, in so far as a character, even if somewhat caricatured, can be ascribed to each of 'rights' and 'regulation' by reference to those scholarly traditions, I suggest they are heuristically useful in considering the potential effect of the proposed merger between the human rights and development projects. To some extent, this heuristic use stands in tension with the ontology of hybridity drawn by some contributors to this volume.

In my argument, and building on the possibility raised in the introduction, rights have a symbolic valence that regulation lacks. This symbolic valence is crucial to the emancipatory, or what I would call 'political', aspect of human rights. This 'political' aspect arises in concrete terms in the gap between the body of human rights norms in international law at a given time, and the imaginative appeal of human rights which will never be coincident with the rights 'on the books'. In other words, at any given moment, there is both a set of positive legal rules laid down in treaties or found in customary international law, and a whole range of people making claims in the name of human rights – either in terms of rights which are yet to be 'recognized' as law, or with respect to the identities which are excluded from the terms of a particular existing right. These two spheres – let us call them the positive and the symbolic – are not co-extensive, but crucially coexist, often in conflictual ways. The effect of one upon the other is to destabilize what would otherwise be a series of rules delimiting a priori, the (human) subject of rights. These rules represent the regulatory

---

Wickramasinghe asserts hopefully that '[t]here is a possibility that the United Nations may play a new role in the formulation of a harmonious, cogent and integrated approach to human rights and development ...' (Wickramasinghe, 1996, p. 322).

aspect of rights. This inherent aspect of rights is at the same time both necessary and dangerous, but is not in itself exhaustive of human rights as a political concept.

In a philosophical sense, rights have the potential to operate as more than 'mere' regulation because they contain the seeds of their own excess in a way that regulation, in the sense of rules plus enforcement mechanisms, does not. This seed arises from the universal claim which human rights must necessarily make by virtue of their investiture in humans. The argument goes something like this. If a right is a 'human' right, it is a universal right. But in what sense is it universal? It is inevitably particular, both in its content (what specific value does it inscribe?) and in its scope (to whom does it apply?). Its 'universality' such that it be, is in its normative, or aspirational claim that it *should* apply to everyone and be a universally endorsed value, but that normative claim is grounded on a descriptive claim about the *actual* universality of human rights. In other words, it *is* universal because it *should be* universal. And why should it be universal? Because it *is* universal. Often this claim is a specifically hegemonic one, for the elevation to the universal of a parochial value is a familiar mode of power (see, for example, Koskenniemi, 2003). But what the paradoxical quality of this operative mode of power means is that when a human right comes up against someone to whom the right does not apply because of the particular 'human' inscribed within the right, that person embodies the limit of the right and presents to the universal an insistent factuality contesting the universal's claim to be such. This clash brings political contestation to the heart of every human right.

As Rancière observes, if human rights did not have this unstable – political – quality at their heart, if they existed only in their positive sense, they would be, as Hannah Arendt feared, either tautological or useless, for if one had them (because they were guaranteed by the state), one would not need them, and if one needed them (because they were not guaranteed by the state), one would not have them. Not dissimilarly, if the universal were stabilized around a particular identity, they could only ever, in Wendy Brown's phrase, 'build a fence' around that identity of the human rights victim at the site of violation, 'regulating rather than challenging the conditions within' (Brown, 2000, p. 231). For both Rancière and Brown, that is simply not the history of human rights. The paradigmatic example they each give is Olympe de Gouges who claims from the scaffold, in the name of the rights of man, that if a woman is entitled to go to the scaffold, she is entitled to go to the assembly (Rancière, 2004. See also Scott, 1996; Douzinas, 2000). This claim – that the subject of human rights is the person who brings to the universal claim of an extant right, evidence in her person of the right's own particularity – is only possible if the value securing the right is open to question. If the 'universal' value is protected in its 'universality' by force, for example, the being who marks its limit will, by definition, be utterly other, or inhuman. This is the place at which rights become purely 'regulatory', and indeed, totalizing. Arguably, an analogous dynamic applies to law, which makes a similarly universal claim and which carries with it a symbolic valence in its imaginative link to justice (see generally Derrida, 2002). In either case, if the space between the symbolic valence and the positive rule is narrowed too much, law and rights lose their capacity to juridify and channel social conflict peacefully. Indeed, some would say that they would lose their hegemonic potential to deradicalize claims which are discordant with the dominant ideology. In either case, however one conceives of what is displaced, without that open space 'law' and 'rights' are reduced simply to rules-plus-violence.

In my argument the transformation of international human rights into (developmental) regulation presents such a danger. As I shall argue, when merged with development, the transcendent space of universality is stabilized and the political quality of human rights is negated. Specifically, human rights become a means by which society is subordinated to the imperative of economic growth through markets. This subordination is effected in concert with many other institutions – institutions more typically the terrain of inquiry of the regulation theorist. However, the extension to human rights deepens and extends that subordination through the formation of the developmental subject, a subject whose very humanity is now delimited according to the demands of market logic.

Arguably of course, a merger with development is not the only means by which a transcendent value is stabilized for human rights. Even in their unmerged guise, human rights law has a regulatory dimension and operates in an imperial mode whenever the 'universality' of the particular values embodied in the human rights laws in place at any given moment are defended by force or coercion (witness the violent 'democratizations' currently taking place in many countries, or war waged in the name of protecting human rights). But in a less conceptual vein, for those who would contest the elevation to the universal of a certain set of parochial values – values which represent the orthodoxy of the powerful – a diminution in political space also occurs simply through the harmonization of the two logics of development and human rights which in the past have provided alternative sites of contestation or claim, often with contrasting goals and modes, the differences between which seemed to offer some strategic potential to the 'developing' world (see Rajagopal, 2006).

In order to make the argument presented here, I will provide a sketch of recent, influential attempts to integrate development and human rights and reveal how these attempts would result in the transformation of rights into regulation instrumental to the goal of growth through markets. I argue that this instrumentalization would occur despite the vociferous insistence by proponents of an integrated approach that human rights should not and need not be instrumentalized in the integration. In my view, if the subordination of rights to market need is to be resisted, the quest for integration must be rejected, no matter how noble the avowed intention of development may be or how certain the champions of human rights are that rights may be maintained as 'trumps'. Instead, strategies must be adopted which emphasize the oppositional or 'political' quality of human rights. Searching for 'relevance' will serve only to enhance the imperial dimension of human rights, sealing their fate as sites of regulation rather than emancipation and increasing the violence of developmental transformations, as well as the likelihood of violent resistance.

A Short Genealogy of the Return of Law in Development and the Inclusion of Rights in Development

Despite earlier attempts by advocates from and for the Third World to assert a 'right to development', moves toward the integration of human rights and development have become part of the mainstream only since the end of the Cold War. For various reasons, after that time, the Bretton Woods institutions in particular turned toward the notion of 'governance' as a key element of the development project and began to revise their understanding of the relationship between development and the state (see for example, Gathii, 1999; Rajagopal, 2003). A key element of that new understanding was a renewed attention to the role of law in development. In my argument, the resurgence of law in development after the Cold War was a key discursive site for the emergence of the conversation about the linkage between rights and development. This is related to the observation made in the introduction to this volume that, aphoristically at least, in the liberal paradigm rights are linked indissolubly with the rule of law. The resurgence of law in development has taken shape as two relatively distinct streams within what I call the 'ideological-institutional complex' known as international law.[4] Each of these two streams had particular laws in mind, and depending on those laws, a differing conception of the relevant human rights which should be regarded as integral to development.

The first group were those who subscribed broadly to the application of the 'New Institutional Economics' to the development concept (Daniels and Trebilcock, 2004, p. 106). This group emanated largely from the Bretton Woods institutions and their fellow travellers. In essence, this group advocated 'substantive laws that provide strong protections of private property rights and alienability, as well as effective enforcement of long term contracts' (Daniels and Trebilcock, 2004, p. 106). The second group – let us call them the 'welfarists', following Trebilcock, were those who came to 'emphasize ... the importance of constitutional reform, an entrenched bill of rights, and strong protection of human rights as necessary preconditions for development' (Daniels and Trebilcock, 2004, p. 106). This group emanated primarily from the United Nations based institutions and their allies, particularly the United Nations Development Programme (UNDP), and various NGOs and civil society groups.[5]

The best way to illustrate the two differing approaches to the 'new' law and development and the question of rights is to engage briefly with two key texts which respectively epitomize those approaches: Hernando De Soto's *The Mystery of*

---

4   I have coined this term in order to overcome the unhelpful dichotomization between the academy and profession in relation to international law. It is my argument that international law, more than other kinds of law, is produced and sustained in the relation and tension between the profession and the academy and that it is appropriate to see this relation as producing a complex of players and practices, ideologies and institutions.

5   Technically, of course, the Bretton Woods Institutions are part of the UN system, being two of the UN's 16 specialized agencies: see generally http://www.un.org/aboutun/chart.html.

Capital (Soto, 2000),[6] connected with the New Institutional Economics school (see, for example, Klasper and Streit, 1998, p. 426), and Amartya Sen's *Development as Freedom* (Sen, 1999), lodestar for the 'welfarist' school.

The Mystery of Capital

A key figure of contemporary inspiration for the 'New Institutional Economics' school in the law and development debate is Peruvian economist, Hernando De Soto. De Soto became enormously influential in the 1990s[7] when his understanding of the relationship between states, markets and development seemed to offer an intermediate position between the two most recent waves of received economic wisdom (Chibundu, 1997, p. 207), both waves being acknowledged failures in terms of the results they promised. The earlier of the two economic orthodoxies was that the state was crucial to modernizing developing countries through eliminating the market failures understood to be endemic to them (Davis and Trebilcock, 1999, p. 4). The more recent orthodoxy of the economically notorious 1980s was to shrink the role of the state dramatically, privatize as much as possible and drastically increase market exposure at both national and international levels (see, for example, Peet, 2003, pp. 204–212) – an orthodoxy known as the 'Washington Consensus' (Fine, 2001).[8] Between these diametrically opposed wisdoms, New Institutional Economics seemed to offer an intermediate position in which 'the state and the institutions that comprise it [could be understood] as endogenous to the development process ...' (Davis and Trebilcock, 1999, p. 4).

De Soto in particular seemed to offer a way to bring the insights of the New Institutional Economics to bear on the quest for development in a way that offered a political compromise. The compromise was between those with an unshaken faith in growth through markets as the key to development and those with a primary concern for poverty alleviation as the main function of development and consequently more alive to the impoverishing consequences of interventions conducted in line with the Washington consensus.[9] In other words, De Soto's approach permitted the reconciliation of the 'broad consensus ... on the kinds of policies that countries ought [still] to follow to achieve economic development' (Clague, 1997, p. 1) with the inescapable recognition that 'when the recommended policies are put into place

---

6   This book was published in 2000 but it represents an elaboration of the ideas in De Soto's earlier book, *The Other Path* (1989).

7   On De Soto's influence, see, for example, former US President Bill Clinton's account of his African tour in 2002: 'I have just come here from a trip to Africa which provided me with all kinds of fresh evidence of the importance of politics ... In Ghana ... a new President is working with a great Peruvian economist, Hernando De Soto, to bring the assets of poor people in to the legal system so they can be collateral for loans ...' (Clinton 2002, cited in Manji 2003, p. 82). As Manji observes, the Bank has been heavily influenced by De Soto's prescriptions, most notably in its land reform initiatives which, Manji remarks, really amount to land *law* reform initiatives (see also Kasper and Streit, 1998, p. 462).

8   For a useful synopsis of critiques of the Washington Consensus, see Florio (2002).

9   On the question of the impoverishment brought by structural adjustment, see generally Chossudovsky (1997), *For an internal (and unwelcome) critique, see World Bank, 1992.*

(often under the guidance of – and pressure from – the International Monetary Fund and the World Bank), the hoped-for results do not materialize' in a way which did not disrupt the core tenets of the consensus (Clague, 1997, p. 1).

Through the numerous empirical studies he led of the 'informal' economy in Peru, De Soto came up with an ingenious justification for both markets, and law and legal institutions by arguing that the market most certainly offered the best way forward, but that poor people were poor not because they were incompetent or less worthy but because they had to operate *outside* the law because of the corrupt and bureaucratic governments of the states in which they lived. This narrative constructed the 'poor person' as a noble and, most importantly, entrepreneurial figure who was doing as well as he could within many constraints but would do much better if the legal system were improved (Soto, 2000, pp. 4–5).

In one-way, De Soto is of course correct that a capitalist economy is not possible without laws which create property rights and transform material realities into discrete, tradable commodities, or indeed, laws which create such commodities out of the immaterial.[10] But what is interesting about his theory and others like it is the way that the idea of a capitalist economy and the commodification of the life world is rendered both universal and axiomatically good. In this technique of universalization, 'the poor person' is reinterpreted as a very specific (legal) subject, the *homo œconomicus*. This subject is understood as a proto-capitalist, possessing an agency which is entrepreneurial, not radical; a subject whose energies can be understood as complementary rather than resistant to capitalist expansion or, as De Soto puts it, the 'globaliz[ation] of capital within [his] own countr[y]' (Soto, 2000, p. 219).

The genius of De Soto's argument, and what makes it politically more palatable than its predecessor theories which locate the sources of developmental failure (yet again) in the orientalized populations of the Third World is that De Soto locates the very source of the generative energy of capitalism within the people of the Third World. Rather than launching yet another reform project which diagnoses the causes of Third World people's misery as residing within themselves, De Soto finds the *homo œconomicus already resident* in the gulleys and favelas, waiting to be liberated properly into capitalist relations. In De Soto's interpretation, this calculating individual already orders his relations pursuant to a rational, cost-benefit analysis but is prevented from lifting himself from poverty because of badly designed (formal) property laws: 'Much behaviour that is today attributed to cultural heritage is not the inevitable result of people's ethnic or idiosyncratic traits but of their rational evaluation of the relative costs and benefits of entering the legal property system' (Soto, 2000, 240). The inhibiting factor preventing the release of this energy is the Third World elites who inhabit a 'bell jar', the interior of which is articulated with

---

10 See Karl Polanyi for the argument that a market economy requires that nature and human activity be commodified into land and labour respectively and that law is the site of that transformation (see generally Polanyi, 2001). Hayek argued something similar but for different political reasons (see generally Hayek, 1944).

global markets but which is impenetrable to those outside its invisible contours.[11] These elites bear an ambivalent relation to government itself which, for De Soto, is both the guardian of the bell jar and the only entity capable of lifting it (Soto, 2000, p. 167).

The question for De Soto then is how to lift the bell jar? In a by now familiar pattern within development studies, the answer to this question resides in the West; 'Western governments succeeded in lifting the bell jar, but it was an erratic, unconscious process that took hundreds of years' (Soto, 2000, p. 167). And because we (still) cannot wait for this organic process to take place elsewhere, De Soto and his colleagues 'have synthesised what [they] think [Western governments] did right into a formula [they] call the "capitalization process", with which [they] are assisting various governments throughout the world.' (Soto, 2000, p. 167.) The structure of the development narrative is therefore retained in so far as the West's past is the Third World's future. What 'the nations of the West had to do to move from pre-capitalist "primitive judgements" to a systematized body of laws' is what the Third World must now do with the assistance of the development agencies (Soto, 2000, p. 173). But instead of effecting a long process of civilizing the savage or modernizing the backward, in this version of the story, universal economic man is discovered to already exist in the Third World and already to be a proto-capitalist with proto-capitalist laws. 'Lifting the bell jar is ... principally a legal challenge' but it is the 'people's laws' which must be given fruit (Soto, 2000, p. 165). This allows the development story to shift conceptually from pedagogical to liberatory. Fortunately for De Soto, the laws which he reads the people as possessing just happen to be rational, efficient, property-centred laws in which land is conceptually commodified and defended by the individuals who 'own' it. Therefore, just as 'Western nations built their formal property systems' by '[d]iscovering "the people's laws"', so must governments of the Third World 'listen to the barking dogs'[12] to discover their own people's laws and integrate those laws into a single integrated property system (Soto, 2000, p. 171).

For De Soto, these immanent laws are the original 'social contract' which is not 'an invisible god-like abstraction that resides only in the minds of visionaries like Locke, Hume and Rousseau,' but also 'arrangements that are explicitly documented by real people' (Soto, 2000, p. 171). The process of lifting the bell jar is therefore about discovering 'the many social contracts "out there" [and integrating them] into one all encompassing social contract' (Soto, 2000, p. 170), 'to integrate the formal legal conventions inside the bell jar with the extralegal ones outside it' (Soto, 2000, p. 164).

---

11 De Soto opens his book with a quote from Ferdinand Braudel evoking the image of the bell jar: 'The problem is to find out why that sector of society of the past, which I would not hesitate to call capitalist, should have lived as if in a bell jar, cut off from the rest; why was it not able to expand and conquer the whole of society? ...' (Braudel (1982), cited in Soto (2000, p. 1).

12 For De Soto, the 'barking dogs' represent a knowledge of the people's law, for as De Soto in Bali 'strolled through the rice fields [he had] no idea where the property boundaries were. But the dogs knew. Every time [he] crossed from one farm to another, a different dog barked. Those Indonesian dogs may have been ignorant of formal law but they were positive about which assets their masters controlled' (Soto, 2000, p. 171).

This 'discovery' of the real 'social contract' and its existence within the sociality of the poor, just like the 'discovery' of the entrepreneurial character of the pauper, is a powerful technology of universalization. This technology is one in which a consonance is posited between an authentic 'people' and the universal value itself, but in circumstances in which some mediating factor has hitherto prevented that value's fulfilment. In this assertion, the normativity of the universal claim is disavowed as it is ostensibly rendered descriptive by the projection of the interference as the reason for the non-realization of that value. In other words, by 'discovering' that the 'people's law' is a 'social contract' about commodified property relations, De Soto can blame the state and improperly conceived property laws for the exclusion of the poor from mainstream capitalist activity and present the radical expansion of commodified property (and by extension, commercial credit) regimes as liberatory rather than transformative or 'modernizing'. Not only this, but the value itself – here an integrated and all encompassing system of property law which replicates the successful system achieved in the West, is given a universal quality through its seeming origin within 'the people'. Thus, the ostensible rediscovery of the 'law of the people' and the solution to the mystery of capital does not lie very far from the economic consensus of the late 1990s which was implicitly secured by the lynchpin of 'well-defined and alienable private property rights and a formal system of contracts' protected by courts (Davis and Trebilcock, 1999, p. 4).

Thus, we see in the universalization of highly specific 'private law' ordering, a consonance being painted between the international community's conception of democracy and 'the people's' conception of democracy. In that vision, external and internal legitimation of the state must inevitably point to the same (universal) thing. Given the structure of international relations, this effectively means that the 'international community' becomes the appropriate arbiter of a state's legitimacy, whatever the wishes of the people inside that state might be. And in both cases, the protection of internally determined political arrangements which the doctrinal respect for formal sovereignty would seem to offer is circumvented by universal character being claimed for the values being asserted and according to which the domestic regulatory setting must be transformed.

Development as Freedom

The second stream in the debate over the appropriate content of law in law and development comprised those who were more concerned with what I will shorthand here as 'justice' and 'equality'. As stated, this group advocated human rights and constitutional reform as essentially and intrinsically related to the rule of law and valuable for their own sake. But this second assertion potentially has a more tenuous relation, if any, to the development project than the first stream. In the first stream, through an acceptance of economic growth as the primary engine of poverty alleviation, a direct connection was maintained between the specific rights being put forward and the normative justification for their connection to development on the grounds that it promotes growth.[13]

However, in the second, 'welfarist' stream, not only was there a resistance to prioritize growth above rights,[14] the risk was always lurking that rights might not promote growth, and indeed, as time passed in the debate it became clearer that there was, at best, ambivalent empirical evidence that human rights and/or constitutional democracy do actually promote growth (Daniels and Trebilcock, 2004, 103). Thus, in order for the welfarists to assert the relevance of rights to the burgeoning (and well funded) field of rule-of-law aid and development, a different approach had to be taken. That approach was to piggy-back on attempts to redefine the concept of *development* as understood within the IEOs in a way which took account of more than economic growth and attributed intrinsic merit to certain substantive values, giving those values normative relevance as themselves being indicators of development. Thus, these groups allied themselves to those advocating what some have called a 'deontological' approach to development epitomized by that taken by Amartya Sen, in which,

> development embraces more than simply income per capita or growth thereof but rather embraces a wide range of dimensions of human well-being that bear on the capabilities of individuals to live lives that they have reason to value, including various freedoms such as freedom of expression, freedom of political association, and freedom of political opposition and dissent (Daniels and Trebilcock, 2004, p. 105. See also Sen, 2000; Farber, 2002).

From this perspective, rights have an intrinsic value and do not need to be justified in terms of developmental goals, seemingly overcoming the problem of growth as neither sufficient nor necessarily supported by their promulgation (see Daniels and Trebilcock, 2004, p. 104).

Sen's vision is more subtle than that of many. It is one which would seem to offer a synthesis between North and South and West and East, as well as offering to the dismal science an aperture through which it can address the richness of culture and human variety. It achieves this latter through a relation between 'development' and 'freedom' which, in Sen's view, are intimately connected to one another. This connection arises from the idea that 'freedom' as Sen defines it is both 'constitutive' of development and 'instrumental' in the achievement of development (see generally Sen, 1999). For Sen, the idea that 'freedom' must be constitutive of development presents a strong challenge to the idea that democracy is a luxury only the rich can afford and that the exigencies of development for the future call for sacrifices now – sacrifices that must usually be borne by the poor. The idea which Sen is challenging, of suffering for future gain, represents a strong current in the development literature from Truman's four point programme (Truman, 1949) to the explicit preference for authoritarian regimes expressed by the Bank and Fund during the 1980s and to the

---

13 This is now accepted as orthodoxy, even though chinks are starting to show since the 'China enigma' – the massive economic growth of China without any identifiable 'rule of law' in the traditions asserted above (see Daniels and Trebilcock, 2004, p. 104).

14 A famous exponent of this is of course Ronald Dworkin (see Dworkin, 1984).

strong arm of 'shock tactics' and austerity programmes which littered the road to development during the 1980s and 1990s (see, for example, Peet, 2003, 87–93). As Sen remarks, he wants to mount an assault on this understanding of development as a '"fierce" process, with much "blood, sweat and tears"', and offer instead a vision compatible with a view 'that sees development as an essentially "friendly" process' of congeniality and mutually beneficial exchange (Sen, 1999, p. 35). This challenge is offered by insisting that development itself must be seen as 'a process of expanding the real freedoms that people enjoy' (Sen, 1999, p. 36). In Sen's approach, the 'expansion of freedom' is viewed as both '(1) the *primary end* and (2) the *principal means* of development' (Sen, 1999, p. 36, emphasis in original).

By asserting freedom as a primary end of development, Sen means that 'basic political freedoms such as civil rights' must be seen as 'constitutive parts of development itself' which overcomes the question of whether such freedoms are 'conducive to development' measured as 'GNP growth or industrialisation' (Sen, 1999, pp. 36–37). However, Sen would also wish to assert that whist these constitutive freedoms have intrinsic importance, they are also 'very effective in contributing to economic progress' (Sen, 1999, p. 37) and can therefore be understood also as a means to development. Sen recognizes that this argument could descend into mere tautology if we were to understand that the extent of his argument was that if freedoms are the ends of development then introducing them is also the means to development. Instead he wants to suggest that the 'the effectiveness of freedom as an instrument lies in the fact that different kinds of freedom interrelate with one another, and freedom of one type may greatly help in advancing freedoms of other types' (Sen, 1999, p. 37).

For Sen, it is clear that a significant number of freedoms are rights-based. In particular, 'the importance of political freedom as part of basic capabilities' is a significant part of his thesis (Sen, 1999, 152). Those political freedoms are not radically open-ended, but consist in 'a general pre-eminence of basic political and liberal rights' (Sen, 1999, p. 148) comprising 'freedom of expression', 'unrestrained participation in political and social activities', 'civil rights' and 'free speech' (Sen, 1999, p. 152). In this embrace of a fairly standard liberal conception of freedom, Sen takes an avowedly universalist position. 'Indeed', Sen writes, 'the overriding value of freedom as the organizing principle of this work has this feature of a strong universalist presumption' (Sen, 1999, p. 244). Sen takes this position in relation to the habitual and seemingly inescapable oscillation familiar to international lawyers between universalism and cultural relativism. The way this debate played out in the development sphere was of course an extension of the arguments in the human rights sphere. In that debate, the intensely problematic claims were made by various Asian governments (most notably Lee Kwan Yew of Singapore) both that political freedoms and rights hamper economic development and that 'Asian Values' require a subordination of the individual to the collective which, in that thesis, authentically manifests itself as the nation-state (Sen, 1999, pp. 148–149). Sen carefully refutes this claim and refuses all authoritarian appropriations of 'Asian values' on the grounds that they neither are, nor can they claim to be, truly 'Asian'. Sen's arguments on this score are erudite and persuasive. The claim to 'authentic' 'Asian' values which not only exist but somehow translate into philosophically coherent props for authoritarian statehood is patently wrong. His response however, is to reiterate the *genuine* 'universality' of *liberal* values, not simply by mere assertion as is often the case, nor by relying implicitly on the development narrative as liberal human rights scholars often do, but by insisting that the West cannot claim a monopoly on (liberal) philosophical attachments to freedom or tolerance of heterodoxy, nor on participation and political debate because those values can be found elsewhere, and earlier than the liberal-occidental origin myths would have it.[15] To this extent, Sen participates in the tradition of attempting to 'refound' the universal on more genuinely universal grounds.[16] Sen, though, has no quibble with the content and scope of liberal values. He does not want to question the values – just the understanding of them *as* solely Western. He presents arguments drawn from Confucianism, Hinduism and Islam to argue that 'the Western traditions are not the only ones that prepare us for a freedom-based approach to social understanding' (Sen, 1999, p. 240). His approach amounts to what we might not entirely facetiously call a 'gentleman's defense of the Orient', in that he refuses to accept an account of the 'Orient' as either unitary, or as primitive or philosophically unsophisticated, but at the same time positions himself within an Enlightenment tradition of reasoned universalism and cosmopolitan exchange.[17] If De Soto's technology of universalization is to find the *homo œconomicus* resident in the gulleys and favelas, then Sen's is to find already living in those same locales, the enlightenment's *homo politicus*.[18]

Politics and Economics Come Together in Law-In-Development

The influence of Sen's understanding of 'development as freedom' and others who take a 'capabilities' approach,[19] as well as De Soto's discovery of the 'mystery of capital' and the insights of the new institutional economics school more broadly, become more visible and increasingly intertwined in the literature of the development

---

15 Sen's recent book, *The Argumentative Indian* is an elaboration of this claim which tries to destabilize the notion of Athens as the cradle of democracy by finding the same and 'properly universal' values in other, older places, including Akbar's Court, etc (see generally Sen, 2005).

16 This resonates with the many Third World responses to international law which have tried to make use of the universal potential of international law both by encouraging broader participation in its formation, and by arguing for a discovery of the 'truly' universal through a more multi-ethnic enquiry. It is carried on in the present day by scholars such as Christopher Weeramantry and Shelly Wright (see, for example, Wright, 2001; Weeramantry, 2004. See also Pahuja, 2004; and see generally the introduction of this volume).

17 He asserts, for example that he does not want 'at all to argue against the unique importance of each culture, but rather to plead in favour of the need for some sophistication in understanding cross-cultural influences ...' (Sen, 1999, p. 244).

18 For an expanded illustration of this kind of thinking and how it relates to gender and development, see Nussbaum (1992).

19 Another prominent exponent of this approach is Martha Nussbaum (see, for example, Nussbaum, 2000).

institutions and beyond, from the late 1990s onwards.[20] The respective and combined influence of each of these ways of thinking has had the effect of significantly expanding the content of law and rights within the development project as a whole[21] and has manifested itself in an increasing attention by the Bank, particularly, to human rights (World Bank, 1998). Whether 'merely' rhetorical or not, this marks something new.

A key site of this expansion is the World Bank's comprehensive development framework (CDF) introduced by Bank President James Wolfensohn in 1999 (Wolfensohn, 1999). The CDF takes a significant step in the direction of an integrated approach to development which is not incompatible with the position taken by Sen. The nascent implementation of ideas of development as freedom produces a necessarily expanded understanding of the role and content of law and rights in development, as well as law's closer integration with the meaning of 'development' itself. In a paper given in the context of the CDF, Sen argues that law and legal institutions bear a similar relationship to development as 'freedom' does in that there is both an intrinsic and instrumental reason for 'legal development' in which legal development cannot be considered to be extrinsic to development per se (Sen, 2000, 2, p. 5). But 'freedom' also bears a relationship to law and legal institutions which is similar to the relationship which, for Sen, it (freedom) bears to development. This relationship is one in which an emphasis on freedom requires that we do not consider the end point of development to be achieved when a (positive) law is enacted or an institution created, but when people have the capabilities to 'realize' those rights. One example Sen gives is of laws which might promote gender equity, but which for him, might remain 'unrealized' if, for example, most women are illiterate. The difference between the emphasis on institution building versus an emphasis on measuring capabilities (and therefore freedoms) is for Sen, the point of both difference and intersection between his approach and that taken in the CDF (Sen, 2000, p. 23).

Thus, for Sen, just as 'legal development' bears an integral relation to development, so do freedoms bear an integral relation to legal development without which they (freedoms) cannot be realized. In the CDF, as in Bank policy generally, this approach translates into an inclusion within the purview of the development agenda of 'the social, structural and human agenda' (Wolfensohn, 1999, p. 3). This

---

20   Both figures have been personally influential at the Bank and the Fund as well as in wider international circles. Indeed, both James Wolfensohn, then World Bank President and Joseph Stiglitz, then World Bank Chief Economist often site Sen as a source of intellectual inspiration, offering his expanded conception of development as a basis for their own. As for De Soto, the Bank has been involved in funding the projects of the Institute for Liberty and Democracy (ILD) of which De Soto is founder and President. See http://web. worldbank.org/wbsite/external/news/0,,contentmdk:20055477~menuPK:-1~pagePK:3437 0~piPK:34424~theSitePK:4607,00.html;   http://web.worldbank.org/wbsite/external/news/ 0,,contentmdk:20019937~menuPK:34460~pagePK:34370~piPK:34424,00.html.   See   also references to De Soto on the IMF website at http://www.imf.org/external/pubs/ft/fandd/2003/12/ pdf/people.pdf; http://www.imf.org/external/pubs/ft/fandd/2001/03/desoto.htm.

21   On the influence of Sen on the rights-based approach to development, see for example, Hamm 2001; Sano 2000. On the influence of De Soto, see for example Manji, 2003; Upham 2002; Kennedy 2003,17; Davis 2006.

agenda not only mandates an expanded domain for development, but requires a closer, more integrated relation with 'the regional development banks, members of the UN system, and other partners in development [and which is also] essential for the IMF which cannot and does not prescribe in a vacuum' (Wolfensohn, 1999, p. 3). Specifically in relation to law and rights, the legacy of both Sen and De Soto is to render integral to development '[a]n effective Legal and Justice System' of which Wolfensohn says in the CDF, '[w]ithout the protection of human and property rights, and a comprehensive framework of laws, no equitable development is possible (Wolfensohn, 1999, pp. 10–11). Further, Sen's emphasis on political freedoms translates into notions of 'broadly participatory processes' (such as 'voice', openness and transparency) which Stiglitz, then Chief Economist and Senior Vice President of the Bank, argued in a paper on the CDF, 'promote truly successful long term development' (Stiglitz, 1999, p. 2).

By the time of the Millennium Development Goals (MDGs), now 'the most prominent initiative on the development agenda' (Alston, 2005, p. 755), not only was the understanding of complementarity rather than conflict between market and state embedded as the new development orthodoxy, but human rights make a significant appearance in the preamble, if not as one of the goals themselves. As Alston has observed, the term 'human rights' makes eight appearances in the text of the *Millennium Declaration*,[22] in which human rights are closely related to democracy and the rule of law. The 147 heads of state and government making the declaration proclaim, for example, that '[w]e will spare no effort to promote democracy and strengthen the rule of law, as well as respect for all internationally recognized human rights.'[23] This declaration and the documents it has generated are not only evidence of a new development orthodoxy in which the meaning of 'development' has yet again expanded, but also marks the burgeoning trend toward institutional integration and coordination between the Bretton Woods and UN based organizations (see, for example, Piron and O'Neil, 2005) – institutions with important differences in voting structure and which, arguably, have maintained at least some productive oppositionality until now. UN Secretary General Kofi Annan, for example, has asserted that the MDGs have 'transformed the face of global development cooperation' and have 'generated unprecedented, coordinated action' on the part of the international monetary fund (IMF), the World Bank, the UN, the

---

22 United Nations, *UN Millennium Development Goals*, available at www.un.org/ millenniumgoals/. The MDGs derive from the Millennium Declaration, a statement adopted by the UN General Assembly in 2000, attended by 147 Heads of State: *United Nations Millennium Declaration*, GA Res 55/2, UN GAOR, 55th sess, Supp 49, UN Doc A/RES/55/2 (8 September 2000), available at www.un.org/millenium/declaration/ares552e.htm.

23 *United Nations Millennium Declaration*, GA Res 55/2, UN GAOR, 55th sess, Supp 49, UN Doc A/RES/55/2 (8 September 2000), available at www.un.org/millenium/declaration/ ares552e.htm; *Implementation of the United Nations Millennium Declaration: Report of the Secretary-General*, UN GAOR, 59th sess, Agenda Item 56, UN Doc A/59/282 (27 August 2004) at [39].

major donors of aid and development assistance and the developing countries at which the goals are targeted.[24]

Post-millennial examples of both the new development, and the new law-in-development, also abound. The Bank's *World Development Report 2002, Building Institutions for Markets* (World Bank, 2002) is but one example. Additionally, the IMF's *World Economic Outlook 2003* (IMF, 2003) not only evinces the shift in development orthodoxy already remarked upon, but includes a broad range of areas within the definition of 'institutions', most of which relate to the role and content of law in development. This definition bears the distinctive traces of the influence of both the 'welfarists' and the 'new institutional economists'.[25] The three 'relatively newly developed and broad measures of institutions', for example, include 'an aggregate governance index', a 'measure of property rights' and 'a variable measuring the "constraint on the executive"'. The 'aggregate governance index' is itself the average of six measures, including (1) 'voice and accountability' defined as 'the extent to which citizens can choose their governments, political rights, civil liberties and independent press; and (5) rule of law – the protection of persons and property against violence or theft, independent and effective judges and contract enforcement (IMF, 2003, p. 120). The 'measure of property rights' indicates 'the degree of protection that private property receives' (IMF, 2003, p. 120) and is incorporated twice – once within the 'aggregate governance index' and once as its own measure.

Widening the Pedagogical Purview and Subordinating Politics to Economics, or why Integration Leads to the Transformation of Rights into Regulation

Struggles over the meaning of the rule of law in the context of development have resulted in the emergence of content-rich, highly specific understandings of 'law' within the law-in-development debate. This has manifested itself in the inclusion of human rights, including civil and political rights, property rights, contractual rights and a whole raft of other substantive areas of law, within the meaning of 'law' in the way it is used within development institutions. Arguably, this coalescence is part of a wider and ever more frequently observed integration and cooperation between the various branches and institutions of international law (Cassese, 2001, p. 45) – an event uniformly interpreted both as something new (see, for example, Cassese, 2001, p. 45) and, as I suggested earlier, something to be welcomed.[26]

---

24 *Implementation of the United Nations Millennium Declaration: Report of the Secretary-General*, UN GAOR, 59th sess, Agenda Item 56, UN Doc A/59/282 (27 August 2004) at [39].

25 In this document the IMF is itself relying on a document which has been widely used and cited throughout the development institutions in relation to measuring the effectiveness of the rule of law as development strategy (this document is Kaufmann and Zoido-Laboton, 1999).

26 In my wider argument made elsewhere, this 'convergence' is not new but the coming to light of a process embedded in the structures of the contemporary international legal order

In contrast to this optimistic understanding, it is my argument that this convergence is problematic at best, and offers us little or no cause to believe that 'human rights' or other politically orientated elements of the rule of law will somehow temper what is arguably the violence of the development project. Instead, in my argument, unpacking the 'new', 'holistic', 'converged' version of law being promulgated by the International Financial Institutions (IFIs) and the consequent integration of development and human rights reveals the transformation of a domain of 'rights' into a rationality or form of ordering we might heuristically think of as 'regulatory'. This transformation has three aspects. The first is that the expanded meaning of law in development and the integration of development and rights has contributed to legitimizing (even legalizing) extensions of the IFI's field of surveillance and intervention within the Third World. The second is that the 'holistic' turn is a manifestation of the spread of 'economics imperialism' as the disciplinary expansion of economics to encompass and subordinate the social, cultural and political to its logic. And the third is that the turn to integration facilitates the juridification and instrumentalization of law and rights to expressions of normative orthodoxy – a negation of the possibility for political contestation which the symbolic valence of those concepts may otherwise carry. The cumulative effect of these three features of the holistic turn is the transformation of rights into regulation. The transformation means that human rights in development are eviscerated of whatever political potential they may have had, becoming sites in which international law can be seen to be imperially operative. That imperium is principally manifest as the generation and maintenance of a particular content for the universal, a content which in this instance is both occidental and captured by economic logic. This containment of the universal through law produces a paradox in which law loses its 'legal' quality, rights lose their 'political' quality, and both become nothing more than a combination of rule(s) and violence – a combination arguably surfacing in current events.

Legitimizing Regulatory Expansion in the Third World

Expansions in the meaning of law-in-development have been a significant factor in cloaking expansions of Fund and Bank conditionality and surveillance in legitimacy. Conditionality is a means through which developmental orthodoxies are made to carry not only normative but also juridical force. And as I have argued elsewhere, conditionality emanating from both the Bank and the Fund has ramifications well beyond their sphere of lending by virtue of their respective roles as a knowledge producer about development (see generally Buchanan and Pahuja, 2004) and as a surveillance mechanism upon which many other development institutions, commercial lenders, state creditors and state and multilateral aid agencies piggyback (see generally Pahuja, 2000. On the incipient extension to non-debtors, see Coffey, 2005). Indeed, not only is it increasingly difficult for states in the Third World to obtain credit unless they subject themselves to some form of Fund/Bank monitoring and comply with their received wisdom (see, for example, Kelsey, 2006), but it

---

since its inception, a process we might call the operationalization of the universal by a ruling rationality – a rationality which is both occidental and increasingly economic in orientation.

seems this requirement is now being extended beyond credit to aid relations, even when debt is rejected by the state in question (Timor Leste is one such example: see Coffey, 2005).

The legitimation of this expanded conditionality occurs in two ways. The first is by providing a method seemingly to circumvent the prohibition on interference in the political affairs of borrowing states through claiming a causal relevance for law in the development project. The second is that once incorporated by the development project, the notion of law then has the capacity to expand to incorporate much of the 'social.'[27]

The Bank and the Fund each have in their respective articles of agreement a prohibition on interfering in the internal politics of borrowing states. The Bank's Articles contain two explicit expressions of its ostensibly non-political character. The first is Article III Section 5(b), which provides that the Bank should lend 'without regard to political or other non-economic influences or considerations'.[28] The second is Article IV Section 10, which expressly prohibits the Bank from engaging in political activity.[29] Similarly, in its Articles, the Fund is exhorted to 'respect the domestic social and political policies of members'[30] in its obligation to exercise surveillance over exchange rates,[31] and although it lacks the explicit prohibition to which the Bank is subject, authoritative interpretations of the Fund's remit have acknowledged such a restriction (such interpretations have included that of Sir Joseph Gold, former General Counsel of the Fund. See Morais, 2000). However, if these provisions ever were respected, and putting to one side the ideological nature of the economics/politics distinction (Wood, 1981), it is clear that the (re)turn to law in development has had the operative effect of authorizing a considerable expansion of the Bretton Woods Institutions' legitimate sphere of interest (see, for example, Rittich, 2004, p. 232). Similarly, human rights and 'governance' have both extended the purview of the Bank, again by an ostensible 'depoliticization' of those matters through an asserted relation between them and the facilitation of development.[32]

---

27 There is a third potential axis of expansion which would arguably be engaged were attempts further to integrate development with other branches of international law to be successful. This is the integration and extension of surveillance and monitoring which would result if the practice of the multitudinous monitoring bodies, both state and multilateral, treaty and non-treaty based, were all to be refracted through the MDGs – a practice as yet barely incipient but with highly influential proponents (see, for example, Alston, 2005, 814–825).

28 *Articles of Agreement of the International Bank for Reconstruction and Development*, opened for signature 22 July 1944, 2 UNTS 134 Article III(5)(b) (entered into force 27 December 1945).

29 *Articles of Agreement of the International Bank for Reconstruction and Development*, opened for signature 22 July 1944, 2 UNTS 134 (1947) Article IV(10) (entered into force 27 December 1945).

30 *Articles of Agreement of the International Monetary Fund*, opened for signature 22 July 1944, 2 UNTS 39, Article IV(3)(b) (entered into force 27 December 1945).

31 There is no express term in the Articles relating to conditionality. On the initiation of, legal basis for and genealogy of conditionality, see Pahuja (2000).

32 For example, Jean-Michel Severino, the Bank's former Vice-President for East Asia and the Pacific, said, referring to Indonesia, that '[i]t is very clear that if we came to a

The nature of the self-authorization effected by asserting a causal relation to development of matters previously regarded as political is evident in statements by James Wolfensohn, former Bank President, as well as Ibrahim Shihata, former Bank General Counsel. Wolfensohn, for example, when admitting that 'just three years ago ... the word "corruption" was never mentioned at the World Bank', pushed aside the warning 'not to talk about the "c" word' with the assertion that 'there was no way to deal with the issue of equity and poverty and development without tackling the question of corruption' (see generally Marquette, 2004, p. 419). So instead of being inhibited by the prohibition being urged upon him, he came out in his Annual Meeting speech and said 'corruption is ... not political but it is social and it is economic and, therefore, I am allowed to talk about it. And if ... politicians think that it is political, that is not my problem. I think it is social and economic. Therefore, I can talk about it.' (Wolfensohn, 2000).

Such redefinition of political issues through connecting them causally to economic growth not only provides a means to circumvent the prohibition on interfering in the internal politics of member states, but also assists in the emasculation of the potentially *international* effect of those concepts. This emasculation helps to stabilize an occidentally generated meaning for these concepts which make a claim to universality. In other words, the overt subsumption within development of notions such as corruption, human rights and the rule of law not only depoliticizes them and authorizes their inclusion with the terrain of IFI intervention, but effectively removes their teeth as concepts which could bite *between* nations, or indeed, between debtor member states and the international organizations themselves.[33] In the past, the Bank for example, has used the prohibition on interfering in politics specifically to avoid the issues of both corruption and human rights. This invocation happened in relation to charges that the Bank's own policies were violating human rights, particularly economic and social rights (see, for example, Anghie, 2004, pp. 225–226); that the Bank was lending to regimes which violated human rights, especially political and civil rights (the most notorious case being that of South Africa under Apartheid); and that the Bank was lending to corrupt regimes which were obviously siphoning off much of the money being lent (Marquette, 2004, p. 414). The Bank's response to each of these charges was that it was not mandated to deal with 'political' matters. However when these matters were recast as integral to *development*, they were no longer externally operative as between states, or between debtors and the IFIs, but as *internal* to the states of the Third World. Moreover, subjected to an economic logic within that discourse, the Bank's (and Fund's) engagement with them became containable as they began to operate as axes of intervention *within* debtor states

---

situation where these governance, democracy and human rights goals were not present in the government, I don't see how there could be any financial, political or technical support from the international community': 'World Bank Ties $ 4.7 BLN Jakarta Support to Democracy, Rights', *Development News* 2 (2) [email newsletter].

33 Though this is complicated by the issue of the legal responsibility of organizations. As Suzuki and Nanwani observe, responsibility of international organizations was added to the work programme of the International Law Commission only in 2000 (Suzuki and Nanwani, 2005, 178).

and were rendered impotent as axes of criticism of the Bank's own conduct. This depoliticization and subjection to economic logic leads us to the second feature of the ostensibly 'holistic' turn and its 'regulatory' effect.

Economics Imperialism

Arguably, both the new institutional economics school and the welfarist approach have contributed to the expansion of economic logic as a way to understand the societies in which they intervene. If De Soto's technology of universalization is to discover the *homo œconomicus* already resident in the gulleys and favelas, then Sen has discovered the same man also to be the enlightenment's *homo politicus* as the basis for asserting the already-universal quality of the values he elevates. This discovery mirrors shifts in the discipline of economics more broadly (see Fine, 2002, p. 2059)[34] which are having significant ramifications in the social sciences and can be felt in institutions full of both such graduands.[35] These shifts not only suppose the autonomous, rational, utility maximizing individual, but now, like Sen and De Soto, find him everywhere, even where his behaviour would contradict the discovery of him as such. For in all of those 'new' fields of economics, what is crucial is that 'non-economic or non-market behaviour is now understood as rational, i.e. individual optimizing behaviour, response to market imperfections' (Fine, 2002, p. 2060). Thus the approach of the 'old' economics was to 'deny the social other than as an aggregation over individuals or as externally given and unexplained' (Fine, 2002, p. 2069). However, through the expansion of the notion of market imperfection these new versions of economics understand the social – and what would otherwise be thought of as 'non-rational behaviour as in customs, trust and norms' and collective social structures such as institutions and the states – as 'appropriate in [the] face of informational, and hence market imperfections' (Fine, 2002, p. 2060). As Fine has observed, these 'simple analytical devices ... expand the capacity of economics to colonize the social sciences' (Fine, 2002, p. 2060) which, because of their formality and abstraction, apply in principle to any non-market, and therefore imperfect, situation. This makes possible the interpretation of people's behaviour as timeless, rootless and optimizing and 'located in history and society only by virtue of the preceding optimizing behaviour of their ancestors' (Fine, 2002, p. 2060). According to this logic, 'the social is the non-market response to market imperfections' (Fine, 2002, p. 2060). This approach provides the analytical tools to do what the old economics did, but in relation to a much expanded sphere of life. For the newly broadened theoretical agenda of development economics still operates 'within the same narrow, reductionist framework of its neo-liberal predecessor' (Fine, Lapavistas and Pincus, 2001, p. xv). As Gary Becker, a Chicago School economist, observes of Milton Friedman during the inexorable rise of economics as the master-

---

34 Fine argues that this shift is present in the new institutional economics, the new economic sociology, the new political economy, the new growth theory, the new labour economics, the new development economics, etc.

35 On the shift from institutions full of economists to institutions turning toward engaging political and social scientists, see Guilhot 2005.

discipline, 'he revitalized my interest in economics and made me see that you can attack social problems with economics. I did not have to move out of economics to deal with relevant problems' (cited in Guilhot, 2005, p. 203). The result, therefore, is not to produce a more heterodox economics, but 'a more aggressive *neo-classical* economics that now possesses the self-confidence ... to [extend] its colonising mission ...' (Fine, Lapavistas and Pincus, 2001, p. xv, emphasis in original.), And in the context engaged in here, with the capacity for juridically enforceable transformation.

The Instrumentalization of Law and Rights to Normative Hegemony

It is clear from recent publications that within the mainstream development institutions, expansions in the meaning of law and the inclusion of rights have not prevented a concerted effort to instrumentalize law. Indeed, as law has been given more scope in this context, so has the scope for instrumentalization grown. By 'instrumentalization' I mean that an effort is made to engage law and rights as essentially in the service of some higher value to which they are subordinate and which they are used to effect or bring about. The relevance of law has now been confirmed within the development orthodoxy[36] as 'play [ing] a critical and all-pervasive role' (Wolfensohn, 2003, p. xi) and attention has turned to 'advanc [ing] the debate through new empirical analysis and ... com [ing] to some conclusions that might be relevant for policymakers' (IMF, 2003, p. 96)[37] as to which 'institutions' (defined, following North, as 'the rules of the game' (IMF, 2003, p. 97; see generally the work of Douglas North including North, 1990)) may be regarded as 'good', in the sense of 'establishing an incentive structure that reduces uncertainty and promotes efficiency – hence contributing to strong economic performance' (IMF, 2003, p. 97). The dual notions of reducing uncertainty and contributing to strong economic performance cast law's importance in two forms. The first is in terms of producing efficiency and economic growth, the second is to suggest that 'certainty' or confidence in a legal system is causally related to growth. The invocation of confidence alludes to the view, deeply embedded within development economics, that foreign investment is of crucial importance to economic growth. Both of these reasons for law's instrumental importance pepper the recent literature. For just two pertinent examples, in the *Global Monitoring Report 2004* (World Bank and IMF Development Committee, 2004, p. ix) – a text written jointly by the Bank and the Fund as the first annual assessment of 'the implementation of policies and actions for achieving the Millennium Development

---

36 This is ironic to say the least, considering the China paradox in which China, a country typically understood in the West as having no rule of law to speak of, has recently undergone extreme economic growth. Contrary to development pundits, the absence of the rule of law does not seem to have created any significant disincentives for foreign investors either, as they have been scrambling over each other to invest in China's expanding economy. To compound the irony, if the MDG goals to halve poverty are met by 2015, it will probably be because of China's rapid growth, perhaps added only to that of India.

37 Given that it is the IMF suggesting that such matters might be 'of relevance to policymakers', it is not unreasonable to think that they will soon find their way into Bank and Fund conditionality if they have not already.

Goals' – law makes two overt appearances. First, improving governance (which it later becomes clear encompasses 'democracy and political governance' as well as the 'rule of law'; World Bank and IMF Development Committee, 2004, 89) is said to 'cut across the reform agenda' (World Bank and IMF Development Committee, 2004, 5) and is 'a key element of the enabling environment for economic growth. Better governance produces better growth outcomes. Growth, in turn, contributes to the reduction of income poverty and to other MDGs' (World Bank and IMF Development Committee, 2004, 81). Further, specific mention of the rule of law appears in the 'Overview' section as part of the subheading 'Reducing Regulation, Strengthening Institutions, especially Property Rights, Rule of Law', tellingly part of the section called 'Improving Private Sector Enabling Environment' (World Bank and IMF Development Committee, 2004, p. 6). In this section, the authors argue that 'a key area of reform is the strengthening of property rights and of institutions that establish and enforce the rule of law, including legal and judicial reform and the reduction of bureaucratic harassment' (World Bank and IMF Development Committee, 2004, p. 7). Both of these appearances cast law's importance in terms of producing economic growth and facilitating private investment. Second, 'serious shortcomings ... in property rights and rule based governance' are perceived to create an environment which 'deters investors, both domestic and foreign' (World Bank and IMF Development Committee, 2004, 7). This echoes the IMF's *World Economic Outlook* which asserts that assessments of institutions defined expansively to include rule of law, political rights, corruption, governance etc., 'may play a major role in determining a country's ability to attract and retain investment flows' (World Bank and IMF Development Committee, 2004, p. 97). This alludes to the perceived importance of law and rights in creating investor confidence.

Why Does Integration Lead to the Instrumentalization of Law and Rights?

But what does this mean for our enquiry here? To put it simply, the problem this poses is that if in order to be law – that is, distinguishable from regulation in the sense of 'rules' combined with a coercive power to enforce them – law must be capable of change (see generally Fitzpatrick, 2001; Derrida, 2002; Koskenniemi, 2003; Koskenniemi, 2005; Pahuja, 2005) then instrumentalizing law to an economic project, as the rule of law as development strategy attempts to do, creates a paradox. That paradox is that if the project succeeds on its own terms, it fails in broader terms, and if it fails on its own terms, it succeeds on broader terms. In other words, if the efforts to instrumentalize law succeed in rendering 'law' abject in the service of 'growth', economic growth would then operate as a transcendent value limiting law's content. This would precisely kill what in a political sense is law's necessary illimitability or capacity for radical change. This capture would thereby perform a kind of reverse alchemy in which auriferous law becomes leaden rules. This may facilitate an authoritarianism of a kind, possibly a rule *by* law, or more exactly a rule by rules, but not, in any sense, a rule of *law*.[38] This would therefore be a failure to subordinate 'law'. Alternatively, the impossibility of containment will reassert itself, refusing law's entry into servitude, bringing the productive instability of law – and so politics – right to the heart of development and negating the possibility of law's containment by growth as a goal. This would amount to a failure to subordinate law. The immediate question arising from the argument being run in this chapter, then, is whether the inclusion within the fold of the 'welfarist' or deontological approaches and the integration of development and human rights, is more likely to push in the first direction – subordinating law – or the second – enhancing the space for politics in development.

Turning first to 'holistic' notions of development, we must return to Sen's near tautology and the idea of 'freedom' as both constitutive of and instrumental to development. As raised earlier, Sen argues that freedom is both constitutive of and instrumental to development in more than the tautological sense which would be invoked if we were to regard his argument as simply one in which the definition of development must be expanded to include the freedoms Sen regards as constitutive. Instead, Sen argues that his conception is not tautological because 'the effectiveness of freedom as an instrument lies in the fact that different kinds of freedom interrelate with one another, and freedom of one type may greatly help in advancing freedoms of other types. The two roles are thus linked by empirical connections, relating to freedom of other kinds' (Sen, 1999, p. 37). It would then seem that in this argument, one kind of freedom brings other kinds of freedoms. It is in this sense that, according to Sen, the various 'freedoms' may be both instrumental and constitutive.

However this seemingly virtuous circle pretends to avoid tautology through being secretly secured by a transcendent value being placed on economic growth and the expansion of markets. Sen's notion of 'capabilities' and the way they relate integrally to the realization of freedoms ultimately boils down to access to markets and the right or opportunity to share in the benefits of economic growth. This becomes clearer still when we consider concrete manifestations of 'freedoms' such as the rights to food, shelter, water and so on. A small number of scholars has persuasively argued that these rights boil down to rights to *access* those things as commodities in a market for them (see, for example, Green, 2005)[39] rather than questioning commodification per se. This precludes supporting actions which may be directed at non-market based economic practices not centring on growth but on subsistence or survival economics, for example, which in some instances may be more effective in securing those rights, if such they be (see for example, Gibson-Graham, 2006).

---

38 One further possibility is that this subjection will enable the myth of the self-regulating market to reassert itself. And if Polanyi is correct, this will ultimately engender corrective self protection by the people subjected to the rule of the market (see Polanyi, 2001).

39 This argument applies also to the De Soto approach to the formalization of title, which assumes an already commodified relation to land and the need to recognize and regularize informal title. Both of these things have been shown by others not simply to be 'givens' in many places, particularly in Africa, and that they also have little to say about those with no land rights, even in a non-formal sense (see, for example, Manji, 2003).

This difficulty, of the inextricability of the instrumental and deontological arguments for a closer relation between human rights and development, is not confined to Sen, but is present in other equally sophisticated attempts to bring human rights to bear on development. Alston, for example, in a recent article arguing for a greater integration between human rights and the MDGs, exhibits a great deal of ambivalence about the question of instrumentalization. On one hand, he insists that human rights must not be limited to those rights which 'can be justified in economic or other instrumental terms' (Alston, 2005, p. 784). However, in attempting to make 'the MDG process ... more human rights friendly ... and human rights standards and procedures ... mobilized so as to enhance the effectiveness of the MDG initiative' (Alston, 2005, p. 800) it would seem that an instrumental character *is* being claimed for human rights in relation to development – a concept which is itself inextricably bound up with economic growth despite protestations to the contrary.

In the quest to insist that human rights are *relevant* to the MDG project, Alston moves uneasily in a position not dissimilar to that of Sen in the wish to maintain the possibility of both the instrumental and the deontological significance of human rights to the MDGs. His own example of women's economic and social rights is a good one (Alston, 2005, p. 766). In this example, he argues that,

> support by human rights groups need not involve tradeoffs by the latter .... There are many ways in which the two can reinforce one another and in which a win-win outcome is possible. Take for example the struggle to ensure that women enjoy their basic economic and social rights. It is widely accepted that these rights have not received the attention they warrant and that many governments are reluctant to treat them as full fledged human rights. The introduction of the MDG rationale for pursuing many economic and social rights brings an important instrumentalist dimension to arguments for achieving the Goals, thereby complementing the principled or normative arguments for these rights (Alston, 2005, p. 766).

This complementarity assumes that there will be no conflict between those rights and the developmental mode of the MDGs. It precludes human rights based contestation for economic equity which challenges the economic orthodoxy of the development institutions, which Alston admits concentrate on the promotion of free-markets which he accepts is legitimate given those institutions' 'self professed focus ... on ... improved economic performance' (Alston, 2005, p. 784) and are arguably disempowering in that the goal is to bureaucratize and secure the granting of those rights rather than facilitate their assertion by those who would claim them.[40]

Additionally, there are frequent references to the fact that the MDGs could be seen as incompatible with human rights but, according to Alston, they need not be. He cites with approbation the *Human Development Report* (2000), in which it was asserted that

> [h]uman development and human rights are close enough in motivation and concern to be compatible and congruous, and they are different enough in strategy and design to

---

40 On the (crucial) difference between the grant of rights by a ruler and the assertion of rights by their subjects, see, for example Rancière 2004; see also Douzinas 2000.

supplement each other fruitfully. A more integrated approach can thus bring significant rewards, and facilitate in practical ways the shared attempts to advance the dignity, well-being and freedom of individuals in general (United Nations Development Programme 2000, 19, cited in Alston, 2005, p. 762).

Their potential compatibility again lies in the production of 'freedom', invoking Sen and accepting the developmentalist vision for such freedom.

Arguably though, it is precisely in the possibility for *incompatibility* that human rights maintain whatever potentially anti-imperial quality they may possess. As Mathews has astutely observed, '[h]uman rights discourse is informed by two very different positions: one built around struggle, with rights used as a vehicle for mobilizing, the other as fundamentally legalistic, centering on the justiciability of rights' (Mathews, 2005, p. 40). As she goes on to suggest, a 'legalistic discourse' of human rights, which instrumentalization to the MDGs would produce, 'tend [s] to reduce human rights to the "technical" and "programmable"' (Mathews, 2005, 40). Arguably in this context, their capacity is diminished twofold. First, such a discourse of human rights disengages itself from structural inequality and in particular the institutional structures of the Bank and the Fund and the political economy in which conditionality, for instance, is embedded. This minimizes the politically useful oppositionality between the exercise of power in Bretton Woods institutions compared with the UN based institutions with their differential voting structures. Secondly such a discourse of rights limits the 'aspirational and strategic potential in struggles' (Mathews, 2005, p. 40) – or in the language of this volume, the symbolic valence – which human rights as a political concept offers (see generally Douzinas, 2000; Rancière, 2004). In this wish to make human rights relevant, concretized in the service of the noble goals of the MDGs, and to limit the (annoyingly) persistent abstraction of human rights, their necessary vacuity – precisely that which may give them a political horizon – is endlessly filled by development. Alston observes that certain human rights scholars have criticized the MDG project on the basis that 'it reflects a one-size fits all approach', a charge he rightly suggests can be 'leveled equally well at the universalist human rights regime' and which therefore causes him little concern because of his own avowedly universalist position. In my argument though, the problem arises precisely here in the concerted effort to make *congruent* those universalities, causing a solidification of a particular content for the universal. This entails a negation of what Žižek calls 'the precise space of politicization proper' which 'universal human rights' may amount to in their radical existence as 'the right to universalisation as such' (Žižek, 2005, p. 131, cited in Fitzpatrick, 2006, p. 16).[41] In other words, a negation of the possibility for those excluded by the value and identity being universalized to present a political challenge to dominant thought by revealing the particularity of the value being elevated to the universal.

On one level, it is my concern that with the nascent convergence between rights and development, not only will law and rights be limited to the extent of their compatibility with prevailing economic orthodoxies, but the possibility of politics

---

41 As I have argued elsewhere, this observation, about the political potential of the instability created by a universal claim for a particular content, can equally be argued to be applicable to law in general, and not only to human rights.

itself would at best be relegated to civil and political rights within a liberal-democratic system with a market economy. In other words, the implicit, and I would argue regulatory, goal of developmental transformation as the production of sameness or the replication of the occidental state, surfaces and intensifies. However, this brings us back to the paradox of instrumentalizing law and rights raised above. For just as there is an aporia between human rights as symbol and (positive) human rights (law) as codified both domestically and internationally, so is there always a gap between the symbolic valence of Law as a political concept (and the relation to justice which that implies) and the codified law 'on the books'. That aporia or gap is precisely the space of politics offered by law and by human rights.

My concern is that if the necessary politics of law, and indeed rights, is ostensibly contained, then that politics will 'out' in some other way. The necessity for sameness driving the instrumentalization will produce either an interventionism of increasing violence, or difference will necessarily reside outside legality, in the manner of the outlaw state beyond law's jurisdiction, or by extension, the denial of rights to those held at Guantánamo Bay. Unfortunately, neither of these possibilities seems to be contradicted by recent events, most notably the war on terror and interventions in the name of 'democratization'. Either way, this enquiry would seem to place us at the doorstep of a much larger question, which is whether the attempt to instrumentalize law and rights is part of the current trajectory of international law in which the transformative project directed toward states outside the 'developed' world is being conducted with ever increasing violence.

Bibliography

AFL-CIO (2004), '13th Annual Report on Occupational Safety'. www.afl-cio.org.

Ali, T. (2003), *The Clash of Fundamentalisms: Crusades, Jihads and Modernity* (London: Verso Press).

Alston, P. (2005), 'Ships Passing in the Night: The Current State of the Human Rights and Development Debate Seen through the Lens of the Millennium Development Goals', *Human Rights Quarterly*, 27, 755–829. [DOI: 10.1353/hrq.2005.0030]

Alston, P. and Robinson, M. (2005), 'The Challenges of Ensuring the Mutuality of Human Rights and Development Endeavours', in Alston and Robinson (eds).

—, eds. (2005), *Human Rights and Development: Towards Mutual Reinforcement* (Oxford: Oxford University Press).

Altman, A. (1990), *Critical Legal Studies: A Liberal Critique* (Princeton: Princeton University Press).

American Textile Mfrs. Inst., Inc. v Donovan (1981) 452 U.S. 490.

Anaya, J.S. (2004), *Indigenous Peoples in International Law* (New York: Oxford University Press).

Anghie, A. (2004), 'International Financial Institutions', in Reus-Smit (ed.).

Annan, K. (2005), *Larger Freedom: Towards Development, Security and Human Rights for All – Report of the Secretary-General, UN Doc A/59/2005 (21 March 2005)*.

Ansell, C. and Vogel, D., eds. (2006), *The Contested Governance Of European Food Safety* (Boston: MIT Press).

Bachrach, P. and Baratz, M. (1963), 'Decisions and Non-decisions: An Analytical Framework', *American Political Science Review*, 57, 632–642. [DOI: 10.2307/1952568]

Bacow, L. (1980), *Bargaining for Job Safety and Health* (Cambridge: MIT Press).

Baer, J. (1999), *Our Lives before the Law* (Princeton: Princeton University Press).

Bagli, C.V. (2005), 'Largesse', in Polner, R. (ed.).

Baldwin, R. and Cave, M. (1999), *Understanding Regulation: Theory, Strategy and Practice* (Oxford: Oxford University Press).

Bardach, E. and Kagan, R. (1982), *Going by the Book: The Problem of Regulatory Unreasonableness* (Philadelphia: Temple University Press).

Barlett, B. (2006), *Impostor: How George W. Bush Bankrupted America and Betrayed the Reagan Legacy* (New York: Doubleday).

Barstow, D. (22 December 2003), 'U.S. Rarely Seeks Charges for Deaths in Workplace', *New York Times*, A1.

Bartley, N.V. (1969), *The Rise of Massive Resistance: Race and Politics in the South During the 1950s* (Louisiana: Baton Rouge).

Bastone, W. (1997), 'Quality of (Night)life Issues', *The Village Voice*, 42(7), 36–37.

Baumle, A.K. and Fossett, M. (2005), 'Statistical Discrimination in Employment: Its Practice, Conceptualization, and Implications for Public Policy', *American Behavioral Scientist*, 48, 1250–1274. [DOI: 10.1177/0002764205274818]

Baym, N.K. (2000), *Tune in, Log onLog On: Soaps, Fandom, and Online Community* (Thousand Oaks, Calif.: Sage Publications).

Beckfield, J. (2003), 'Inequality in the World Polity: The Structure of International Organization', *American Sociological Review*, 68, 401–424. [DOI: 10.2307/1519730]

Black, J. (2001), 'Proceduralizing Regulation: Part II', *Oxford Journal of Legal Studies*, 21, 33–58. [DOI: 10.1093/ojls%2F21.1.33]

— (2002), Critical Reflections on Regulation in CARR Discussion Paper, DP 4.

— (2002), 'Critical Reflections on Regulation', *Australian Journal of Legal Philosophy*, 27, 1–37.

Blomley, N. (2003), 'Law, Property, and the Geography of Violence: The Frontier, the Survey, and the Grid', *Annals of the Association of American Geographers*, 93(1), 121–141. [DOI: 10.1111/1467-8306.93109]

Bourdieu, P. and Thompson, J. (1991), *Language and Symbolic Power* (Cambridge, MA: Harvard University Press).

Boyle, E.H. and Meyer, J.W. (1998), 'Modern Law as a Secularized and Global Religious Model: Implications for the Sociology of Law', *Soziale Welt*, 49, 213–232.

Boyle, E.H., Songora, F. and Foss, G. (2001), 'International Discourse and Local Politics: Anti-Female-Genital-Cutting Laws in Egypt, Tanzania, and the United States', *Social Problems*, 48, 524–544. [DOI: 10.1525/sp.2001.48.4.524]

Braithwaite, J. (1985), *To Punish or Persuade: Enforcement Of Coal Mine Safety* (Albany: State University of New York Press).

Braudel, F. (1982), *The Wheels of Commerce* (New York: Harper and Rowe).

Brenner, N. and Theodore, N. (2002), 'Cities and the Geographies of "Actually Existing Neoliberalism"', *Antipode*, 34(3), 349–379. [DOI: 10.1111/1467-8330.00246]

Breyer, S. (1982), *Regulation and its Reform* (Cambridge: Harvard University Press).

Bridges, R.L. and Nelson, W.P. (1999), *Legalizing Gender Inequality: Courts, Markets and Unequal Pay for Women in America* (New York: Cambridge University Press).

Brown, W. (2000), 'Suffering Rights as Paradoxes', *Constellations*, 7(2), 230–241. [DOI: 10.1111/1467-8675.00183]

Brysk, A. (2000), *From Tribal Village to Global Village: Indian Rights and International Relations in Latin America* (Stanford: Stanford University Press).

Buchanan, P. (1992), Republican National Convention Speech, Houston, Texas, 17 August 1992.

Buchanan, R. and Pahuja, S. (2004), 'Legal Imperialism, Empire's Invisible Hand?', in Dean and Passavant (eds.).

Buckley, W.F., Jr (1985), 'End Reverse Discrimination', *National Review*, 20 September 1985, 17–18.

— (1988a), 'Everything Goes Under Civil Rights', *National Review*, 13 May 1988, 69.

— (1988b), 'Doubletalk on Civil Rights', *National Review*, 29 April 1988, 57.

— (1994), 'Starting Again in California', *National Review*, 7 February 1994, 78–79.

— (1996), 'For Dole: The Educational Challenge', *National Review*, 30 September 1996, 74–75.

— (1998), 'Answer Me, Yes or No', *National Review*, 26 January 1998, 58.

— (2003), 'Civil Rights Pandemonium', *National Review*, 27 January 2003, 57.

Bureau of Labour Statistics (2004), Press Release, Union Members Summary, (published online 27 January 2005) http:// stats.bls.gov/news76elease/union2. NR0.htm

Burger, J. (1987), *Report from the Frontier: The State of the World's Indigenous Peoples* (London: Zed Books).

Bush, G.W. (2001), 'Statement on the Anniversary of the Americans with Disabilities Act of 1990', 26 July 2001, . http://findarticles.com/p/articles/mi_m2889/is_30_37/ai_77875883, Last Accessed on 15 November 2006.

— (2006), 'Remarks on Signing the Fannie Lou Hamer, Rosa Parks, and Coretta Scott King Voting Rights Act Reauthorization and Amendments Act of 2006', 27 July 2006, . http://www.gop.com/News/Read.aspx?ID=6448; Last Accessed 15 November 2006.

Cain, M. (1979), 'Trends in the Sociology of Police Work', *International Journal of the Sociology of Law*, 7, 143.

Calabresi, G. and Melamed, A.D. (1972), 'Property Rules, Liability Rules and Inalienability: One View of the Cathedral', *Harvard Law Review*, 85, 1089–1128.

Canadian Broadcasting Corporation, 'Axworthy Casts Lot with Inuit on Climate Change' (8 December 2005). www.cbc.ca/north/story/inuit-axworth-08122005. html, Accessed on 18 May 2006.

Carter, D.T. (1995), *The Politics of Rage: George Wallace, the Origins of the New Conservatism, and the Transformation Of American Politics* (New York: Simon & Schuster).

Cassese, A. (2001), *International Law* (Oxford: Oxford University Press).

Chevigny, P. (1991), *Gigs: Jazz and the Cabaret Laws in New York City* (New York: Routledge).

Chibundu, M.O. (1997), 'Law in Development: On Tapping, Gourding and Serving Palm-Wine', *Case Western Reserve Journal of International Law*, 29, 167.

Chossudovsky, M. (1997), *The Globalisation of Poverty: Impacts of IMF and World Bank Reforms* (London: Zed Books).

Christopherson, M. (1994), 'The Fortress City: Privatized Spaces, Consumer Citizenship', in Amin, A. (ed.).

Cingranelli, D.L. (1988), *Human Rights: Theory and Measurement* (New York: St Martin's Press).

Civil Rights Act (1964), *Title VII*, 42 U.S.C. § 2000e.

Clague, C. (1997), *Institutions and Economic Development: Growth and Governance in Less-Developed and Post-Socialist Countries* (Maryland: Johns Hopkins Press).

Clark, D.L. (2002), 'The World Bank and Human Rights: The Need for Greater Accountability', *Harvard Human Rights Journal*, 15, 205.

Clinton, B. (2002), 'Address to the British Labour Party Conference', *October*, 2002. http://politics.guardian.co.uk/labour2002 (cited in Manji 2003).

Coates, K.S. (2004), *A Global History of Indigenous Peoples: Struggle and Survival* (New York: Palgrave Macmillan).

Coffey, L. (2005), '"To Govern Our Own Destiny": Sovereignty, Debt and the International Institutions in Timor-Leste' (unpublished manuscript, written December 2005 in partial satisfaction of the requirements of the Master of Laws degree, University of Melbourne) (copy on file with the author).

Collins, H. (1999), *Regulating Contracts* (Oxford: Oxford University Press).

Comprehensive Regulatory Reform Act (1995)*S*. 343, 104th U.S. Congress.

Convention on Biological Diversity, Multilateral Convention No30619 Concluded at Rio de Janeiro (5 June 1992).

Convention on the Elimination of All Forms of Discrimination against Women (1979). http://www.un.org/womenwatch/daw/cedaw/.

Convention on the Rights of the Child (1989). http://www.unhchr.ch/html/menu3/b/k2crc.htm.

Cover, R.M. (1983), 'The Supreme Court, 1982 Term – Foreword: *Nomos* and Narrative', *Harvard Law Review*, 97(4), 4–25.

Cowan, J.K., Dembour, M. and Wilson, R.A., eds. (2001), *Culture and Rights: Anthropological Perspectives* (Cambridge: Cambridge University Press).

Crenshaw, K. (1988), 'Race, Reform, and Retrenchment: Transformation and Legitimation in Antidiscrimination Law' *Harvard Law Review*, 101, 1331.

Daes, E.A. (1996), *'Working Paper on the Concept of "Indigenous People"'*, United Nations Economic and Social Council Commission on Human Rights, Sub-Commission on Prevention of Discrimination and Protection of Minorities, Working Group on Indigenous Populations (E/CN.4/Sub.2/Ac.4/1996/2).

Daniels, R. and Trebilcock, M. (2004), 'The Political Economy of Rule of Law Reform in Developing Countries', *Michigan Journal of International Law*, 26, 99.

Dañino, R. (2006), 'Legal Opinion on Human Rights and the Work of the World Bank', 27 January 2006, New York: World Bank.

Davis, K. and Trebilcock, M. (1999), 'What Role do Legal Institutions Play in Development?' (Draft paper prepared for the International Monetary Fund's Conference on Second Generation Reforms, 8–9 November 1999) (copy on file with the author).

Davis, M. (1992), *City of Quartz: Excavating the Future in LA* (UK: Vintage).

— (2006), *Planet of Slums* (UK: Verso).

De Soto, H. (1989), *The Other Path* (New York: Harper Collins).

— (2000), *The Mystery of Capital: Why Capitalism Triumphs in the West and Fails Everywhere Else* (London: Black Swan).

Dean, J. and Passavant, P. (2004), *Empire's New Clothes* (New York: Routledge).

Decker, K., McInerney-Lankford, S. and Sage, C. (2005), 'Human Rights and Equitable Development: "Ideals," Issues, and Implications', background Paper for the World Development Report 2006, http://siteresources.worldbank. org/INTWDR2006/Resources/477383-1118673432908/Human_Rights_and_ Equitable_Development_Ideals_Issues_and_Implications.pdf.

Department of the Environment Property Advisory Group (1981), *Planning Gain* (London: HMSO).

Derrida, J. (2002), 'Force of Law: The Mystical Foundation of Authority', in *Acts of Religion*. Derrida, J. (ed.), in Anidjar (ed.) (New York: Routledge).

Dezalay, Y. (1995), 'Professional Competition and the Social Construction of Transnational Markets' in Dezalay, Y. and Sugarman, D. (eds.), *Professional competition and professional power* (New York: Routledge).

Dicken, P. (1992), *Global Shift: Internationalization of Economic Activity* (London: Paul Chapman Publishing Ltd).

Dixon, D., Bottomley, A., Coleman, C., Gill, M. and Wall, D. (1989), 'Reality and Rules in the Construction and Regulation of Police Suspicion', *International Journal of the Sociology of Law*, 17, 185.

Douzinas, C. (2000), *The End of Human Rights: Critical Legal Thought at the Turn of the Century* (Oxford: Hart).

Drori, G., Meyer, J.W., Ramirez, F.O. and Schofer, E. (2003), *Science in the Modern World Polity: Institutionalization and Globalization* (Stanford: Stanford University Press).

Dudas, J. (2004), 'Review of "The Politics of Rights"', *Law and Politics Book Review*, 14(10), 788–793.

— (2005), 'In the Name of Equal Rights: "Special" Rights and the Politics of Resentment in Post-Civil Rights America', *Law and Society Review*, 39, 723. [DOI: 10.1111/j.1540-5893.2005.00243.x]

— (2008), *The Cultivation of Resentment: Treaty Rights and the New Right* (Palo Alto, California: Stanford University Press).

Dunlap, D.W. (1983), 'Two-thirds of City's Cabarets Violating the Fire Safety Law', *New York Times*, 28 March, 1983.

Durham Morning Herald (1956a), 'Hodges Releases School Plan Details', 15 July 1956, 1.

Durham Morning Herald (1956b), 'Text of Gov. Luther Hodges' Speech to General Assembly', 24 July 1956, 1.

Durham Morning Herald (1956c), 'Operation or Closing is Made Local Option', 15 July 1956, 1.

Durham Morning Herald (1957a), '12 Negro Families Ask Entry to White Schools', 1 September 1957, 1.

Durham Morning Herald (1957b), 'Hodges Convinced Integration Error', 4 September 1957, 1.

Dworkin, R. (1984), 'Rights as Trumps' in Waldron (ed.).

Edelman, L.B. (1992), 'Legal Ambiguity and Symbolic Structures: Organizational Mediation of Law', *American Journal of Sociology*, 97, 1531–1576. [DOI: 10.1086/229939]

Edelman, M. (1964), *The Symbolic Uses of Politics* (Chicago: University of Chicago Press).

Edgeworth, B. (2003), *Law, Modernity, Postmodernity: Legal Change in the Contracting State* (Aldershot: Ashgate).

Edsall, T.B. and Edsall, M.D. (1992), *Chain Reaction: The Impact of Race, Rights, and Taxes on American Politics* (New York: W. W. Norton and Company).

Emmett, R. (1982), 'VNET or GRIPENET', *Datamation*, 4, 48–58.

Engel, D.M. and Munger, F.W. (2003), *Rights of Inclusion: Law and Identity in the Life Stories of Americans with Disabilities* (Chicago: University of Chicago Press).

Epp, C.R. (1998), *The Rights Revolution: Lawyers, Activists, and Supreme Courts in Comparative Perspective* (Chicago: University of Chicago Press).

Epstein, C.F. (1970), 'Encountering the Male Establishment: Sex-Status Limits on Women's Careers in the Professions', *American Journal of Sociology*, 75, 6.

Espeland, W.N. (1998), *Struggle For Water: Politics, Rationality, and Identity In the American Southwest* (Chicago: University of Chicago Press).

Evans, M., ed. (2003), *International Law* (Oxford: Oxford University Press).

Ewick, P. and Silbey, S. (1998), *The Common Place of Law: Stories from Everyday Life* (Chicago, Ill.: University of Chicago Press).

Fainstein, S.S. (1994), *The City Builders: Property and Planning in London and New York* (Oxford: Blackwell).

Farber, D.A. (2002), 'Rights as Signals', *Journal of Legal Studies*, 31, 83.

— (1995), 'There's Trouble in Clubland', *Daily News (New York)*, May, 15 (1995).

Feagin, J. and Eckberg, D. (1980), 'Discrimination: Motivation, Action, Effects, and Context', *Annual Review of Sociology*, 6, 1–20.

Felstiner, W.L.F., Abel, R.L. and Sarat, A. (1980–81), 'The Emergence and Transformation of Disputes: Naming, Blaming, Claiming ....', *Law and Society Review*, 15, 631–654. [PubMed 11614870]

Fernback, J. (1999), 'There Is a There There: Notes Toward a Definition of Cybercommunity', in Jones, S.G. (ed.).

Fine, B. (2001), 'Neither the Washington nor the Post-Washington Consensus: An Introduction', Fine, Lapavitsas and Pincus (eds).

— (2002), 'Economics Imperialism and the New Development Economics as Kuhnian Paradigm Shift?', *World Development*, 30, 2057–2070.

Fine, B., Lapavitsas, C. and Pincus, J. (2001), 'Preface', in Fine, Lapavitsas and Pincus (eds.).

Fine, B., Lapavitsas, C. and Pincus, J., eds. (2001), *Development Policy in the Twenty-First Century: Beyond the Post-Washington Consensus* (London: Routledge).

Finholt, T. and Sproull, L. (1990), 'Electronic Groups at Work', *Organizational Science*, 1, 41–64.

Finkin, M. (2003), 'Law Reform American Style: Thoughts on a Restatement of the Law of Employment', *Labour Lawyer*, 18 (Winter/Spring), 405–416.

Fitzpatrick, P. (2001), *Modernism and the Grounds of Law* (Cambridge: Cambridge University Press).

— (2006), 'Is Humanity Enough: The Secular Theology of Human Rights' (Paper delivered at the Human Rights and Global Justice Conference, University of Warwick 29–31 March 2006) (copy on file with the author).

Fleming, S.H. (1996), 'Charting a New Course Toward Workplace Safety and Health', *Job Safety and Health Quarterly*, 7, 10.

Florio, M. (2002), 'Economists, Privatization in Russia and the Waning of the "Washington Consensus"', *Review of International Political Economy*, 9, 2, 374.

Flusty, S. (2001), 'The Banality of Interdiction: Surveillance, Control and the Displacement of Diversity', *International Journal of Urban and Regional Research*, 25, 658–664.

Ford Motor Company v Huffman (1953) 345 U.S. 330.

Fox, J.A. and Brown, D.L., eds. (1998), *The Struggle for Accountability: The World Bank, NGOs, and Grassroots Movements* (Boston: MIT Press).

Francis, S. (1993), 'Message from MARs: The Social Politics of the New Right', in Schneider, G. L. (ed.).

Frank, D.J. and Meyer, J.W. (2002), 'The Profusion of Individual Roles and Identities in the Postwar Period', *Sociological Theory*, 20, 86–105.

Frank, D.J., Hironaka, A. and Schofer, E. (2000), 'The Nation State and the Natural Environment, 1900–1995', *American Sociological Review*, 65, 96–116.

Frank, T. (2004), *What's the Matter with Kansas? How Conservatives Won the Heart Of America* (New York: Metropolitan Books).

Freedman, S. (1986), 'Musicians Taking City Cabaret Law to Court', *New York Times*, 4 June 1986, A1.

Fukuda-Parr, S. (2002), *'Operationalising Amartya Sen's Ideas on Capabibilites, Development, Freedom and Human Rights – The Shifting Policy Focus of the Human Development Approach'*, (UNDP) http://hdr.undp.org/docs/training/oxford/readings/fukuda-parr_HDA.pdf.

Fyfe, N. and Bannister, J. (1998), 'The Eyes upon the Street: Closed-Circuit Television Surveillance and the City', in Fyfe, N. (ed.).

Gall, G. (1988), *The Politics of Right to Work: The Labour Federations as Special Interests* (Westport: Greenwood Press).

Gamble, B. (1997), 'Putting Civil Rights to a Popular Vote', *American Journal of Political Science*, 41, 245–269.

Gathii, J.T. (1999), 'Good Governance as a Counterinsurgency Agenda to Transformative Social Projects in International Law', *Buffalo Human Rights Law Review*, 5, 118–174.

Gatson, S.N. and Zweerink, A. (2000), 'Choosing Community: Rejecting Anonymity in Cyberspace', *Research in Community Sociology 10, 105–137.*

— (2004), *Interpersonal Culture on the Internet: Television, the Internet, and the Making of a Community* (Lewiston: The Edwin Mellen Press, Ltd.).

Gazette, G. (2005), 'Giuliani – Savior of the City, or Its Enemy?', 8 August 2005. www.gothamgazette.com/article/20050808/202/1508.

Gearey, A. (2005), *Globalization and Law: Trade, Rights, War* (Oxford: Rowman and Littlefield).

Gibson-Graham, J.K. (2006), *A Postcapitalist Politics* (Minnesota: University of Minnesota Press).

Gillin, K. (2006), 'Whither Indigeneity? Bougainville, Secession, and the Transnational Indigenous Peoples' Movement', Macalester College, unpublished manuscript.

Gilmer v Interstate Johnson Lane Corp (1991) 500 U.S. 20.

Glendon, M.A. (1991), *Rights Talk: The Impoverishment of Political Discourse* (USA: Free Press).

Goldberg-Hiller, J. and Milner, N. (2003), 'Rights as Excess: Understanding the Politics of Special Rights', *Law and Social Inquiry*, 28, 1075–1118.

Goldstein, A. and Cohen, S. (2004), 'Bush Forces a Shift in Regulatory Thrust: OSHA Made More Business-Friendly', *Washington Post*, August 15.

Goldwater, B. (1960), 'The Conscience of a Conservative', in Schneider, G. L. (ed.).

— (1964), 'Extremism in the Defense of Liberty: The Republican National Convention Acceptance Address', in Schneider, G.L. (ed.).

— (1970), *The Conscience of a Majority* (New Jersey: Prentice-Hall).

Goluboff, R. (2003), '"We Live's in a Free House Such as it Is"': Class and the Creation of Modern Civil Rights', *University of Pennsylvania Law Review*, 151, 1977–2018.

Government Accountability Office (2004), Report. Available at http://www.gao.gov/docsearch/date.php.

Grant, M. (1982), *Urban Planning Law* (London: Sweet & Maxwell).

Green, M. (2001), 'What We Talk About When We Talk About Indicators: Current Approaches to Human Rights Measurement', *Human Rights Quarterly*, 23, 1062–1097.

Green, A. (2005), '"A Healthier Worker is a More Productive Worker": Biopower and the Present Moment of Food Security' (unpublished manuscript on file with the author).

Greenhouse, C.J., Yngvesson, B. and Engel, D.M. (1994), *Law and Community in Three American Towns* (New York: Cornell University Press).

Gregory, D. (1994), *Geographical Imaginations* (Oxford: Blackwell).

Grey, T. (1980), 'The Disintegration of Property', in Pennock and Chapman (eds).

Griggs v. v Duke Power (1971) 401 U.S. 424.

Gross, M. (1985), 'The Party Seems to Be Over for Lower Manhattan Clubs', *The New York Times*, 26 October, 1985.

Gruskin, S. and Tarantola, D. (2002), 'Human Rights and HIV/AIDS: Current Thinking and Approaches. http://hivinsite.ucsf.edu/InSite.jsp?page=kb-08-01-07.

Guilhot, N. (2005), *The Democracy Makers: Human Rights and International Order* (New York: Columbia University Press).

Haas, D.J. (2003), '*Falling Down* on the Job: Workers' Compensation Shifts from a No-Fault to a Worker-Fault Paradigm', *North Dakota Law Review*, 79, 203-287.

Hafner-Burton, E.M. and Tsutsui, K. (2005), 'Human Rights in a Globalizing World: The Paradox of Empty Promises', *American Journal of Sociology*, 110, 1373–1411.

Hagan, J. (2003), *Justice in the Balkans: Prosecuting War Crimes in The Hague Tribunal* (Chicago: University of Chicago Press).

Halliday, S. and Schmidt, P., eds. (2004), *Human Rights Brought Home: Socio-Legal Perspectives on Human Rights in the National Context* (Oxford: Hart).

Hamm, B. (2001), 'A Human Rights Approach to Development', *Human Rights Quarterly*, 23, 1005–1031.

Hampson, F., Intervention at 21st Session of Working Group on Indigenous Peoples (25 July 2003).

Harlow, C. and Rawlings, R. (1992), *Pressure Through Law* (London: Routledge).

Hart, M. (2006), 'Skepticism and Expertise: The Supreme Court and the EEOC', Fordham Law Review. 74, *March, 1937–62*.

Harvey, D. (1989a), 'From Managerialism to Entrepreneurialism: The Transformation of Urban Governance in Late Capitalism', *Geografiska Annaler*, 71B, 3–17.

— (1989b), *The Condition of Postmodernity* (Oxford: Blackwell).

— (2005), *A Brief History of Neoliberalism* (Oxford: Oxford University Press).

Hatchard, J. and Perry-Kesaris, A., eds. (2003), *Law and Development: Facing Complexity in the 21st Century* (London: Cavendish).

Hathaway, O.A. (2002), 'Do Human Rights Treaties Make a Difference?', *Yale Law Journal*, 111, 1935–2042.

Hawkins, K. (1984), *Environment and Enforcement: Regulation and the Social Definition of Pollution* (Oxford: Clarendon Press).

Henrard, K. (2002), *Minority Protection in Post-Apartheid South Africa: Human Rights, Minority Rights, and Self-Determination* (Westport: Praeger).

Henshaw, J.L. (2004), Speech by Head of OSHA, 21 April 2004.

Hertogh, M. and Halliday, S. (2004), *Judicial Review and Bureaucratic Impact: International and Interdisciplinary Perspectives* (Cambridge: Cambridge University Press).

'History of the EEOC', at http://www.eeoc.gov/abouteeoc/35th/thelaw/index.html (accessed 3 May 2006).

Hodges, L. (1962), *Businessman in the Statehouse: Six Years as Governor Of North Carolina* (Chapel Hill: University of North Carolina Press).

Hogler, R. (2005), 'The Historical Misconception of Right to Work Laws in the United States: Senator Robert Wagner, Legal Policy, and the Decline Of American Unions', *Hofstra Labour and Employment Law Journal*, 53(fall), 101–52.

Holmström, B. (1998), Courts and Democracy: the Political Role of the Judiciary in England, France and Germany, Published in Swedish as *Domstolar och demokrati – Den tredje statsmaktens politiska roll i England, Frankrike och Tyskland*, (Uppsala: Acta Universitatis Upsaliensis).

Horsley, C.B. (1978), 'The Impact of Disco Mania on Nightspots is Growing', *New York Times*, 9 July 1978, R1, R4.

— (1979), 'Zoning Controls on Discos Planned: Zoning Controls Being Planned to Cover Discos in the City', *New York Times*, 4 November 1979, R1, R8.

Horta, K. (2003), 'Rhetoric and Reality: Human Rights and the World Bank', *Harvard Human Rights Journal*, 15, 227.

Hubbard, P. and Hall, T. (1998), 'The Entrepreneurial City and the "New Urban Politics"' in Hall, T. and Hubbard, P. (eds.).

Human Rights Council (2006a), *'Human Rights Council Adopts Texts for Protection from Enforced Disappearance, Rights of Indigenous Peoples'*, (Information Service, United Nations Office at Geneva), accessed 29 June 2006.

Human Rights Council (2006b), *'Implementation of General Assembly Resolution 60/251 of 15 March 2006 Entitled "Human Rights Council"'*, (United Nations Office at Geneva) (A/HRC/1/L.3), accessed June 23 2006.

Hunter, J.D. (1991), *Culture Wars: The Struggle to Define America* (USA: Basic Books).

Huntington, S.P. (1968), Political Order in Changing Societies (New Have: Yale University Press).

Hutter, B.M. (1997), *Compliance: Regulation and Environment* (Oxford: Clarendon Press).

IBLF/IFC/UN Global Compact (2006), A Guide to Human Rights Impact Assessment, Draft http://www.unglobalcompact.org/docs/issues_doc/human_rights/2006_HRIA_draft_June1.pdf.

Implementation of the United Nations Millennium Declaration: Report of the Secretary-General, UN GAOR 59th sess, Agenda Item 56, UN Doc A/59/282 (27 August 2004).

Indus. Union Dept. v Am. Petroleum Inst. (1980) 448 (1980), 448 U.S. 607.

International Covenant on Economic, Social and Cultural Rights (1976). http://www.unhchr.ch/html/menu3/b/a_cescr.htm.

International Guidelines on HIV/AIDS and Human Rights (1997), UNHCR res. 1997/33, UN Document E/CN.4/1997/150.

International Labor Organization (1957), 'Concerning the Protection and Integration of Indigenous and Other Tribal and Semi-Tribal Populations in Independent Countries', Convention 107.

International Labor Organization (1989), 'Concerning Indigenous and Tribal Peoples in Independent Countries', 'Convention 169', http://www.unhchr.ch/html/menu3/b/62.htm.

International Monetary Fund (2003), *World Economic Outlook 2003: Growth and Institutions* (Washington, DC: International Monetary Fund) http://www.imf.org/External/Pubs/FT/weo/2003/01/pdf/front.pdf.

Inuit Circumpolar Conference (2005), 'Petition to the Inter-American Commission on Human Rights Seeking Relief from Violations Resulting from Global Warming Caused by Acts and Omissions of the United States. http://www.ciel.org/Publications/ICC_Petition_7Dec05.pdf.

Issacharoff, S. and Nelson, J. (2001), 'Discrimination with a Difference: Can Employment Discrimination Law Accommodate the Americans with Disabilities Act?', *North Carolina Law Review*, 79(January), 307–58.

Jabine, T. and Claude, R. (1992), *Human Rights and Statistics* (Philadelphia: University of Pennsylvania Press).

Jackson, K.T. (2005), 'The Second Most Effective Mayor of the 20th Century', *Gotham Gazette*. Available at http://www.gothamgazette.com/commentary/91.jackson.shtml.

Johnston, R.J. et al., eds. (2000), 'Regulation School. Available at http://www.xreferplus.com.libezproxy2.syr.edu/entry/734652.

Jolls, C. (2001), 'Antidiscrimination and Accommodation', *Harvard Law Review*, 115: December, 642–99.

Jones, S.G., ed. (1999), *Doing Internet Research: Critical Issues and Methods for Examining the Net* (Thousand Oaks, Calif.: Sage Publications).

— (1998), 'Are We Witnessing a Kinder, Gentler EEOC? The EEOC's Task Force Report on Best Private Sector EEO and Diversity Practices and Other Agency Trends', *Labour Lawyer*, 14(fall), 317–38.

Jordan, W. (2000), 'Ossification Revisited: Does Arbitrary and Capricious Review Significantly Interfere with Agency Ability to Achieve Regulatory Goals Through Informal Rulemaking?', *Northwestern University Law Review*, 94(winter), 393–450.

Jordana, J. and Levi-Faur, D., eds. (2004), *The Politics of Regulation: Institutions and Regulatory Reforms for the Age of Governance* (Cheltenham: Edward Elgar).

Judd, D. (1995), 'The Rise of the New Walled Cities', in Liggett, H. and Perry, D. (eds.).

Kagan, R. (2004), 'Regulators and Regulatory Processes' in *The Blackwell Companion to Law and Society*. Sarat, A. (ed.) (Oxford: Blackwell Publishing).

Kagan, R. and Axelrod, L. (2000), *Regulatory Encounters: Multinational Corporations and American Adversarial Legalism* (Berkeley: University of California Press).

Karst, K. (1989), *Belonging to America: Equal Citizenship and the Constitution* (New Haven: Yale University Press).

Kaufmann, D., Kraay, A. and Zoido-Laboton, P. (1999), 'Governance Matters', '(Working Paper No. 2196, World Bank)'. Available at http://www.worldbank.org/research (this report has been updated regularly since then).

Kazin, M. (1995), *The Populist Persuasion: An American History* (New York: Basic Books).

Keck, M. and Sikkink, K. (1998), *Activists Beyond Borders: Advocacy Networks in International Politics* (Ithaca: Cornell University Press).

Keck, T.M. (2004), *The Most Activist Supreme Court in History: The Road to Modern Judicial Conservatism* (Chicago, Illinois: University of Chicago Press).

Keleman, D. (2006), 'Suing for Europe: Adversarial Legalism and European Governance', *Comparative Political Studies*, 39(1), 101–127.

Kelsey, J. (2006), 'Confronting Trade-Related Human Rights in a *GATS* Compatible World' (Paper delivered at the Human Rights and Global Justice Conference, University of Warwick, 29–31 March 2006) (copy on file with the author).

Kendall, L. (2000), "Oh No! I'm a NERD!" Hegemonic Masculinity on an Online Forum, *Gender and Society*, 14, 256–274.

Kennedy, D. (1982), 'The Stages of the Decline of the Public/Private Distinction', *University of Pennsylvania Law Review*, 130(June), 1349–1357.

— (2003), 'Laws and Developments', in Hatchard and Perry-Kesaris (eds).

Klarman, M.J. (2004), *From Jim Crow to Civil Rights: The Supreme Court and the Struggle for Racial Equality* (New York: Oxford University Press).

Klasper, W. and Streit, M.E. (1998), *Institutional Economics: Social Order and Public Policy* (Chelteham, UK: Edward Elgar for the Locke Institute).

Klug, F., Starmer, K. and Weir, S. (2005), *The Three Pillars of Liberty* (London: Taylor & Francis Group).

Kluger, R. (1975), *Simple Justice: The History of Brown v Board of Education and Black America's Struggle for Equality* (New York: Vintage).

Knox, P.L. (1993), *Urbanization: An Introduction to Urban Geography* (Englewood Cliffs, N.J.: Prentice-Hall).

— (1998), *The Restless Urban Landscape* (Englewood Cliffs, N.J.: Prentice-Hall).

Koskenniemi, M. (2003), 'What is International Law for?', in Evans (ed.).

— (2005), 'Formalism, Fragmentation, Freedom: Kantian Themes in Today's International Law' (Paper delivered in Frankfurt, 25 November 2005), . Available at http://www.valt.helsinki.fi/blogs/eci/Frankfurt-Formalism-05h[1].pdf.

Kousser, M. (1974), *The Shaping of Southern Politics: Suffrage Restriction and the Establishment of the One-Party South, 1880-1910* (New Haven, Yale University Press).

Larson, E. (2004), 'Institutionalizing Legal Consciousness: Regulation and the Embedding of Market Participants in the Securities Industry in Ghana and Fiji', *Law and Society Review*, 38, 737–767.

— (2005), 'Partial International Judicialization: The Dynamics of CERD's Consideration Of Fiji', *paper presented at Annual Meeting s of Law and Society Association, Las Vegas.*

Larson, E. and Aminzade, R. (forthcoming), 'Nation-States Confront the Global: Discourses of Indigenous Rights in Fiji and Tanzania', *The Sociological Quarterly.*

Lee, O. (2001), 'Legal Weapons for the Weak? Democratizing the Force of Words in an Uncivil Society', *Law and Social Inquiry*, 26, 847–892.

Lee, R. (2003), 'Indigenous Rights and the Politics of Identity in Post-Apartheid South Africa', in Dean, B. and Levi, J. (eds.) (2003) *At the Risk of Being Heard: Identity, Indigenous Rights, and Postcolonial States* (Ann Arbor: University of Michigan Press).

Lefebvre, H. (1991), *Production of Space* (Cambridge, Massachusetts: Blackwell).

Levin, J. and Levin, W. (1982), *The Functions of Discrimination and Prejudice* (New York: Harper & Row).

Li, T.M. (2000), 'Articulating Indigenous Identity in Indonesia: Resource Politics and the Tribal Slot', *Comparative Studies in Society and History*, 42, 149–179.

Lieberman, J. (1995), 'Lieberman on Affirmative Action. http://www.newmassmedia.com/lieberman/affirm.html, (Accessed on 5 September 2006).

Lipietz, A. (1986), 'New Tendencies in the International Division of Labor: Regimes of Accumulation and Modes of Regulation', in Scott, A. J. and Storper, M. (eds.).

Liu, D. and Boyle, E.H. (2001), 'Making the Case: The Women's Convention and Equal Employment Opportunity in Japan', *International Journal of Comparative Sociology*, 42, 389–404.

Lobel, O. (2003), 'Orchestrated Experimentalism in the Regulation of Work', *Michigan Law Review*, 101(May), 2146–2162. [DOI: 10.2307/3595349]

— (2004a), 'The Renew Deal: The Fall of Regulation and the Rise in Governance in Contemporary Legal Thought', *Minnesota Law Review*, 89(December), 342–470.

— (2004b), 'Setting the Agenda for New Governance Research', *Minnesota Law Review*, 89(December), 498–508.

— (2005), 'Interlocking Regulatory and Industrial Relations: The Governance of Workplace Safety', *Administrative Law Review*, 57(fall), 1071–1151.

— (2006), 'The Four Pillars of Work Law', *Michigan Law Review*, 104(May), 1539–1557.

Lochner v New York (1905), 198 U.S. 45.

Loughlin, M. and Scott, C. (1990), 'The Regulatory State', in Dunleavy, P. et al. (eds.), *Developments in British Politics* (3rd ed) (Basingstoke: Macmillan Press).

MacKay, F. (2002), 'Universal Rights or a Universe Unto itself? Indigenous Peoples' Human Rights and the World Bank's Draft Operational Policy 4.10 on Indigenous Peoples', *American University International Law Review*, 17, 527.

— (2005), 'The Draft World Bank Operational Policy 4.10 on Indigenous Peoples: Progress or 'More of the Same', *Arizona Journal of International and Comparative Law*, 22, 65–98.

MacLeod, G. (2002), 'From Urban Entrepreneurialism to a "Revanchist City"? On the Spatial Justices of Glasgow's Renaissance', *Antipode* 34(3).

MacKinnon, C.A. (1979), *Sexual Harassment of Working Women: A Case of Sex Discrimination* (New Haven: Yale Press).

Maiguashca, B. (1994), 'The Role of Ideas in a Changing World Order: The International Indigenous Movement, 1975 – 1990', CERLAC Occasional Paper Centre for Research on Latin America and the Caribbean (York University).

Majone, G. (1994), 'Paradoxes of Privatisation and Deregulation', *Journal of European Public Policy*, 1(1), 53–69.

Mamdani, M. (1996), *Citizen and Subject: Contemporary Africa and the Legacy of Late Colonialism* (Princeton: Princeton University Press).

Manji, A. (2003), 'Commodifying Land, Fetishising Law: Women's Struggles to Claim Land Rights in Uganda', *Australian Feminist Law Journal*, 19, 81–92.

Marquette, H. (2004), 'The Creeping Politicisation of the World Bank: The Case of Corruption', *Political Studies*, 52, 413–430. [DOI: 10.1111/j.1467-9248.2004.00488.x]

Marshall, A. (2005), *Confronting Sexual Harassment: Law and Politics in Everyday Life* (Dartmouth: Ashgate Publishing).

— (2005), 'Idle Rights: Employees' Rights Consciousness and the Construction of Sexual Harassment Policies', *Law and Society Review*, 39, 83–123. [DOI: 10.1111/j.0023-9216.2005.00078.x]

Marshall, A. and Barclay, S. (2003), 'In their Own Words: How Ordinary People Construct the Legal World', *Law and Social Inquiry*, 28, 617–628. [DOI: 10.1111/j.1747-4469.2003.tb00209.x]

Marshall, T.H. (1950), *Citizenship and Social Class and Other Essays* (Cambridge: Cambridge University Press).

Martínez Cobo, J.R. (1981), *Study of the Problem of Discrimination against Indigenous Populations, Final Report*, Vol. 1 (Geneva: UN Economic and Social

Council, Commission on Human Rights, Sub-Commission on Prevention of Discrimination and Protection of Minorities).

— (1987), Study of the Problem of Discrimination against Indigenous Peopulations, *Volume 5 – Conclusions, Proposals, and Recommendations*, (E/CN.4/ Sub.2/1986/7/Add.4), United Nations.

Mary and Carrie Dann (United States) (2002), Inter-American Commission on Human Rights, Report 75/02 (Case 11.140).

Mashaw, J. (1996), 'Reinventing Government and Regulatory Reform: Studies in the Neglect and Abuse of Administrative Law', *University of Pittsburg*, 57: Winter, 405–22.

Mathews, S. (2005), 'An Occasion for Fuzzy Convergence: Human Rights, Millennium Development Goals and Poverty Strategy Reduction Papers' (unpublished paper on file with the author).

Mayagna (Sumo) Awas Tingni Community v Nicaragua (2001), Inter-American Count of Human Rights, (Ser. C) 79.

McArdle, A. and Erzen, T. (2001), *Zero Tolerance: Quality of Life and the New Police Brutality in New York City* (New York: New York University Press).

McCann, M. (1994), *Rights at Work: Pay Equity Reform and the Politics of Legal Mobilization* (Chicago: The University of Chicago Press).

McCann, M. and Dudas, J.R. (2006), 'Retrenchment … and Resurgence?, Mapping the Changing Context of Movement Lawyering in the United States', in Sarat, A. and Scheingold, S. (eds.).

McCrudden, C. and Chambers, G. (1994), *Individual Rights and the Law in Britain* (Oxford: Clarendon Press).

McGarity, T. and Shapiro, S. (1993), *Workers at Risk: The Failed Promise of the Occupational Safety and Health Administration* (Westport: Praeger Publisher).

McGirr, L. (2001), *Suburban Warriors: The Origins of the New American Right* (Princeton, N.J.: Princeton University Press).

McHugh, C. (1989), 'For Night Crawlers, Are City's Glamour, Excitement Fading?', *New York Observer*, 11 December, 1989.

McKenzie, E. (1994), *Privatopia: Homeowner Associations and the Rise of Residential Private Government* (New Haven: Yale University Press).

McMillen, N.R. (1971), *The Citizens' Council: Organized Resistance to the Second Reconstruction, 1954-1964* (Urbana: University of Illinois Press).

Mele, C. (2000), *Selling the Lower East Side: Culture, Real Estate, and Resistance in New York City* (Minnesota: University of Minnesota Press).

Mendeloff, J. (1984), 'The Role of OSHA Violations in Serious Workplace Accidents', *Journal of Occupational Medicine*, 26, 353–360. [PubMed 6726484] [DOI: 10.1097/00043764-198405000-00009]

Metcalf, C. (2003), 'Indigenous Rights and the Environment: Evolving International Law', *Ottawa Law Review*, 35, 101–140.

Meyer, J.W. (2004), 'The Nation as *Babbit*: How Countries Conform', *Contexts*, 3(3), 42–47.

Meyer, J.W. and Jepperson, R.L. (2000), 'The "Actors" Of Modern Society: The Cultural Construction of Social Agency', *Sociological Theory*, 18, 100–120. [DOI: 10.1111/0735-2751.00090]

Meyer, J.W., Boli, J., Thomas, G.M. and Ramirez, F.O. (1997), 'World Society and the Nation-State', *American Journal of Sociology*, 103, 144–181. [DOI: 10.1086/231174]

Meyer, J.W., Ramirez, F.O. and Soysal, Y.N. (1992), 'World Expansion of Mass Education, 1870 – 1980', *Sociology of Education*, 65, 128–149. [DOI: 10.2307/2112679]

Michael, J. and Wechsler, H. (1937a), 'A Rationale of the Law of Homicide. I', *Columbia Law Review*, 37, 701. [DOI: 10.2307/1116597]

— (1937b), 'A Rationale of the Law of Homicide. II', *Columbia Law Review*, 37, 1261. [DOI: 10.2307/1116597]

— (1940), *Criminal Law and Its Administration: Cases, Statutes and Commentaries* (Chicago: Foundation Press).

Mill, J.S. (1978), 'On Liberty' in Rappaport, E. (ed.).

Milner, N. and Goldberg-Hiller, J. (2002), 'Reimagining Rights', *Law and Social Inquiry*, 27, 339–368. [DOI: 10.1111/j.1747-4469.2002.tb00807.x]

Ministry of Health, Eleventh Annual Report (1929-30) Cmd. 3667 (June 1930) (London: HMSO).

—, Seventeenth Annual Report (1935-36) Cmd. 5287 (Oct 1936) (London: HMSO).

Minutes of Informal Meeting of the Temporary Commission (29 November 1962), Box 2, Folder 1, 2.

Mitchell, D. (2001), 'Postmodern Geographical Praxis?, Postmodern Impulse and the War against Homeless People in the "'Postjustice" City', in Minca, C. (ed.).

— (2003a), *The Right to the City: Social Justice and the Fight for Public Space* (New York: The Guilford Press).

— (2005), 'Property Rights, the First Amendment, and Judicial Anti-Urbanism: The Strange Case of *Hicks V. Virginia*', *Urban Geography*, 26(7), 565–586.

Mizrach, S., 'What Is Cyberanthropology?', http://www.fiu.edu/~mizrachs/Cyber Anthropology.html, accessed 20 April 2003.

Morais, H. (2000), 'The Globalization of Human Rights Law and the Role of International Financial Institutions in Promoting Human Rights', *George Washington International Law Review*, 33, 71.

Moran, M., Rein, M. and Goodin, R.E., eds. (2006), *The Oxford Handbook of Public Policy* (Oxford: Oxford University Press).

Morgan, B. (2003), 'The Economisation of Politics: Metaregulation as a Form of Nonjudicial Legality', *Social and Legal Studies*, 12, 489–523. [DOI: 10.1177/09 64663903012004004]

Morgan, R. (2004), 'Advancing Indigenous Rights and the United Nations: Strategic Framing and its Impact on the Normative Development of International Law', *Social and Legal Studies*, 13, 481–500. [DOI: 10.1177/0964663904047330]

Narvaez, A.A. (1976), 'When Bars Close, Night Is Young At Illegitimate but Abundant Clubs; When Bars Close, Night Is Still Young at Illegal Clubs', *New York Times*, 26 December, 1, 46.

National Labour Reform Act (2000), § 7, 29 U.S.C. §§ 157-69.

Nelson, R.L. and Bridges, W.P. (1999), *Legalizing Gender Inequality: Courts, Markets, and Unequal Pay for Women in America* (New York: Cambridge University Press).

New York Times (2000), *Transcript of Presidential Debate*, 12 October 2000, A22.

New York Times, 'State Picks Panel on Criminal Law (21 June 1961), 39.

Nielsen, L.B. (2000), 'Situating Legal Consciousness: Experiences and Attitudes of Ordinary Citizens About Law and Street Harassment', *Law and Society Review*, 34, 1055–1090. [DOI: 10.2307/3115131]

Niezen, R. (2003), *The Origins of Indigenism: Human Rights and the Politics of Identity* (Berkeley: University of California Press).

North Carolina Session Laws (1955), An Act to Provide for the Enrollment of Pupils in Public Schools, Chapter 366, 310.

North, D. (1990), *Institutions, Institutional Change and Economic Performance* (Cambridge: Cambridge University Press).

Nussbaum, M. (1992), Human Functioning and Social Justice: In Defense Of Aristotelian Essentialism, *Political Theory*, 20, 202–246.

— (2000), *Women and Human Development: the Capabilities Approach* (Cambridge: Cambridge University Press).

Office of the High Commissioner for Human Rights, *Leaflet No. 2: indigenous peoples, the UN, and human rights*, http://www.sdnpbd.org/sdi/international_days/Indigenous-people/2004/indigenous_people/document/indi_un_human.pdf.

Ogus, A. (1994), Regulation: Legal Form and Economic Theory, (Oxford: Oxford University Press).

Oloka-Onyango, J. (2001), *Constitutionalism in Africa: Creating Opportunities, Facing Challenges* (Kampala: Fountain Publishers).

Omi, M. and Winant, H. (1994), *Racial Formation in the United States, from the 1960s to the 1980s* (New York: Routledge).

Osin, N. and Porat, D., eds. (2005), *Legislating against Discrimination: An International Survey Of Anti-Discrimination Norms* (Leiden: Martinus-Nijhoff Publishers).

Owen, F. (1997a), City Hall is Changing the Rules of Nightlife in New York, *Village Voice*, 18 February 1997, 42(7).

— (1997b), Dry Zone, *Village Voice*, 42(24), 26.

— (2003), *Clubland: the Fabulous Rise and Murderous fall of Club Culture* (New York: St Martin's Press).

Pahuja, S. (2000), 'Technologies of Empire: IMF Conditionality and the Reinscription of the North South Divide', *Leiden Journal of International Law*, 13, 749. [DOI: 10.1017/S0922156500000479]

— (2004), '"This is the World: Have Faith"', *European Journal of International Law*, 15(2), 381–393. [DOI: 10.1093/ejil%2F15.2.381]

— (2005), 'The Postcoloniality of International Law', *Harvard International Law Journal*, 46, 459–469.

Papayanis, M.A. (2000), 'Sex and Revanchist City: Zoning out Pornography in New York', *Environment and Planning D: Society and Space. 18*(3), 341–353.

Parker, C., Scott, C., Lacey, N. and Braithwaite, J. (2004), *Regulating Law* (Oxford: Oxford University Press).

Passavant, P.A. (2002), *No Escape: Freedom of Speech and the Paradox of Rights* (New York: New York University Press).

Peck, J. and Tickell, A. (1994), 'Searching for a New Institutional Fix: The After-Fordist Crisis and Global-Local Disorder' in Amin, A. (ed.).

— (2002), 'Neoliberalizing Space', *Antipode*, 34(3), 380–404. [DOI: 10.1111/1467-8330.00247]

Peet, R. (2003), *Unholy Trinity: The IMF, The World Bank and the WTO* (London: Zed Books).

Penner, J.E. (1996), 'The "Bundle of Rights" Picture of Property', UCLA Law Review, 43: February, 711–820.

Permanent Forum on Indigenous Issues (2005), *Report on Fourth Session (16 – 27 May 2005),* U.N. Economic and Social Council Official Records, Supplement No. 23. (E/C.19/2005/9).

Pew Research Center (2006), 'March 2006 News Interest Index Final Topline, 8 – 12 March 2006', . http://people-press.org/reports/questionnaires/271.pdf, Last Accessed on 15 November 2006.

Pierce, J.L. (1995), *Gender Trials: Emotional Lives in Contemporary Law Firms* (Los Angeles: University of California Press).

Piron, L. and O'Neil, T. (2005), *Integrating Human Rights into Development: A Synthesis of Donor Approaches and Experiences* (London: Overseas Development Institute for the OECD/DAC Network on Governance).

Pliskin, N. and Romm, C. (1994), 'Empowerment Effects of Electronic Group Communication: a Case Study', Work. Pap. Dep. Manage., Faculty Commerce, University of Wollongong, Australia.

Polanyi, K. (2001), *The Great Transformation: The Political and Economic Origins of our Time* (Boston: Beacon Press) (originally published 1944).

Pritchard, J. Robert S., (1983), *Crown Corporations in Canada: The Calculus of Instrument Choice* (Toronto: Butterworth).

Prosser, T. (1983), *Test Cases for the Poor* (London: Child Poverty Action Group).

Quinn, B.A. (2000), 'The Paradox of Complaining: Law, Humor, and Harassment in the Everyday Work World', *Law and Social Inquiry*, 25, 1151–1185. [DOI: 10.1111/j.1747-4469.2000.tb00319.x]

Radin, M. (1938), 'A Restatement of Hohfeld', *Harvard Law Review*, 51, 1141–1164.

Rajagopal, B. (2003), *International Law from Below: Development, Social Movements and Third World Resistance* (UK: Cambridge University Press).

— (2006), 'Counter-Hegemonic International Law: Rethinking Human Rights and Development as a Third World Strategy', *Third World Quarterly*, 27(5), 767–783. [DOI: 10.1080/01436590600780078]

Rancière, J. (2004), 'Who is the Subject of the Rights of Man', *South Atlantic Quarterly*, 103(2/3), 297–310. [DOI: 10.1215/00382876-103-2-3-297]

Reagan, R. (1968), *The Creative Society: Some Comments of Problems Facing America* (New York: The Devin-Adair Company).

Reiss, A.J. (1974), 'Discretionary Justice' in Glaser, D. (ed.), *Handbook of Criminology* (Chicago: Rand McNally College Publishing Company).

Reus-Smit, C., ed. (2004), *The Politics of International Law* (Cambridge: Cambridge University Press).

Rheingold, H. (1993), *The Virtual Community: Homesteading on the Electronic Frontier* (Reading, Mass.: Addison-Wesley).

Rhode, D.L. (2001), *The Unfinished Agenda: Women in the Legal Profession* (Chicago, Ill.: American Bar Association Commission on Women in the Profession).

Rhodes, R. (1997), *Understanding Governance* (Buckingham: Open University Press).

Rittich, K. (2004), 'The Future of Law and Development: Second Generation Reforms and the Incorporation of the Social', *Michigan Journal of International Law*, 26, 199.

Roedinger, D. (1997), 'White Workers, New Democrats, and Affirmative Action' in Lubiano, W. (ed.).

Rogin, M.P. (1987), *Ronald Reagan, the Movie: and Other Episodes in Political Demonology* (Berkeley, California: University of California Press).

Rohde, D. (1998), 'Vowing Noise Crackdown, City Shuts Four East Side Bars', *New York Times*, 7 April 1998, B3.

Romano, T. (2002), 'The Safety Dance: You Can't Dance if You Want To', *Village Voice*; (27 November 2002–03 December) 2002.

— (2004), 'The Next Brooklyns: New York's DJs Flee Overseas to Berlin', *Village Voice*; (22 July 2004).

Rosenberg, J., Perlstadt, H. and Phillips, W. (1993), 'Now That We Are Here: Discrimination, Disparagement, and Harassment at Work and the Experience of Women Lawyers', *Gender and Society*, 7(3), 415–433. [DOI: 10.1177/0891243 93007003006]

Rosenburg, G.N. (1991), *The Hollow Hope: Can Courts Bring about Social Change?* (Chicago: University of Chicago Press).

Ross, M.W., Mansson, S., Daneback, K., Cooper, A. and Tikkanen, R. (2005), 'Biases in Internet Sexual Health Samples: Comparison of an Internet Sexuality Survey and a National Sexual Health Survey in Sweden', *Social Science and Medicine*, 61, 245–252. [PubMed 15847976] [DOI: 10.1016/j.socscimed.2005.01.019]

Rothman, R. (1999), 'Sites Unscene', *Village Voice*; (28 September 1999).

Rubin, E. (2005) 'The Conceptual Explanation for Legislative Failure', *Law and Social Inquiry*, 30, 583-606.

Sanders, A. (1987), 'Constructing the Case for the Prosecution', *Journal of Law and Society*, 14, 229. [DOI: 10.2307/1409943]

Sano, H. (2000), 'Development and Human Rights: The Necessary, but Partial Integration of Human Rights and Development', *Human Rights Quarterly*, 22, 3, 734. [DOI: 10.1353/hrq.2000.0037]

Sarat, A.D. and Felstiner, W. (1988), 'Law and Social Relations: Vocabularies of Motive in Lawyer/Client Interaction', *Law and Society Review*, 22, 737–770. [DOI: 10.2307/3053708]

Sarfaty, G.A. (2005), 'The World Bank and the Internalization of Indigenous Rights Norms', *Yale Law Journal*, 17, 1792.

Scheingold, S.A. (1974), *The Politics of Rights: Lawyers, Public Policy, and Political Change* (New Haven, Conn.: Yale University Press).

Schlein, L. (2006), 'UN Rights Body Adopts Indigenous Rights Declaration Despite Canada's No Vote', Canadian Newswire (June 29), available through LexisNexis.

Schneider, E.M. (1990), 'The Dialectic of Rights and Policies: Perspectives from the Women's Movement' in Gordon (ed.).

Schofer, E. and Hironaka, A. (2005), 'World Society and Environmental Protection Outcomes', *Social Forces*, 84, 25–47. [DOI: 10.1353/sof.2005.0127]

Schofer, E. and Meyer, J.W. (2005), 'The World-Wide Expansion of Higher Education in the Twentieth Century', *American Sociological Review*, 70, 898–920.

Schrag, P. (1969), 'The Forgotten American' in Chafe, W.H. and Sitkoff, H. (eds.).

Scott, C. (2006), 'Privatisation and Regulatory Regimes' in Moran, M., Rein, M. and Goodin, R.E. (eds.).

Scott, J. (1996), *Only Paradoxes to Offer* (Cambridge: Harvard University Press).

Sellers, M., ed. (1996), *The New World Order: Sovereignty, Human Rights and the Self-Determination of Peoples* (Oxford: Berg).

Sen, A. (1981), *Poverty and Famines* (Gloucestershire: Clarendon Press).

— (1999), *Development as Freedom* (Oxford: Oxford University Press).

— (2000), 'Role of Legal and Judicial Reform in Development', '(Address delivered at The World Bank Legal Conference, Washington DC, US, 5 June 2000)'. Available at http://www1.worldbank.org/publicsector/legal/legalandjudicail.pdf (copy on file with the author).

— (2005), *The Argumentative Indian: Writings on Indian History, Culture and Identity* (London: Allen Lane).

Senator Hutchison (1995), Testimony before Congress.

Sered, S. and Ferandopulle, R. (2005), *Uninsured in America: Life and Death in the Land of Opportunity* (Berkeley, California: University of California Press).

Sharf, B. (1997), 'Communicating Breast Cancer On-Line: Support and Empowerment on the Internet', *Women and Health*, 26, 65–84. [DOI: 10.1300/J013v26n01_05]

Silberman, S. (1998), 'First Amendment?', 'Not on the Job', 'Wired News', http://www.wired.com/news/politics/0,1283,10217,00.html, Accessed on 11 November 2003.

Silbey, S.S. (2005), 'After Legal Consciousness', *Annual Review of Law and Social Science*, 1, 323–368. [DOI: 10.1146/annurev.lawsocsci.1.041604.115938]

Simon, H. and Sparrow, M. (1997), Regulatory Reform at OSHA (C102-97-1371.0) Kennedy School of Government Case Program.

Sissons, J. (2005), *First Peoples: Indigenous Cultures and their Futures* (London: Reaktion Books).

Skocpol, T. (1996), *Boomerang: Clinton's Health Security Effort and the Turn Against Government in U.S. Politics* (New York: W.W. Norton & Co).

Sleeper, J. (1987), 'Days of the Developers, Boom and Bust with Ed Koch', *Dissent*, 1987 (fall), 437–452.

Smith, N. (1996), *The New Urban Frontier: Gentrification and the Revanchist City* (New York: Routledge).

— (1998), 'Giuliani Time: the Revanchist 1990s', *Social Text*, 57, 16(4), 1–20.

'Snare speech, American Bar Association OSH Law Committee Key West, Florida' (2 March 2005), at http://www.osha.gov/pls/oshaweb/owadisp.show_document?p_table=SPEECHES&p_id=838.

Snyder, C.R. (2005), 'Waking up in the "City that Never Sleeps": a Solution for Nighttime Noise in West Chelsea', *Columbia Journal of Environmental Law*, 30, 249–291.

Sorkin, M., ed. (1992), *Variations on a Theme Park: The New American City and the End of Public Space* (New York: Hill and Wang).

Sowell, T. (1984), 'The Civil Rights Vision: From Equal Opportunity to "Affirmative Action"' in Buckley, W.F., Jr and Kesler, C.R. (eds.).

— (1989), 'Affirmative Action: A Worldwide Disaster' in Gerson, M. (ed.).

Span, P. (1998), 'On a Cleaning Spree: Nightclubs the New Target', *The Washington Post*, 20 February, 1998.

Special NGO Committee on Human Rights (1981), *Report on International NGO Conference on Indigenous People and the Land* (Geneva: Women's International League of Peace and Freedom).

Stavenhagen, R. (2003), 'Report of the Special Rapporteur on the Situation of Human Rights and Fundamental Freedoms of Indigenous People', United Nations Economic and Social Council, Commission on Human Rights (E/CN.4/2003/90).

Steele v Louisville & N.R. Co. (1944), 323 U.S. 192.

Steiner, H. (1998), 'Social Rights and Economic Development: Converging Discourses?', *Buffalo Human Rights Law Review*, 4, 25.

Steinman, E.W. (2005), 'Legitimizing American Indian Sovereignty: Mobilizing the Constitutive Power of Law through Institutional Entrepreneurship', *Law and Society Review*, 39, 759–791. [DOI: 10.1111/j.1540-5893.2005.00244.x]

Stiglitz, J. (1999), 'Participation and Development: Perspectives from the Comprehensive Development Paradigm' (Paper delivered in Seoul, South Korea, 27 February 1999) (copy on file with the author).

Stone-Sweet, A.S. (2000), *Governing with Judges: Constitutional Politics in Europe* (Oxford: Oxford University Press).

Sturm, S. (2001), 'Second Generation Employment Discrimination', *Columbia Law Review*, 101(April), 458–567.

— (2006), 'The Architecture of Inclusion: Advancing Workplace Equity in Higher Education', *Harvard Journal of Law and Gender*, 29(summer), 247–334.

Suchman, M.C. and Edelman, L.B. (1997), 'Legal Rational Myths: The New Institutionalism in the Law and Society Tradition', *Law and Social Inquiry*, 21, 903–941.

Suk, J. (2006), 'Antidiscrimination Law in the Administrative State', *University of Illinois Law Review*, 2006, 406–473.

Sunstein, C. (1990), *After the Rights Revolution: Reconceiving the Regulatory State* (Cambridge: Harvard University Press).

Suzuki, E. and Nanwani, S. (2005), 'Responsibility of International Organizations: The Accountability Mechanisms of Multilateral Development Banks', *Michigan Journal of International Law*, 27, 1, 177.

Temporary Commission to Revise the Penal Law of New York, *Minutes of Public Hearing* (New York City: New York Supreme Court Criminal Law Library), Box 2, Folder 1.

Teubner, G. (ed.) (1987), *Juridification of Social Spheres: A Comprehensive Analysis in the Areas of Labor, Corporate, Antitrust, and Social Welfare Law* (Berlin: Walter de Gruyter).

Thernstrom, A. and Blum, E. (2005), 'Voting Rights Act: After 40 Years, It's Time for Virginia to Move On', *Richmond Times-Dispatch*, 1 August 2005.

Tilley, V.Q. (2002), 'New Help or New Hegemony? The Transnational Indigenous Peoples' Movement and "Being Indian" in El Salvador', *Journal of Latin American Studies*, 34, 525–554.

TNA, 'HLG 52/592, *Town and Country Planning Act, 1932: Agreements*' (1933).

—, 'HLG 71/267 *Comments on the Town and Country Planning Act, 1932 and the Town and Country Planning (Interim Development) Act, 1943*' (1942–47).

—, 'HLG 95/52 *Precedent Books; Precedent Cases Arising under the Town and Country Planning Act, 1932 and Various Acts in Relation to Planning Questions: A to L.*', Vol. I.

Tocqueville, A. (1966), *Democracy in America, Trans. Lawrence G.* (New York: Harper & Row).

Truman, H. (1949), 'Inaugural Address', '20 January 1949', . Available at http://www.trumanlibrary.org/whistlestop/50yr_archive/inagural20jan1949.htm (administered by the National Archives and Records Administration, Harry S. Truman Library and Museum).

Tushnet, M. (1984), 'An Essay on Rights', *Texas Law Review*, 62(May), 1363–1403.

Tyson, T.B. (1999), *Radio Free Dixie: Robert F. Williams and the Roots of Black Power* (Chapel Hill: University of North Carolina Press).

Unger, R. (1989), *The Critical Legal Studies Movement* (Boston, Mass.: Harvard University Press).

United Nations, *UN Millennium Development Goals*, Available at www.un.org/millenniumgoals.

United Nations Development Programme (2000) in Human Development Report (ed.). *United Nations Millennium Declaration, GA* Res 55/2, UN GAOR, 55th sess, Supp 49, UN Doc A/RES/55/2 (8 September 2000), available at www.un.org/millenium/declaration/ares552e.htm.

Universal Declaration of Human Rights (1948). http://www.un.org/Overview/rights.html.

Upham, F. (2002), 'Mythmaking in the Rule of Law Orthodoxy' (Paper Number 30, Carnegie Endowment for International Peace Working Papers, Rule of Law Series, Democracy and the Rule of Law Project).

Viscusi, W. (1983), *Risk by Choice: Regulating Health and Safety in the Workplace* (Cambridge: Harvard University Press).

Von Hayek, F. (1944), *The Road to Serfdom* (London: Routledge).

Waldron, J., (ed.) (1984), *Theories of Rights* (Oxford: Oxford University Press).

Warf, B. and Grimes, J. (1997), 'Counterhegemonic Discourses and the Internet', *Geographical Review*, 87, 259–274.

Warhol, R. (1999), 'The Inevitable Virtuality of Gender: Performing Femininity on an Electronic Bulletin Board for Soap Opera Fans' in Farrell, M., Vallone, L. and Arbor, A. (eds.).

Wasserman, I.M. and Richmond-Abbott, M. (2005), 'Gender and the Internet: Causes of Variation in Access, Level, and Scope of Use', *Social Science Quarterly*, 86, 252–270.

Weber, M. (1968), *Economy and Society: An Outline of Interpretive Sociology*. Roth, G. and Wittich, C. (eds.) (Berkeley: Univeristy of California Press).

Wechsler, H. (1940), *Criminal Law and Its Administration: Cases, Statutes and Commentaries* (Chicago: Foundation Press).

— (1952), 'The Challenge of a Model Penal Code', *Harvard Law Review*, 65, 1097.

— (1956), 'Legal Scholarship and Criminal Law', *Journal of Legal Education*, 9, 18.

— (1968), 'Codification of Criminal Law in the United States: The Model Penal Code', *Columbia Law Review*, 68, 1425.

Weeramantry, C. (2004), *Universalising International Law* (Leiden: Brill).

Weil, D. (1992), 'Building Safety: The Role of Construction Unions in the Enforcement of OSHA', *Journal of Labor Research*, 13(1), 121–132.

Weissbrodt, D., Fitzpatrick, J. and Newman, F. (2001), *International Human Rights: Law, Policy, and Process* (Cincinnati: Anderson Publishing).

Wellman, B., Salaff, J., Dimitrova, D., Garton, L., Gulia, M. and Haythornwaite, C. (1996), 'Computer Networks as Social Networks: Colaborative Work, Telework, and Virtual Community', *Annual Review of Sociology*, 22, 213–238.

Wickramasinghe, N. (1996), 'From Human Rights to Good Governance: The Aid Regime in the 1990s' in Sellers (ed.).

Williams, P.J. (1991), *The Alchemy of Race and Rights: Diary of a Law Professor* (Cambridge, Mass.: Harvard University Press).

Wills, G. (1970), *Nixon Agonistes: The Crisis of the Self-Made Man* (New York: Houghton Mifflin Co.).

— (1987), *Reagan's America: Innocents at Home* (New York: Doubleday).

— (1992), 'The Born-Again Republicans', *The New York Review of Books* (24 September 1992).

Wilson, J.Q. and Kelling, G.L. (1982), 'Broken Windows', *Atlantic Monthly*, 249(3), 29–38.

Wolfensohn, J.D. (1999), 'A Proposal for a Comprehensive Development Framework (A Discussion Draft)'. Available at http://www.worldbank.org/cdf/cdf-text.htm (copy on file with the author).

— (2000), 'NGO Meeting with Mr Wolfensohn', '(Transcript of meeting, Prague, Czech Republic, 22 September 2000)', Available at http://web.worldbank.org/WBSITE/EXTERNAL/NEWS/ontentMDK:20025788~menuPK:34476~pagePK:34370~piPK:42771~theSitePK:4607,00.html.

— (2003), 'Foreword' in *The World Bank Legal Review: Law and Justice for Development*. World Bank (ed.) (The Hague: Kluwer Law International) Volume 1.

Wood, E.M. (1981), 'The Separation of the Economic and the Political in Capitalism', *New Left Review*, I(127), 66–95.

Working Group Established in Accordance with Commission on Human Rights Resolution 1995/32 of 3 March 1995, (2006), 'Report on its Eleventh Session to the Commission on Human Rights' (Geneva: United Nations Office at Geneva) (E/CN.4/2006/79).

Working Group on Indigenous Populations (1982), *Report to the Sub-Commission on Prevention of Discrimination and Protection of Minorities,'* (Geneva: United Nations Office at Geneva).

— (1994), *Report on its Twelfth Session to the Sub-Commission on Prevention of Discrimination and Protection of Minorities,'* (Geneva: United Nations Office at Geneva) (E/CN.4/Sub.2/1994/30).

World Bank (1992), *Effective Implementation: Key to Development Impact* (Portfolio Management Taskforce Report) (Washington DC: World Bank) (Also known as the 'Wappenhams Report').

—(1998), *Development and Human Rights: The Role of the World Bank* (Washington, DC: International Bank for Reconstruction and Development).

— (1999), Principles and Good Practice in Social Policy: Issues and Areas for Public Action: http://lnweb18.worldbank.org/ESSD/sdvext.nsf/60ByDocName/ PrinciplesandGoodPracticeinSocialPolicyIssuesandAreasforPublicAction preparedbytheWorldBankfortheWorldBankIMFDevelopmentCommitteeApril 1999alsoavailableinFrenchandSpanish/$FILE/PrinciplesEng.pdf

— (2002), World Development Report 2002: Building Institutions for Markets (New York: Oxford University Press for the World Bank).

— (2003), 'Project Appraisal Document on a Proposed Loan to the Russian Federation for a Tuberculosis and AIDS Control Project', Report 21239-RU.

— (2003), Implementation of Operational Directive 4.20 on Indigenous Peoples: An Independent Desk Review,' (Operations Evaluation Department), Report 25,332 http://indianlaw.org/MDB_WorldBank_OD420_Desk_Review.pdf.

— (2004), 'Project Appraisal Document on a Proposed Loan to St'. 'Lucia for HIV/AIDS Prevention and Control Project', Report 29129. http://www-wds. worldbank.org/servlet/WDSContentServer/WDSP/IB/2004/06/17/000012009_ 20040617132504/Rendered/INDEX/291290SL.txt.

— (2005a), Legal Note on Indigenous Peoples, April 8 2005.

— (2005b), Staff Response to Public Comments, Revised Draft Policy on Indigenous Peoples (OP 4.10), 1 December 2004.

— (2005c), Operations Manual: Bank Procedure 4.10 – Indigenous Peoples.

— (2005d), Operations Manual: Operational Procedure 4.10 – Indigenous Peoples.

—(2005e), 'Empowering People by Transforming Institutions', 'Social Development Strategy', http://lnweb18.worldbank.org/ESSD/sdvext.nsf/62ByDocName/ EmpoweringPeopleByTransformingInstitutions/$FILE/SD+Strategy+Board+ver sion+01+12+05+Final.pdf.

World Bank and IMF Development (2004), 'Committee' in Policies and Actions for Achieving the Millennium Development Goals and Related Outcomes. Global Monitoring Report (ed.) (Washington, DC: International Bank for Reconstruction and Development).

World Bank, 'World Bank Ties $4.7 BLN Jakarta Support to Democracy, Rights', Development News [email newsletter], 2(2).

Wright, S. (2001), International Human Rights, Decolonization and Globalization: Becoming Human (London: Routledge).

Yeager, P.C. (1991), *The Limits of Law: The Public Regulation of Private Pollution* (Cambridge: Cambridge University Press).

Zaring, D. (2006), 'Best Practices', New York University Law Review, 81(April), 294–350.

Žižek, S. (2005), 'Against Human Rights', New Left Review, 34, 115–131.

Zuboff, S. (1988), The Age of the Smart Machine (New York, NY: Basic Books).

Zukin, S. (1989), Loft Living: Culture and Capital in Urban Change (New Jersey: Rutgers University Press).

— (1991), Landscapes of Power: From Detroit to Disneyworld (Berkeley, California: University of California, Los Angeles Press).

Index